Connecting with children: developing working relationships

Working together for children

This innovative series brings together an interdisciplinary team of authors to provide an accessible collection of ideas, debates, discussions and reflections on childhood, practice and services for children. The books have been designed and written as illustrative teaching texts, giving voice to children's and practitioners' own accounts as well as providing research, policy analysis and examples of good practice. These books are aimed at students, practitioners, academics and educators across the wide range of disciplines associated with working with children.

There are three books in the *Working together for children* series:

- *Connecting with children: developing working relationships*, edited by Pam Foley and Stephen Leverett
- *Promoting children's wellbeing: policy and practice*, edited by Janet Collins and Pam Foley
- *Changing children's services: working and learning together*, edited by Pam Foley and Andy Rixon

Connecting with children:

developing working relationships

Edited by Pam Foley and Stephen Leverett

The Open University

Published by

The Policy Press
University of Bristol
Fourth Floor, Beacon House
Queen's Road, Clifton
Bristol BS8 1QU
United Kingdom
http://www.policypress.org.uk

in association with

The Open University
Walton Hall, Milton Keynes
MK7 6AA
United Kingdom

The Open University

First published 2008

Edited and designed by The Open University.

Typeset in India by Alden Prepress Services, Chennai.

Printed and bound in the United Kingdom by The Alden Group, Oxford.

This book forms part of an Open University course KE312 *Working together for children*. Details of this and other Open University courses can be obtained from the Student Registration and Enquiry Service, The Open University, PO Box 197, Milton Keynes MK7 6BJ, United Kingdom: tel. +44 (0)845 300 60 90, email general-enquiries@open.ac.uk

http://www.open.ac.uk

British Library Cataloguing in Publication Data

A catalogue record for this book is available from the British Library.

Library of Congress Cataloging-in-Publication Data

A catalog record for this book has been requested.

ISBN 9781847420589

1.1

Contributors

Janet Collins is a Senior Lecturer in Primary Education at The Open University's Faculty of Education and Language Studies. Her practice background is in teaching and learning in primary schools.

Gill Crow is a Consultant Clinical Child Psychologist working in the Child and Adolescent Mental Health Services in Sheffield.

Pam Foley is a Senior Lecturer in Children and Families at The Open University's Faculty of Health and Social Care. Her practice background is in women's and children's health.

Stephen Leverett is a Lecturer in Children and Young People at The Open University's Faculty of Health and Social Care. His practice background is in social care and social work in both the statutory and voluntary sectors.

Andy Rixon is a Lecturer in Children and Young People at The Open University's Faculty of Health and Social Care. His practice background is as a social worker and in local authority training and development.

Other contributors

This series of three books forms part of The Open University course *Working together for children* and has grown out of debates and discussions within the course team working at the University. We would like to thank the following for their critical reading and invaluable feedback: Judith Argles, Brigitte Beck-Woerner, Sheila Campbell, Maurice Crozier, Hasel Daniels, Trevor Evans, Louise Garrett, Gill Goodliff, Glo Potter, Lin Miller, Kate New, Janet Seden and our developmental testers. We would also like to thank our focus group, our Editors Carol Price, Alison Cadle and Kate Hunter, our Course Team Assistant Val O'Connor, and our External Assessor, Denise Hevey, who has provided insightful and timely comments at every turn.

We should especially like to acknowledge the contribution of our Course Manager, Tabatha Torrance, who has guided, assisted and supported the course team throughout.

Contents

Introduction

Pam Foley and Stephen Leverett

This book is about examining, challenging and developing ideas and conceptions that affect the lives of children. It includes arguments and information that could help change how the capabilities and requirements of children are perceived and responded to: how adults think about children and how children think about themselves. It is equally concerned with how these ideas and debates are followed through into policy and practice.

Each society's response to the needs of children is intricately bound up with the way it sees itself and its hopes and fears for the future. In our society, powerful interest groups, social commentators, politicians, academics and children's charities debate the importance of family integrity, social trends and the impact of the state on children's lives. Children and young people are central to many questions, debates and decisions, including those about education, crime, poverty, childcare and child abuse. Many of these debates are fuelled by uniquely raw emotions, such as those associated with the protection of children, and raise difficult questions about individual and collective futures. People find it hard to accept that a state with advanced health and social care systems apparently remains unable to adequately provide for, or protect, its most vulnerable citizens, children. When compared to the other rich industrialised countries of the world, the UK performs poorly in supporting children's wellbeing (UNICEF, 2007). Such comparative approaches describe many British children as experiencing a poor quality of life. This may be a reminder of the division between children as human becomings and as human beings (as described by Qvortrup in 1994); investing in tomorrow's society, without investing in children's lives today, comes at a cost.

Everyone is aware of the powerful feelings generated by children, both individually and collectively, which lead many adults to question whether they share the same values and goals. For many adults, children hold the key to the future and each generation can be driven by a sense of responsibility to make things better for those which follow. The importance of children is not just to their parents but to all of us; as adults we are aware that what we sow, we reap, both as individuals and as societies. And while we may see children and young people as a source of social dislocation, we have no choice but to rely on them for the continuity of what we most value.

Uncertainty about the status of childhood as a period of life with its own particular qualities is evident in the rhetoric of much public policy, and in the provision of children's services. To pessimistic observers modern childhood has become institutionalised, subject to media manipulation and a troubling mode of consumption. In their view, many children have become disconnected from families, society and even childhood itself. More optimistic observers consider that childhood remains a prolonged and protected phase but now with considerable rights and consumer powers. Others emphasise children's individuality and connectedness as interdependent, evolving and context-specific. This can be understood by applying an ecological model which places children at the heart of a range of interrelationships from the micro- through to the macro- level. Rather than make judgements about aspects of an individual child (for example, their learning needs, behaviour, the style of parenting within their family) an ecological model helps us carefully consider the influence of additional factors located in families, peer groups, communities or a wider society.

At a time when the children's workforce is evolving to accommodate a wide and varied set of expectations, we consider it more than ever important to put children at the centre of practice. Throughout this book, and the others in the series *Working together for children*, children are given a voice in a variety of contexts and relationships. We aim to encourage practitioners to work together to build patterns of holistic support with children, both individually and in groups, based on skills and specific resources.

Throughout the 1990s, a new sociology of childhood mounted a vigorous challenge to established thinking about children (James and Prout, 1997; Hutchby and Moran Ellis, 1998; Mayall, 2002). The influence of these ideas in the first part of the twenty-first century is evident in examples of practice that recognise the capacity of children to act, as having agency. As with the ecological model, the idea of agency means recognising that children and young people influence, as well as being influenced by, their familial and social world; that children act on others as well as being acted upon. Children's social and personal development comes about as the result of active participation in the social relationships of their familial and social groupings, rather than being the subject of a gradual and accumulated socialisation 'process'. The new sociology overlapped with social constructivist theories about how children learn, which view knowledge as constructed through a child's interconnections with adults and peers rather than within the individual child (Vygotsky, 1978). Similar ideas are also evident in the influential Reggio Emilia approach to early years learning.

These theories complement the ideology and methods behind the growing number of children's participation initiatives across a range of health, education and social care services. By referring to such examples in this book we challenge readers, particularly those involved in the children's workforce, to reflect on their own engagement with children and to develop confidence in using theoretical ideas as a basis for improving practice.

The new sociology has also directly encouraged research that pays close attention to the everyday lives of children in differing contexts (Hutchby and Moran Ellis, 1998). This includes adult-controlled settings, such as children's centres, nurseries and schools, various social care and healthcare settings, and also less regulated contexts or spaces, such as the street or community play areas. Much of this research has given a voice to children themselves, providing an insight previously hidden or assumed not to exist. This too is reflected in this book. Collectively, this research has shown that childhood is constructed within socially and historically situated discourses, and is both variable and relative. Childhood can be understood as a structural concept, a category alongside other social categories, with political, economic, social and environmental parameters, and influenced by ethical debate, polemic and history. This also helps us to understand that 'childhood' is not a universal experience but can take many different forms.

Children's activities, and their connectedness and interactions with the peers and adults with whom they live, contribute to the diversity of micro-cultures that exist within families, schools and neighbourhoods. Such micro-cultures, or social spaces, shape social interactions and processes and can support different views of children (Moss and Petrie, 2002). The fact that children live in such hugely differing circumstances, and have such widely different experiences, has led some sociologists to refer to 'childhoods', plural. However, to make meaningful commentaries, and to have any hope of providing services which are responsive and successful, we may still need to refer to a childhood, singular, that has a number of meaningful characteristics in common (for example, girlhood or boyhood or a childhood lived apart from parents).

Throughout the twentieth century, childhood was increasingly marked out as a distinct and separate phase of life. Now, complex, overlapping, and often unspoken, ideas about children and childhood feed into policies, services and practices. The media reflects this ambivalence, both mythologising and pathologising children and young people: sometimes villains, sometimes victims, sometimes the hope for the future, at other times a cause for despair.

Is a modern concept of 'childhood' and children discernible as a result of these social and political debates? Should we be sanguine about the right of the state to regulate and intervene in certain families in the public interest and in the interest of the child? How much are childhoods shaped and differentiated by inequalities of class, gender, disability and ethnicity?

Most children's lives are now much more about play and learning than working or contributing in other ways to their families' wellbeing. This has had consequences for how we understand children's levels of competency and dependency, but have these changes also affected the evolution of child–adult relations? To what extent should our educational system be expected to work with families to raise children to be self-reliant, resilient individuals who are law-abiding, economically active, politically engaged and at ease with the socio-economic structural status quo?

These are not just abstract issues; questioning the politics and status of childhood with ideas about competence, voice, agency and rights has real potential to bring about change. But this has to start with the destabilisation and deconstruction of existing thinking and practices. The differentials in the positioning of children and adults need to be reassessed and more widely understood, before changes are reflected and enacted in any political and social agenda.

Some of the ideas in this book (including those about relationships, participation and transitions) are already well-developed and well-served by literature focused on young people. We challenge our readers to assess the suitability of applying and adapting these ideas to a younger age group. We believe that middle childhood is in particular danger of being overlooked at a time when many state resources are being invested in early intervention initiatives. Our upper age threshold also approximates with the age of transition within a number of children's services, such as education.

This series of books focuses on the 0–12 age group but we have decided to omit identifying children's ages unless they seem to be particularly relevant. By bracketing childhood in this way we run the risk of reproducing the 'age and stage' thinking that has often obscured children's individual capacities and capabilities. In fact, we hope to encourage people with an interest in childhood to look outwards and consider how this important period in children's lives connects with the rest of the life course. We have drawn together writers and practitioners from a variety of disciplines to contribute to this book and this is reflected in the diversity of language and terminology; both 'disabled children' and 'children with disabilities' are used here for example. We have decided not to standardise language when it reflects a considered and valid viewpoint.

The first chapter of this book examines communication as fundamental to the development of positive relationships, good practice and effective services for children. Knowing how to interact with children in ways that support the development of their abilities to think, learn and form good relationships with the people around them is a core skill for everyone working with children. The authors offer guidance for improving communication skills and explain just how this can contribute to children's social and emotional development.

The second chapter examines the significance and development of positive relationships for children within families and within services for children. Children's own accounts reveal that bullying relationships are widespread and cause a great deal of distress. We look at how adults working with children can identify and prevent bullying and at how children might be supported to deal with it when it occurs.

In Chapter 3, 'Positive relationships with children and families', the author looks at how practitioners can learn from the views of children and their families and how this impacts on agencies, practitioners and services for children. The chapter examines what we mean by 'relationship-based' approaches to practice and how reflective practice can contribute to developing and sustaining positive working relationships with children for practitioners in a variety of contexts and settings.

Chapter 4, 'Listening across generations', considers the evolving changes to child–adult relations that frame policy and practice developments. Care, dependency and interdependency between adults and children are examined. The chapter also looks at ways in which recognition of children's agency, together with evolving competence and confidence, has the potential to improve many children's quality of life.

Chapter 5 critically examines the ideological and political basis for *children's participation* and presents examples of innovative good practice. It also highlights the dangers of tokenism and the need for evaluative evidence to show that children actually are successfully influencing policy and practice. The reader will be encouraged to examine, reflect upon and develop their own skills in terms of engaging with and involving children.

Although emphasised in some areas of policy and practice, transitions are frequently narrowly understood as movements between one service area and another. Chapter 6, 'Understanding transitions', encourages the reader to take a broader perspective, viewing transitions as common experiences across the life course which require people to adapt to, and come to terms with, losses and changes. For children, early transitions are an opportunity to develop their capacities for dealing with changes associated with status, space and time. Examining childhood transitions within an ecological context makes it possible to identify how they occur from the interrelationship between children and different environmental systems. This helps to identify the impact of unexpected life events, as well as more common, culturally produced, transitions at both the macro- and micro-levels. The reader is encouraged to reflect on how a sensitivity towards, and an understanding of, transitions can enhance the development of positive adult–child relationships.

Chapter 7, 'Working with children and transitions', builds on the material in Chapter 6 to present and critically examine practical support skills associated with different types of transition. It challenges adults working with children to critically reflect and provide support with transitions that complement children's own agency and capacity. 'Working with children and transitions' also highlights the importance of universal and specialist services working together to provide different types of support. The importance of interpreting children's behaviour associated with transitions is highlighted, as is creating space in which children can express, and come to terms with, their feelings. Practical activities are suggested that can be adapted by adults working with children to support different types of transition.

There exists a mixture of past and present thinking about children but there persists discernible confidence in schools and the family as key institutions which can be used as a means of governance or control. British policies and practices continue a balancing act between concern, care and control in relation to children. More recent thinking, introducing questions about competency, voice, rights and participation, has contributed new insights into what it means to be a child, and what it means to be a child or young person in contemporary western European society. This thinking has informed policies and practices for children with a more complex and varied set of causes and consequences. Although the recognition of childhood as a social construction still leaves many of the barriers to change intact, we can recognise and respond to this period of change by acting on a range of choices concerning why, when and how to connect with children.

References

Hutchby, I. and Moran Ellis, J. (eds) (1998) *Children and Social Competence: Arenas of Action*, London, Falmer Press.

James, A. and Prout, A. (eds) (1997) *Constructing and Reconstructing Childhood: Contemporary Issues in the Sociological Study of Childhood* (2nd edn.), London, Falmer Press.

Mayall, B. (2002) *Towards a sociology for childhood: thinking from children's lives*, Buckingham, Open University Press.

Moss, P. and Petrie, P. (2002) *From Children's Services to Children's Spaces. Public Policy, Children and Childhood*, London, Routledge Falmer.

Qvortrup, J. (1994) 'Childhood Matters: An Introduction' in Qvortrup, J., Bardy, M., Sgritta, G. and Wintersberger, H. (eds) *Childhood Matter: Social Theory, Practice and Politics*, Aldershot, Avebury.

UNICEF (2007) *Child Poverty in Perspective: An Overview of Child Well-being in Rich Countries*, Innocenti Report Card 7, UNICEF, Florence, Innocenti Research Centre.

Vygotsky, L.S. (1978) *Mind and society: The Development of Higher Mental Processes*, Cambridge MA, Harvard University Press.

Chapter 1

Communicating with children

Gill Crow, Pam Foley and Stephen Leverett

Introduction

To connect with children, develop good working relationships and deliver good services, people who work with children need to understand how and why they communicate and what affects that communication.

Everyone in the children's workforce needs to be able to form, develop and sustain relationships not only with children but also with parents, carers, and other people who work with children. We believe that children have a right to, and are able to, communicate their views about the world in which they live. Good communication and listening skills, as well as specific knowledge, are vital in many different roles, contexts and settings.

> (Communication) is important because these are the people that you go to for advice so you should be able to talk to them about anything.
>
> (Child quoted in Turner, 2003, p. 30)

Communicating with children can involve touch, listening, tone of voice, gesture, playing, observing, reassuring, signing, explaining, receiving and transmitting information and interpreting and reflecting. It is a complex and value-laden process that draws on theoretical knowledge, cultural understanding and experience. When done badly it can be confusing, discriminatory, alienating, deflating, cause harm or create problems. When done well it can support positive relationships, support learning and development and contribute significantly to children's wellbeing. It can keep them safe, empower them, affirm their identity, encourage their creativity and help them to build sustaining and pleasurable relationships with other people – as well as inform the development and evaluation of children's services.

We cannot hope to cover everything, or even most things, associated with communicating with young children in this chapter. We will also be looking at communication and positive relationships later in this book (in Chapters 2 and 3), at the wider issues associated with child–adult relations (in Chapter 4) and at listening to children and children's participation (in Chapter 5). In this chapter we focus on why good communication is fundamental to good care and education, and on what affects communication. In the final section we will look at the different ways children communicate.

While most of our examples relate to work in education, play-work and health and social care practice, many of the skills we discuss and describe are relevant to other relationships, including relationships between children, and between children and other adults including their parents and carers.

Core questions

- How does communication support children's development?
- How do children communicate?
- What skills do practitioners need to be able to communicate effectively with children?
- What role does communication play in supporting children with different experiences and in different contexts?

1 Why is good communication important?

Good communication is frequently seen as key to solving problems and there are many reasons why communication skills need to be developed by people working with children. Some of these reasons are pragmatic, others more philosophical.

People working with children will need to communicate with them about generalities and specifics, about easy and difficult subjects, as individuals and in groups, in formal, semiformal and informal settings. Children's views are increasingly sought by adults; hearing the voices of children and involving them in decision making has become part of policy and practice for working with children in the UK. Making this widespread commitment to listening to children integral to workplace settings means making it part of the ethic of working, a way of working that permeates all practice and working relationships (Moss et al., 2005).

Listening is crucially important to children. It is easy to overlook the fact that, at times, the most important task of any parent, carer, or service provider is to relate directly and receptively, with attention and respect, to a child.

> Working with groups of children is an engrossing experience. Its almost constant business leads one to at times feel in a fusillade of noise, tempo and activities. Through this I became aware of the importance of 'looking and listening' when the children asked me to. I developed a determination not to let myself be interrupted by something or somebody else until a child had completed what he or she wanted me to see or hear.
>
> (Christensen, 2004, p. 169)

Anxieties about modern childhood include a concern that children now have poorer language development and are less able to communicate than children of previous generations. Some children now spend an increased amount of time outside their families which makes them more reliant on their ability to talk to their carers, on their carers' ability to communicate with them and on children's services to be responsive to their opinions, needs and aspirations. Such concerns have prompted a focus on communication within early intervention programmes and the improvement of communication skills amongst members of the children's workforce.

Communication may benefit groups of children who have, in the past, been perceived as vulnerable or marginalised. Most service provision for disabled children, for example, is still based on what adults and 'able-bodied' people provide for them; disabled children have yet to routinely take the lead in identifying and developing solutions for their own life problems (Davis et al., 2003).

> Monica went away to a school for Deaf children when she was five. 'I was saying no I want to stay home. My mum said no, you stay here and do your work, I'm going home, and I was miserable and said goodbye and gave her a hug and a kiss and my mum went off and I felt very shy and it was different.'
>
> (Morris, 1998, p. 8)

> People let me speak and say what I feel because they have to, but then ignore what I say because it's not what they want to do.
>
> (Disabled child quoted in Turner, 2003, p. 9)

Developing good communication skills and channels in children's services can also protect children. Children's dependency on adults to communicate their concerns and feelings leaves some children vulnerable; in particular, those cared for within state institutions. A failure to engage and communicate directly with the children themselves about their feelings, experiences and circumstances has been recognised as a common thread through a series of inquiries into child abuse and neglect (Parton, 2006).

Turner (2003) asked disabled children and young people to describe the world's worst health, education and social work professional. They compiled a list of the different views:

> Someone who **doesn't listen**
>
> Someone who thinks what is best for you **instead of asking** you
>
> Someone who talks to your parents **instead of you**
>
> Someone who **isn't very friendly** or happy and doesn't smile
>
> Someone who wants you to do things that you know **you can't do**
>
> Someone who **doesn't explain** what they are doing to you
>
> Someone who is **rude** and swears at you
>
> Someone who has **not got any manners**
>
> Someone who is **not caring** or helpful
>
> Someone who doesn't give you the right **information**
>
> Someone who **doesn't follow support** through
>
> Someone who is **unapproachable**

Someone who doesn't have enough time and is always **too busy**

Someone who **isn't interested** in you

Someone who **isn't dedicated** to their job

Someone who talks to you but you **can't understand** them

Someone who **only talks to your parents** because they think that you would not understand but hasn't bothered to find out if you can

Someone who is **boring**

(Turner, 2003, p. 19)

Thinking point 1.1   Most of the points in this list relate to poor communication. Can you transform it into a list of desirable communication skills for working with children?

If policy makers and practitioners decide to view children as developing but effective communicators, the great variety of practitioners now working with children will need to re-examine their workplace roles and relationships (Clark, 2005).

Children want practitioners to be 'kind', 'friendly', 'gentle', 'fair', 'respectful, 'trustworthy', 'patient' and 'reliable'. They also want them to tell the truth, to listen, understand, explain well and get things done on their behalf. Effective communication has to do with being as well as doing, how you are as a person as well as what you do (Luckock et al., 2006).

1.1 Communication and communication skills

Communication is fundamental to development; it is one of the ways in which children develop cognitively, socially, emotionally. Children need communication to develop their own communication skills and their understanding of their society and culture.

Communication between carer and baby plays a key role in the development of the infant's brain (Gerhardt, 2004). Through reciprocal interactions – the adult responding to a baby's movements, gestures, sounds, and direction of gaze – first **dyadic** relationships are the building blocks for connections in the brain. Soothing communications help build self-soothing skills, consistent communication patterns help build an understanding of cause and effect, early exposure to child-directed language lays the foundation for developing language, empathic responses help the child understand their own and others' emotions.

Dyadic – combining two people.

The early organisation within the brain underpins future learning, so early relationships have a profound impact on all aspects of development. Children who have not had an early experience of building a relationship with a carer who is tuned-in and responsive, particularly those who have suffered severe neglect or abuse, show restricted brain growth. They may experience difficulties in all areas of development due both to their failure to establish important neural pathways and their understanding of the world.

Children are primed to communicate from babyhood. Newborn babies will gaze intently at other people's faces, mimicking their gestures, and they respond to being held; right from the start, infants are using skills to connect with others. We expect the development of language, but many other skills are acquired before and during more complex communications. These gradually include attending to another person, listening, being able to take turns, using and responding to the subtleties of voice, gestures and facial expressions, understanding/interpreting other people's non-verbal communications and learning about social roles and rules.

Children are born into a social world

However, Hart and Risley's observational study of communication in families with young children showed some marked differences in the extent and nature of communication with children. They found that socioeconomic status made a highly significant difference to how much talking goes on in a family. In the families in which the parents were in professional and managerial occupations, the average number of parent utterances per hour when the baby was 11–18 months old, and had barely begun to speak, was 642, of which 482 were addressed to the baby. Among families receiving state benefits, the parents averaged 394 utterances per hour, of which 197 were addressed to the baby. They also observed that a child in a professional family was accumulating, on average, 32 affirmatives and 5 prohibitions per hour, while among families on state benefits, the average child experienced 5 affirmatives and 11 prohibitions. The authors made the point that, to redress this early and important imbalance, childcare outside the family needs to provide, from infancy, a substantial amount of additional hours of language and affirmative feedback (Hart and Risley, 1995).

This widely quoted study was undertaken to discover what in children's early experience could account for the wide differences in vocabulary extent among four-year-olds. Hart and Risley emphasised that vocabulary extent profoundly contributes to breadth of knowledge, analytic and symbolic competencies, self-confidence and problem-solving which are among the interlocking 'soft skills' needed for entry into an increasingly educated and skilled world. Studies such as theirs have been used to support the political argument that the first years of life are when good communication is most important and supportive skilled interventions most likely to be effective.

Acquiring communication skills and using them effectively not only needs awareness and knowledge of verbal and non-verbal communication, but also an understanding of cultural and social conventions. These include the use of metaphor and idiom, the range of language and its use in different situations, the use of jokes, puns and slang, and what might be called social conventions within conversation (for example the distinction between social 'white' lies and lying). Children learn these skills through experience of communicating, initially with their families. Children watch and learn from communications between other people – they directly observe their friends and peers, older children, family members, strangers and the practitioners who are involved in their care and education. Their experience includes interactions at an individual and group level, with adults and with other children, and using a range of different methods and techniques.

> Monica [a girl with a hearing impairment starting a new school] hadn't learnt to sign at her first school: 'I didn't understand signing and I was feeling a bit lost and I was wondering what was going on. The children tried to help me with the signing, teaching me to sign and slowly I started to learn to sign.'
>
> (Morris, 1998, p. 8)

1.2 Communication and cognitive development

Theories of learning from Piaget, Bruner, Vygotsky and others, suggest that children need to interact with their environment in order to construct schemas or mental models. The 'internal working model' children construct enables them to understand, interact, anticipate and plan in relation to their particular world.

Children's cognitive development is active, not passive: they take meaning from what they see, hear and experience and make sense of it within their own world view. Bruner (1966) suggests that it is an adult's task to provide an environment that stimulates inquiry, builds on previous experiences and facilitates extended thinking without overstretching the child. In Bruner's view, learning occurs through active dialogue.

One of the drivers to teaching and learning is the quality of dialogue between mentor and learner. In dialogue, as a joint enquiry through which all participants learn, children may learn new perspectives and the mentor/teacher may learn new things about the child. To explore children's understanding the mentor first listens and then may respond and prompt, explore or expand. Thus communication through action and conversation stimulates the development of thinking, placing the instructor in a learning role alongside the child.

One of the perennial questions in discussions about communication is whether language comes before thought, or vice versa, and how the two are interconnected.

Which comes first?

There is not room to explore it in detail here, but it is worth raising some key issues as they relate to the care and education of children. Vygotsky (1962) explored the interrelationship of language development and thought in his seminal work *Thought and Language*. He suggested that infants learn meaning through interaction with others and that thought therefore develops socially. Children use language as a social tool and to guide their own activities ('self-talk') then the self-talk evolves and becomes internalised as 'inner speech'. Vygotsky drew the distinction between normal 'external' speech and 'inner speech' which allows meanings and understandings to develop in thought. He did not suggest that thinking cannot take place without language, but that language as inner speech helps develop more sophisticated thinking and reasoning.

Debate over the links between language and thought was continued by, among others, Pinker (1998), who argued that language has an evolutionary basis and is created by the mind to express understandings we already have, and Turner (1996), who suggested that language follows from the use of story and parable and is created in order to understand our environment. Pinker's stance has been supported by experiments indicating that infants have concepts (that is, they can distinguish between objects on the basis of conceptual differences) before they have language (Hespos and Spelke, 2004). In other instances, children may use language before understanding the concepts it encompasses. Children may use the term 'river' but not understand the key concepts underlying the word: that water runs downhill for example (Platten, 1995). Exploring the meaning of a concept necessarily extends language.

It has also been suggested that different types of intelligence are linked to preferred ways of organising information about the world; for example Gardner (1983) proposed seven intelligences – linguistic, mathematical, musical, spatial, **kinetic**, interpersonal and intrapersonal. A non-linguistic way of thinking, for example, is described by Daniel Tammet who has Asperger syndrome. He sees numbers, time and words as colours and patterns and 'thinks' in this mode rather than through language (Tammet, 2007). There has been further debate on whether language shapes or constrains thought: the Sapir-Whorf hypothesis, for example, contends that the structure of their mother tongue influences the way individuals perceive the world (Kay and Kempton, 1984).

Kinetic – relating to motion.

These distinctions may seem largely academic, if interesting, but the debate is important when we consider the impact of language. Is thinking constrained or influenced by the language we use? For example it seems peculiar to some people (especially girls and women!) that animals are automatically referred to as 'he' unless their being female is particularly evident. It seems important to some to challenge assumptions that being male is the default position.

Thinking point 1.2   What do you think about challenges that are made about the use of the word 'black' – in terms such as 'black mark', 'black mood', 'black day' – to mean bad or negative? Does your workplace consider the language that it habitually uses because of the way language impacts on the way people think?

Children may be affected by these distinctions and become aware of them. One black pupil commented on the use of language in his school:

'around the school when it's white boys it's a group but when it's black boys it's a gang, and I think it's wrong'

(London Development Agency, 2004, p. 63)

The interplay of language and thought suggests that communication plays an important role in the development of cognitive schemas and thinking, and cognitive schemas and understandings shape people's day-to-day experience of the world. We are all building our own understanding of the world based on our experience, and will give different weight to, or perceive different relationships according to, the constructs we use (Kelly, 1991). Practitioners cannot therefore make assumptions about the understanding, perspective or abilities of children – nor for that matter of the children's parents and carers, or work colleagues. They can, however, use communication to understand, test or challenge their own perceptions or the assumptions of others.

1.3 Communication and emotional literacy

There are, of course, important overlaps between cognitive development and social and emotional development. Some aspects of social and emotional development require cognitive understandings, for instance, understanding different role categories and what you might expect from different people, such as an aunt, a teacher or a friend. However, the development of social/emotional and cognitive skills seems to be different, because we know that some children struggle with one area while being competent in another. Some children may have good social skills, and be comfortable interacting with a wide range of people, even if their ability to think and plan is compromised. Other children may be able to think and plan but lack the understanding of emotions and social rules to interact effectively.

Through their interaction with the world children are not only building an understanding of the material world, but also an understanding of people, their actions, emotions and relationships. They will be internalising ideas about love, trust, power, friendship and worthiness from their experience of others, participating in and observing communications. Communication plays a key part in every child's social and emotional development. Prioritising the development of social and emotional literacy can be one way in which individual settings develop their services for children.

Thinking point 1.3   The phrase 'emotional literacy' has gained widespread use. What do you understand this phrase to mean?

We not only communicate about things and events, we communicate about thoughts and feelings too – so communication provides a means to learn about your own internal worlds and those of others. The ability to understand and manage emotions in oneself and in others is often referred to as 'emotional literacy', or 'emotional intelligence'. There are a number of aspects of emotional literacy that may usefully be grouped, such as recognising your own emotional state, managing your own emotions, recognising others' emotions, being able to be explicit about feelings, and being able to talk about talking. These skills and understandings are important components with which to build and sustain relationships with others. Here a child describes how, in her school, a simple bully box can encourage children to communicate worries and feelings:

> 'Here at Wheatcroft School we show our feelings. For instance, we have a bully box where if anything is wrong or we are not sure about something, we write it down and then post it in the box. Normally the next day it would be sorted out. Me and my friends are proud of this because if we didn't have things like this we wouldn't be able to work as well because our problem would be stuck in our mind and we would be fidgeting and we wouldn't be concentrating on our work.'
>
> (Peacock and Wheatcroft School, 2001, p. 53)

Notice how she describes the bully box as useful for feelings which 'we are not sure about'. This illustrates the extent to which children sometimes require help to use language that identifies and names feelings and emotions. It also illustrates how, without help, children's emotions can get 'stuck in the mind' and subsequently impact on other areas of their life. The emotional content of communications and relationships – both verbal and non-verbal – can teach the child about their own and others' feelings, and caring relationships can model emotional connectedness, care and empathy.

Practitioners and policy makers have become more aware of the need to be explicit about supporting the development of emotional literacy in children, and a number of techniques and programmes have been developed. While there is some evidence that interventions have been effective in the short term, to be most effective, the ideas need to be embedded in the culture of the setting (Greenberg et al., 2003). It helps if an environment respects and values relationships and is itself emotionally literate. It is, it seems, not so much a case of teaching emotional literacy as modelling and developing it. This requires a whole school or community approach, capitalising on opportunities throughout the setting (Weare, 2004) and depends on a level of connectedness and sense of belonging with others (Gilmour, 2005). Even severe emotional trauma can, in some cases, be tackled through emotional relearning. With time, reassurance and careful support the effects of abuse, violence or neglect can, for some children, be reduced by looking at the source of their distress, revisiting the experience and developing other aspects of their emotional portfolio.

I: When you look back, can you think of any not-so-good things?

T: Making me talk about my Dad. It just made me bad tempered, and upset. [But] it got things, it cleared my head and I didn't have to worry.

(Interviewer and child in play therapy session, Carroll, 2002, p. 183)

I: When you look back on it now, what did you really like about it?

L: Explaining all my problems. She'd sort of like say everything would be alright, and I believed her; and everything was alright, so after I thought, well yea.

I: Was it you talking about it that made it feel better or her saying it was going to be alright?

L: Her saying it was going to be alright.

(Interviewer and child in play therapy session, Carroll, 2002, p. 183)

Learning emotional control is another dimension of emotional literacy. Children frequently experience feelings of happiness, sadness, loneliness, anger, fear, surprise and disgust; these are universal emotions, but part of being human is to learn to manage these and other complex emotions. This is a difficult task that often takes a lifetime. Many adults remain unaware of their feelings, have emotional outbursts that are unproductive and can be destructive of relationships. Through observing others' skills in communicating feelings, and being guided to develop individual skills and coping strategies, children can learn to control or channel their emotions. So practitioners who shout and 'lose it' while frequently reprimanding children for the same thing, who panic and 'fall to pieces' or who manipulate others, are teaching children and, in effect, communicating the acceptability of these strategies. Practitioners who can express their feelings effectively and demonstrate positive coping strategies are communicating a wealth of information to children about emotional control:

- the practitioner who can *demonstrate* social rules and understandings through their actions is communicating them to others

- *teaching* children what to do, when, helps them to develop behaviours that are socially acceptable

- *explaining* to a child social rules such as sharing, being polite, being fair, or letting everyone have a say, helps them see what is to be gained by such rules

> - *supporting children's communication* with others creates opportunities for them to develop and practise their social skills and emotional literacy.

Intricately linked to the ability to understand the emotions and standpoint of others, is the development of social skills. Through interaction and communication with others, children watch, learn and absorb the values and rules of social interaction.

Many of the social skills needed to function effectively in a complex world are difficult, and this is particularly so in relation to managing conflict and negotiating what we want. When children are arguing over a toy, or who should go first or when they are 'breaking up friends' they experience conflict and develop ways to manage conflict. Practising solving conflict can help them develop skills of negotiation and conflict resolution: if an adult solves it, the experience is distanced. On the other hand, when adults stop bullying, or even violence, the children involved may need to observe how someone else resolves things.

The way people communicate with us, and what they communicate, also tells us about ourselves. The information we receive contributes to the development of our identity or self-image.

Thinking point 1.4   Can you recall being assigned an identity that did not match your own opinion of yourself? How was this communicated to you? What impact did this have on you at the time? Does it still affect you today?

People communicate judgements when they communicate with a child, including what kind of person they consider the child to be. 'Oh, you are so untidy', 'you stupid girl', 'you haven't forgotten your coat again, have you?', 'don't be so fussy', 'I wish you were more like your brother' – many things carry (often unintended) negative messages. Other messages may contribute to the development of a positive identity: 'how kind you are', 'you have drawn that beautifully', 'you learnt that very quickly', 'what a lovely singing voice you have'. Some messages may be ambiguous, and rely much more on the context for their interpretation – for example 'you don't give up easily, do you?' could mean 'you are pestering me, you're a nuisance', if it is said in a tone that conveys irritation, or 'you have kept going to reach your goal, your determination is great', if it is said in an admiring tone.

1.4 Communication, cultural understandings and social identity

Cultural understandings are embedded in communication. These include assumptions and expectations about how people will behave and relate to one another, such as attitudes to authority, autonomy and responsibility, independence and conformity, relationships between men and women, girls and boys and about generations. All these are transmitted through communications within the child's peer group and family, within institutions, community and the media. Everyone has internalised some cultural values and identity and some of the assumptions and opinions of different nations, religions and ethnic identities. The ways in which practitioners communicate will contribute further to the cultural understandings and identities of individuals and groups – and many practitioners broaden concepts and discuss differences to explore different values and beliefs.

Societal assumptions, albeit based on stereotypes and prejudices, can impact upon a child's identity and self-esteem. An artistic child may be valued and encouraged in one milieu, developing a positive identity and self-esteem, but be ridiculed and feel a disappointment to others in another family or environment. Contradictory expectations arise across different environments. A child from a family that believes that boys are more important than girls, for example, may become confused and angry in an environment where girls and boys are expected to compete on equal terms.

Gender identity is very clearly assigned by cultures, as are many other aspects of identity that are communicated to children and may affect their feelings of self-worth, including how different religions, ethnicities and sexualities are represented. (Consider how children are sometimes told to 'act your age', 'girls can't play football', 'boys don't care about what they wear', 'that's not the behaviour we expect of you'.) Groups with identities and, often, labels, assigned by cultures may include different ethnic minorities, travellers, Looked After children, refugees, children with special educational needs and disabled children. Communications can unwittingly reinforce a perception in a child that 'they', as part of a particular culture, class or group, are different or 'other'.

We know that the identities communicated to a child can affect their wellbeing and development. Expectations are communicated covertly through tone of voice, the extent and kind of attention given and the experiences to which children are guided (Rosenthal, 2003). Some high-achieving Looked After children interviewed about their education, for example, thought that negative stereotypes and low expectations were major obstacles to their educational success within the care system (Martin and Jackson, 2002). Low expectations within the education system of Black and minority ethnic children, particularly those of African-Caribbean heritage, have also been shown to affect their outcomes. From the 1960s onwards, studies have identified some key issues for African-Caribbean children in UK schools:

- Low expectations of academic success
- High expectations of challenges to authority
- Unequal behaviour management with harsher reprimands
- Excessive levels of control, provoking conflict
- Repression of attempts to contribute (for example, ignoring raised hands, not giving response times to allow the expression of views; one study found that white pupils had up to three times the opportunity to initiate talk than black pupils)
- Failure to tackle institutional racism
- Communications received within school experienced as devaluing, unfair and undermining.

(London Development Agency, 2004).

Children have their own individual and collective identity. It is a practitioner's task, in order to connect with children, to learn about the child's world, to be able to interpret their experience. This remains true as children get older.

Key points

1   Building relationships through communication is a major part of caring for, and educating, children and has a significant impact on all areas of their wellbeing.

2   Communication can reinforce children's self-esteem and contribute to cultural understandings and the reinforcement of identities.

3   Emotional literacy is an increasingly widespread concept, supported through early years and schools, but this needs to be modelled rather than simply taught.

4   Communication can have an effect on identity and the identity development of children.

5   Effective communication can enable the fulfilment of children's rights to protection, provision and participation.

2 What affects communication?

In addition to social and cultural influences, personal history will have shaped the 'internal working model' children and adults have of how the world works, upon which they base their expectations of others. For instance, if a child has been very frequently shouted at by the adults in their life, they will expect all adults to shout. They will therefore approach adults with that expectation, and if they are not shouted at, they might not take requests seriously. Perhaps they will not be able to listen well because they are anxiously waiting for the shouting to start; or perhaps they will be suspicious of an adult who is being 'nice' and not trust them.

Language is a means to express yourself through forming opinions and describing experiences. Equally it can provide a learning experience through constructive encounters with the needs, values, rights and opinions of others. Power relations and inequalities are also an important feature of communication. Power and powerlessness are not fixed to categories such as 'child' or 'adult' but rather in the social representations of these that are made, disputed, negotiated and worked out (Christensen, 2004).

Moss et al. (2005) identified several ways in which power relations can distort and undermine attempts to genuinely listen to children. Listening can be a method of directing and defining what can and cannot be discussed, and may thereby serve to bring children under more adult management. Similarly, the language of participation may be substituted for conflict, effectively dissipating pressure and thereby supporting existing power differentials.

The kinds of things that may affect your communication skills are physical and emotional states, personalities, disabilities, cultural diversity, the environment in which the communication takes place and the circumstances in which the communication takes place. But studies of communication skills and processes have suggested these three key skills that may be vital to model in work with children:

- *expressive skills* for stating a point of view non-defensively – including emotional skills to express feelings

- *listening skills* for learning about another's point of view – which requires being able to postpone voicing your own concerns and opinions to understand those of others

- *process skills* to understand and manage the overall interaction – negotiating the rules of the interaction, identifying what information is needed and appropriate, interpreting the information received in its context, and ending the interaction.

(Dick, 1986)

Thinking point 1.5 Think about your own communication skills in these three categories. Are some of your key skills stronger than others? What do you think affects your expressive, listening and processing skills?

2.1 Physical and emotional factors

How you feel physically will also affect how you communicate. Children have less experience and skill in coping with physical adversity than adults – they may be more affected by tiredness, hunger and thirst, illness and pain, and unable to interact effectively with others when in these states.

Some schools take direct action to reduce the possible effect of hunger on the school day: this is a breakfast club

Lack of sleep may be another issue, as many children's sleep patterns do not meet their physical and physiological needs. Sadeh (2000) found that twenty per cent of primary school age children have serious sleep problems; in another study, ten per cent of children were found to fall asleep at school (Owens et al., 2000).

Often feelings affect the ability to communicate; children or adults who are anxious, stressed, alienated or angry can't communicate well. There is a clear physiological explanation for this: the perception of threat causes the release of the hormones cortisol and adrenalin which block cognitive and memory processes and trigger the fight, flight or freeze reaction. High emotions can block thought. We say and do things we would not normally say or do, we are less in control of ourselves. Emotions also tend to interfere with our ability to concentrate – we don't listen so well and so we easily miss information or misinterpret the message.

> 'I think it's when something's said that sort of affects me or I feel upset about I think that from then on it's really difficult for me to concentrate and listen to what anyone else is saying because I'm just sort of going through in my head all my thoughts and I'm not really paying attention ...'
>
> (Child quoted in Strickland-Clark et al., 2000, p. 330)

Adults working with children need to be particularly aware of both children's and their own emotional state, and the way this impacts on communication. If something the child does or says pushes a particular button for us and we suddenly get angry, we may do or say something unusual – our emotion has overwhelmed our ability to be thoughtful or logical. If we, as adults, are affected by our emotions to that extent, think how much more children are likely to be affected, because they have much less experience of understanding what is going on, or of recognising and managing their emotions.

Inevitably practitioners will, at some point, work with children who are experiencing, among other things, loss, neglect, grief, family illness, bullying, family violence, or family separation. Good communication can support children through many sad or traumatic experiences. It can also enable them to take part in decision making in particular stressful circumstances, such as family law cases or medical investigation or treatment.

For children in physical states, emotional states, or a combination of physical and emotional states, the most helpful communication is clear and calm:

- *Containing emotions*: remaining calm and confident, using a firm but neutral/positive tone of voice and body language. This gives a strong message that the carer is in control of themselves and is not frightened or overwhelmed by the child's emotions.

- *Acknowledging and understanding the emotion*: acknowledging the emotion shows empathy, and an understanding that emotions occur whether you want them or not. Carers can refer to the emotion, or communicate empathy through body language and voice: 'I know you really want to go out', 'I think you're having a difficult time today', 'You set your heart on that toy didn't you?'.

- *Making it clear that certain behaviour is not acceptable*: by explaining that the behaviour is not OK: 'Screaming and crying/hitting people/fighting over the toy is not acceptable here', 'We can't sort out problems like that'.

- *Helping with recurring problems*: show you care by speaking to them privately in a non-threatening way. Discuss the problem and ways to solve it.

- *Helping to calm down and manage or express feelings in appropriate ways*: depending on the child or the context, specific strategies may help, for example, using Makaton symbols, drawing or playing.

Children who have been traumatised or who have experienced upsetting events may present as active and aggressive or they may react in the opposite way, by withdrawing, becoming quieter, less involved, less inclined to join in and easily upset. Childcare settings and schools can be havens for children, providing a safe, calm and predictable environment away from the difficulties they may be experiencing elsewhere. Communicating to children that they are welcome in this haven, and continuing to provide care and predictability, can be of great help. There is a school of thought that settings should not get involved at all with outside events that affect the child, but should carry on as always, acting as if everything is all right, believing that this provides the child with a haven. The opposite viewpoint is that children's experiences are real and that to act as though everything is all right is to deny reality and their feelings about it. Places or practitioners taking this stance might make considerable allowances and try to create opportunities to talk.

Understanding behaviour helps establish effective communication. We have already alluded to the 'fight or flight' reactions that are prompted when people feel under threat. These reactions are reflexes – the person does not 'think' about them – and whilst people's lives are rarely under threat, their feeling of safety may be threatened by many things. If a child or adult feels their safety or personal integrity is under threat, they may respond instinctively by fighting, running away or freezing.

A child's behaviour might therefore be a message that they feel that their safe world is under threat. There are many things that can threaten a child's safe world: being bullied at home or outside home, parents arguing or fighting, adults in their life who are out of control or unavailable, being told off for things they do not understand, the family under threat, for example, of eviction or violence, someone ill, dying or disappearing, new people coming into the picture. In these circumstances the child is not behaving badly by choice. Are they behaving badly because they feel anxious, scared, lonely, confused, rejected or bad about themselves?

While providing 'sameness' is very comforting to children, trauma and upset may make it difficult for them to meet usual expectations. Allowances may therefore be appropriate – but if you change the rules for them too much, you remove the certainty and safety that is so valuable. People can be helped to recognise cause and effect between behaviour and context and find new understandings and, maybe, solutions. This is, of course, no easy task in the complex world of real and everyday parenting, everyday practice and everyday lives.

2.2 Disabilities and communication

If a child has a disability in any area of functioning (physical, sensory, cognitive or social), their communication is likely to be affected. There are a number of common themes to consider in connection with communicating with disabled children:

- Understanding their communications – difficulties identifying and understanding communication can lead to avoidance.

- Finding new ways to communicate – using other means of communication may require creativity, training and resources – for example, signing, visual displays, using computer technology.

- Using materials that are age-appropriate, are chosen by the child and suit the child's communication skills.

The particular communication solutions will depend on the particular impairment, but, whatever the situation, it is essential for practitioners to seek and find ways to connect with disabled children (Sigafoos et al., 2006; Beukelman and Mirenda, 2005).

Children need to be able to use a wide variety of communication methods

Children with cerebral palsy, for example, may be unable to coordinate or use their body sufficiently to communicate their thoughts through speech. These children may need communication aids (for example, electronic word keyboard or translator).

Communication systems that use an individual child's strengths, using a modified or unmodified computer, for example, may be appropriate. However, a child may not have symbolic understanding, meaning that their communication is directly through sounds and movement. Amaral (2003) found that carers often missed opportunities to respond to children's non-symbolic communication because they were not attending to the cues: analysing communication that had been videoed raised awareness and improved communication.

Children with social and communication difficulties, such as those on the autistic spectrum, can pose different challenges (Browne, 2006). Many of these children have sensory sensitivities, being unable to cope with loud noise, bright lights, or touch. Their inability to understand their social world often causes them very high anxiety, as they cannot make sense of their surroundings. For this reason, communication that is based on concrete impersonal systems, such as the Picture Exchange Communication System (PECS) (Bondy and Frost, 2001), is effective, and effective teaching may require finding motivations other than social praise and encouragement. Picture sequences can help children follow and learn routines, and children with language and/or cognitive difficulties can be helped significantly in this way.

Communication aids can help children express themselves

Children, such as those with Asperger syndrome, may use language but get the pragmatics of communication wrong. They can be helped through teaching communication skills that other children would pick up naturally, and perhaps through gaining an intellectual understanding of their own difficulties.

Communication can be impeded when practitioners rely on adult or practitioner-centred verbal or narrowly focused methods. This is particularly true when communicating with children with impairments if practitioners fail to use the child's primary mode of communication, do not accept help from others who know the child well, do not use observation to make sense of indirect communication, or do not appreciate a child's frustrations and show respect for them (Luckock et al., 2006).

2.3 Personality and communication

The personality and temperament of a child affect their communication, and the kind of communication styles that are most effective for them (Pauley et al., 2002). As parents know, all children are different: some are calm and placid, others are shy, some are born optimists, others have masses of self-esteem. Childhood presents many opportunities for emotional learning and change, so characteristics such as these may become more or less pronounced. There may be marked differences between children in terms of activity levels, regularity of sleeping and eating patterns, adaptability, intensity of emotion, mood, distractibility, persistence and attention span, and sensory sensitivity. Added to this, of course, is the fact that the practitioners with whom they are communicating all have different personalities and temperaments too.

Aspects of children's personalities fluctuate according to the people they are with. Certain combinations of people may inhibit the communication of some individuals within the group. Calmer children do not get upset easily, they manage change well, they don't get anxious – but they may need active engagement and stimulating experiences to engage them effectively. Some children may be quickly overexcited, or anxious, which leads them to cut off from stimuli; they may need a quieter, low-stimulation environment to enable them to focus and engage. All these factors combine to make the simultaneous care and education of large groups of children so difficult to do well.

2.4 Social and cultural differences

Attitudes to those in positions of responsibility, the relationship of individuals to society, ways of resolving conflict, expressing thoughts and feelings and behaviour in social institutions are, to a considerable extent, embedded in culture. For example, a classroom in Japan might look very different to a classroom in the UK. A child from Japan might come into a British classroom expecting quiet study, rote learning and a respectful distance from the teacher; the teacher might interpret the new student's behaviour as socially withdrawn and consider them reluctant to participate in learning (Samovar et al., 1999).

A practitioner may need to be proactive in finding out about the different perspectives of children and families; identifying cultural references within various communities, and talking to children and parents about their experiences and expectations of the people who work with them, for example.

Children's 'culture' takes a variety of fast-changing forms through which they can connect with others

Thinking point 1.6   How are ideas about a school's culture (primary or secondary) communicated to a child before they start school? What effect could this have on communication between the child and people at school on the first day?

Children learn about life in school, for example, through listening to other children, including their siblings, through television programmes and books, through their own experiences, and through the way their primary carers and people in their social networks communicate verbally and non-verbally about school.

Children develop their own language, signs and symbols through which they communicate – their words, choice of hairstyle, dress, music, activities and so on are all used to communicate messages to their peer group. Adults sometimes find this cultural difference bewildering, and can be nervous of communicating with children and young people. So culture can inhibit as well as influence communication. This may also be due to language acquisition, linguistic differences or different mother tongue. Establishing the communication choices of others, rather than making assumptions, is respectful and shows a willingness to communicate well. Other useful strategies for effective communication in the children's setting include using interpreters, translating materials, checking understanding and adapting, or offering opportunities to increase understanding of the language used. There is controversy about using a variety of languages, for example, exposing children to literature that is written in colloquial language or patois. Some argue that this maintains barriers between people while others argue that adopting different languages signals inclusivity, a willingness to embrace cultural difference and an acknowledgement of the validity of the experience of different cultural groups. In the USA controversy has focused on 'Ebonics' – understanding and using the language style or patois of the black population in the classroom (Bohn, 2003).

2.5 Environmental factors

The factors affecting communication considered so far have concentrated on *internal* states and understandings. Yet the external environment also has a considerable impact on how we communicate – factors such as how hot or cold the room is, what the seating arrangements are or how bright the light is. Noise can be a particular problem for both children and adults in children's settings. Some people can filter out background noise to focus on speech while others struggle to distinguish between meaningful and non-meaningful sounds and some children are particularly sensitive to noise. Other factors may be more subtle, but can still have a significant effect, for example some children are sensitive to light and others find it difficult to cope with close proximity to peers. These sensory sensitivities are commonly recognised in autistic children, but may be much more prevalent than is generally thought (Greenspan and Wieder, 2006). The importance of linking children to the natural environment has been emphasised by others because connection to the natural world can reduce stress.

The Reggio Emilia approach to early learning places a high emphasis on the environment, using natural light, natural materials and found objects

Seating arrangements within the environment can also have a significant effect on communication. Have you ever had an appointment to see someone who sat in a large important chair behind a desk, while you sat in a smaller, perhaps lower chair? This is a fairly common experience for adults visiting the doctor and for parents going to talk to teachers. What messages are communicated through the seating arrangement? What effect might this have on the communication between these adults?

Within children's settings seating arrangements are often variable: children sit on the floor for some activities, and may be grouped around tables for others. Children have differing views on these arrangements, which may impact on their ability to listen and communicate well (Kershner and Pointon, 2000). Practitioners should also consider how settings are decorated and cared for, and the impact this might have on the way adults and children communicate. A child in a room with formal furniture, delicate china ornaments and dark paintings on the wall is likely to communicate with the adults present in a different way than if they met the same adults in an environment with more relaxed, modern furniture and children's toys and games. It may benefit adults to consult with children about environments in order to effectively communicate; for example, a social worker could ask a child how they would like a meeting room organised prior to a multi-professional review meeting (to discuss the child's current and future care). A child might prefer something different from offices, desks and chairs. The environment is one area about which children can be consulted; it is clear that children can and do 'read' settings (Ruddock et al., 1996; Kershner and Pointon, 2000).

Key points

1   Communication is affected by various factors which need to be considered: physical and emotional states, personality, disability, cultural diversity and the environment, and the circumstances in which the communication takes place.

3 Communicating in different ways

There are many other channels and modes of communication apart from language. Appreciating the many ways in which people can communicate can help you to capitalise on the range of opportunities available to communicate with children. A pluralistic approach is one that will be most likely to positively affect the greatest number of children.

3.1 Play

Children can use play and games to explore and communicate their understanding of the world. Providing time and space, maybe toys for play can enable children to explore different feelings, roles and experiences and communicate the things that are important to them. Dressing-up clothes, farm and zoo animals (including family groups), scary toys, domestic equipment, puppets and dolls are all useful for facilitating communication between children and between children and adults. If children feel safe when playing they will be able to choose to explore what is important.

Dolls can help children cope in difficult circumstances, to absorb information, to prepare themselves and to make choices

Even older children, given a safe space, can use games to communicate feelings that are difficult to articulate. Watching a child at play can tell you a lot about their understanding of the world, and playing alongside them provides opportunities for communication. Genuine interest, a belief in its value to children, and letting the child, or children, take the lead are key skills to enabling play.

Play can also be used to build communication with very young children and with those who struggle to use speech, whether due to developmental or emotional difficulties. Through sharing in play, showing through play and talking about play the practitioner can connect to the child and strengthen their communicative skills.

3.2 Visual methods of communication

Art communicates visually. From simple scribbles to detailed drawings or making models, what children make, and how they make it, can communicate something of their understanding, experiences and feelings.

Children often express feelings about their friendships, family and wider social circumstances through art. If a child draws a picture of their family, the drawing may convey information not only about the composition of the family but also about how those people relate to each other, their relative importance and their roles.

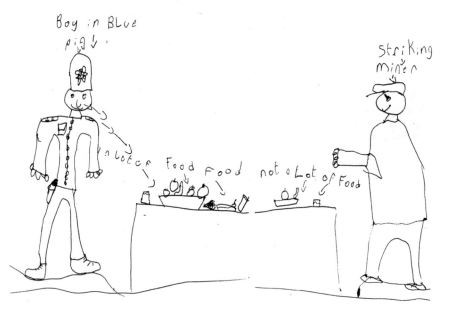

Here a boy from a mining family represents aspects of the world as he saw it during the 1984 miners' strike (Hoyles and Hemmings, 1985)

A child scribbling all over a piece of paper in black pen may be communicating something very different from a child scribbling with a red or a green pen, or a child doing a very small black scribble in one corner. Interpreting visual communication is a bit of an art in itself, and practitioners should not attempt to read too much into children's offerings – it's often enough to just share, and sometimes being alert can help you understand and tune in to children.

Pictures can also be used to aid communication. Many nurseries have picture labels by children's coat hooks which communicate ownership. Pictures on drawers can tell children what is in there, pictures in the cloakroom can remind children to wash their hands, and so on.

3.3 Books and stories

Books, their language and pictures, are highly effective methods of communication. Most obviously books contribute to children's vocabulary and language development. However, books can also be a wonderful stimulus for exploring social and emotional issues and coping with new experiences. Books about transitions and key life events such as starting nursery, having a new baby in the family or going to the doctor or dentist are useful in this respect. Some books specifically aim to address social and emotional issues relevant to children with stories that mirror some children's experiences. Adults can use these to help children reflect on their experience of the world: the story distances the child from the personal and can free them to both appreciate different perspectives and feel that their own situations and feelings are acknowledged. However, it can often be difficult to find a book that meets the needs of a particular situation, in which case the practitioner can make up stories, or involve children in making up a story, to mirror events and feelings (Sunderland, 2000).

Narrative theory suggests that humans create a narrative of their life, constructing a view of themselves and locating themselves in time and context (Gergen and Gergen, 2003). Stories can help children anticipate difficult events, understand the consequences of actions, and consider and accommodate feelings. In this way, story-telling can be seen as a type of discourse for making meaning. Stories, both written and spoken, can help children create and amend their personal narrative so that it is coherent and meaningful. Children particularly enjoy hearing stories of past events in which they were involved and the history of their familiar environment.

3.4 Humour

Children appreciate humour; they tend to laugh more than adults, and while their use of jokes and humour depends on their age and the setting, they can delight in surprise and sounds from a very early age. As they begin to know more about the world around them, and about how humour works, they enjoy language and games rooted in humour and will enjoy their own jokes as well as those of other children and of adults.

Humour has been identified as a key component of effective communication and is sometimes described as a 'social lubricant'.

Introducing humour appropriately enables both adults and children to feel on the same level, share meanings and experiences, and establish or maintain relationships. Humour humanises and personalises communication in many situations where communication is difficult. Humour can reduce stress, create positive connections and establish a good atmosphere within which other interactions can take place. The following line was taken from a poem written collectively by a group of children. They cannot resist the temptation to have a joke at the expense of their teacher, yet the humour also appears to be communicating a level of trust and fondness for Mrs Wills:

> Boredom is having nothing to do, poetry with Mrs Wills (only joking!)
>
> (Foster Care Associates, 2000, p. 12)

It is recognised by all the professions working with children as highly beneficial to developing working relationships. This child is responding positively to the way her play therapist used humour and mild teasing:

> She'd say how pretty I looked in my school uniform, how cheerful I was; I lost one of my teeth once and she said, she kept saying "Have you been kissing a lot of boys lately?" and I went "No".
>
> (Child quoted in Carroll, 2002, p. 183)

Thinking point 1.7   Humour can also be deflating, even cruel at times. Can you think of an example of when humour was used to support rather than challenge stereotypes?

3.5 Words and music

> The Park
>
> I play on the seesaw and swings,
>
> I see the grass and trees,
>
> The park smells of fire,
>
> When I am on my own it is quiet,
>
> When I am with my friends I shout and call,
>
> That is when I like the park.
>
> (Child's poem in Foster Care Associates, 2000, p. 36)

As children become more competent with written language, writing can be used as an effective medium for communication. This can be through poems, stories, letters, or electronic methods. The written word can carry more weight than speech; a written criticism or compliment, for example, may have greater power than a spoken one. Creative writing can enable children to explore feelings and experiences with the safety of distance through using fictitious figures. Stories do not have to be logical, they can use metaphor and myth to explore alternative narratives and futures (Fisher, 1987). Keeping a diary can help children record and reflect on their daily lives, with beneficial impact on their wellbeing (Reynolds et al., 2000). And children can also initiate and sustain friendships using the technology to which increasing numbers have access.

Music can also help engage children, provide a medium for exploring experience and be used therapeutically (Lefevre, 2004). For these reasons it is used by play therapists, child psychotherapists and family therapists as well as by practitioners who know how much pleasure music can give children and adults alike.

3.6 Old technologies, new technologies

Communication methods change and develop constantly. In the last few decades there have been many significant changes to methods of communication, including the advent of email, texting and instant messaging.

Many children are adept at using modes of communication less familiar to older generations

Children can lead the way in adopting new forms of communication that are significant for friendships and establishing and maintaining children's culture and identities.

Example of texting language:

> Hi hun wt r u up 2? RoFL dis guy @ skewl iz wel anoyin bcos he kept askin me 2 go up da city 2 a movie lol. I thort mayb we cud go up dere dis sat? kk ring me c u @ skewl btw cn u tel me hv we gt ne hmwrk 4 2moro? Cyaz

Translation:

> Hello friend, what are you up to? It was really funny (Rolling on Floor Laughing) this guy at school is very annoying because he kept asking me to go up to the city to a movie, laughing out loud. I thought maybe we could go up there this Saturday? Okay cool. Ring me. See you at school. By the way can you tell me have we got any homework for tomorrow? See you.

Electronic communication does not have to be emotionless. New conventions for expressing feelings have developed in parallel with new modes of communication, notably the creative punctuation and emoticons used online and in text messaging:

> :-) or ☺ (smiley)
>
> :-(or ☹ (sad)
>
> :s or :-S (confused)

Some argue that information technology is damaging children's ability to communicate articulately and effectively. Others maintain that many different communication media and styles can be used effectively and that ignoring children's communication experiences using new technologies is to ignore their skills, interests and how they respond to new opportunities.

Key points

1 Appreciating the many ways in which children communicate is a key skill for those in the children's workforce. A pluralistic approach is one that will be most likely to positively affect the greatest number of children.

Conclusion

Understanding the nature of children's communication will support the growth of adult skills aimed at connecting with children, keeping children informed and involved, and developing a positive working relationship. A knowledge of barriers to communication and how to overcome them could support a practitioner to actively listen, avoid assumptions and increase practice inclusivity.

Children, like adults, use a wide range of methods of communication about a wide range of issues. Good communication skills are fundamental to building a rapport with children, to knowing how to present and provide genuine choices and key information and to empathy and making them feel valued.

References

Amaral, I. (2003) 'Analysing teacher/child interactions', *Deafblind International Review*, no. 32, pp. 12–18, available online at <http://www.deafblindinternational.org/standard/review1_b.html >, accessed 2 August 2007.

Beukelman, D.R. and Mirenda, P. (2005) *Augmentative and Alternative Communication: Supporting Children and Adults with Complex Communication Needs*, Baltimore, MD, Brookes Publishing Co.

Bohn, A.P. (2003) 'Using Ebonics communication techniques in the classroom', *Urban Education*, vol. 38, no. 6, pp. 688–707.

Bondy, A. and Frost, L. (2001) 'The Picture Exchange Communication System', *Behaviour Modification*, vol. 25, pp. 725–744.

Browne, M.E. (2006) 'Communicating with the child who has autistic spectrum disorder: a practical introduction', *Paediatric Nursing*, vol. 18, no. 1, pp. 14–18.

Bruner, J. (1966) *Toward a Theory of Instruction*, Cambridge, MA, Harvard University Press.

Carroll, J. (2002) 'Play therapy: the children's views', *Child & Family Social Work*, vol. 7, no. 3, pp. 177–187.

Christensen, P. (2004) 'Children's participation in ethnographic research: issues of power and representation', *Children & Society*, vol. 18, pp. 165–176.

Clark, A., Kjorholt, A.T. and Moss, P. (2005) *Beyond Listening: Children's Perspectives on Early Childhood Services*, Bristol, The Policy Press.

Davis, J., Watson, N., Corker, M. and Shakespeare, T. (2003) 'Reconstructing disability, childhood and policy in the UK' in Hallett, C. and Prout, A. (eds) *Hearing the Voices of Children. Social Policy for a New Century*, London, Routledge Falmer.

Dick, B. (1986) *Learning to Communicate*, Brisbane, University of Queensland.

Fisher, W.R. (1987) *Human Communication as Narration: Toward a Philosophy of Reason, Value, and Action*, Columbia, University of South Carolina Press.

Foster Care Associates (FCA) (2000) *It's Mad That's All. A Collection of Poems about Being Looked After*, Bromsgrove, Foster Care Associates.

Gardner, H. (1983) *Frames of Mind: The Theory of Multiple Intelligences*, New York, Badic Books.

Gergen, K. and Gergen, M. (2003) *Social Construction: A Reader*, London, Sage.

Gerhardt, S. (2004) *Why Love Matters*, London, Brunner-Routledge.

Gilmour, K. (2005) 'Maximising the potential of pastoral care groups', AHIGS Conference Shore School, cited in Nemec, M. and Roffey, S. (2006) 'Emotional literacy and the case for a whole-school approach to promote sustainable educational change', *Australian Educational Researcher*, available online at <http://www.aare.edu.au/05pap/nem05355.pdf>, accessed 2 August 2007.

Greenberg, M., Weissberg, R., O'Brien, M., Zins, J. and Fredericks, L. (2003) 'Enhancing school-based prevention and youth development through coordinated social, emotional and academic learning', *American Psychologist*, vol. 58, nos 6–7, pp. 466–474.

Greenspan, S. and Wieder, S. (2006) *Infant and Early Childhood Mental Health: A Comprehensive Developmental Approach to Assessment and Intervention*, Washington DC, American Psychiatric Publishing.

Hart, B. and Risley, T.R. (1995) *Meaningful Differences in the Everyday Experience of Young American Children*, Baltimore, MD, Brookes Publishing Co.

Hespos, S. and Spelke, E. (2004) 'Conceptual precursors to language', *Nature*, vol. 430, no. 6998, 22 July, pp. 453–456.

Hoyles, M. and Hemmings, S. (1985) *More Valuable than Gold. A Collection of Writings on the Miner's Strike of 1984–1985 by Striking Miners' Children*, London, Martin Hoyles.

Kay, P. and Kempton, W. (1984) 'What is the Sapir-Whorf hypothesis?', *American Anthropologist*, vol. 86, no. 1, pp. 65–79.

Kelly, G. (1991) *The Psychology of Personal Constructs; Volume 1: A Theory of Personality*, London, Routledge.

Kershner, R. and Pointon, P. (2000) 'Children's views of the primary classroom as an environment for working and learning', *Research in Education*, vol. 64, November, pp. 64–77.

Lefevre, M. (2004) 'Playing with sound: the therapeutic use of music in direct work with children', *Child & Family Social Work*, vol. 9, no. 4, pp. 333–345.

London Development Agency (LDA) (2004) *The Educational Experiences and Achievements of Black Boys in London Schools 2000–2002*, London, LDA.

Luckock, B., Lefevre, M., Orr, D., Jones, M., Marchant, R. and Tanner, K. (2006) *Teaching, Learning and Assessing Communication Skills with Children and Young People in Social Work Education*, Social Care Institute for Excellence, Bristol, The Policy Press.

Martin, P. and Jackson, S. (2002) 'Educational success for children in public care: advice from a group of high achievers', *Child & Family Social Work*, vol. 7, no. 2, pp. 121–130.

Morris, J. (1998) *Still Missing, Volume 1. The Experience of Disabled Children and Young People Living Away from Their Families*, London, JRF and Who Cares Trust.

Moss, P., Clark, A. and Kjorholt, A.T. (eds) (2005) *Beyond Listening. Children's Perspectives on Early Childhood Services*, Bristol, The Policy Press.

Owens, J.A., Spirito, A., McGuinn, M. and Nobile, C. (2000) 'Sleep habits and sleep disturbance in elementary school aged children', *Journal of Developmental Behavioural Paediatrics*, vol. 21, no. 1, pp. 27–36.

Parton, N. (2006) *Safeguarding Childhood: Early Intervention and Surveillance in a Late Modern Society*, Basingstoke, Palgrave Macmillan.

Pauley, J.A., Bradley, D. and Pauley, J.F. (2002) *Here's How to Reach Me – Matching Instruction to Personality Types in Your Classroom*, Baltimore, MD, Brookes Publishing Co.

Peacock, A. and Wheatcroft School (2001) 'Working as a team: children and teachers learning from each other', *FORUM*, vol. 43, no. 2, pp. 51–53.

Pinker, S. (1998) *How the Mind Works*, London, Penguin.

Platten, L.B. (1995) 'Talking geography: young children's understandings of geographical terms', *International Journal of Early Years Education*, vol. 3, pp. 174–179.

Reynolds, M., Brewin, C.R. and Saxton, M. (2000) 'Emotional disclosure in school children', *Journal of Child Psychology and Psychiatry*, vol. 41, no. 2, pp. 151–159.

Rosenthal, R. (2003) 'Covert communication in laboratories, classrooms and the truly real world', *Current Directions in Psychological Science*, vol. 12, no. 50, pp. 151–154.

Ruddock, J., Chaplain, R. and Wallace, G. (eds) (1996) *School Improvement: What Can Pupils Tell Us?*, London, Fulton.

Sadeh, A. (2000) 'Sleep patterns and sleep disruptions in school age children', *Developmental Psychology*, vol. 36, May, pp. 291–301.

Samovar, L.A., Porter, R.E. and McDaniel, E.R. (1999) *Communication Between Cultures* (6th edn), Belmont, CA, Wadsworth Publishing.

Sigafoos, J., Arthur-Kelly, M. and Butterfield, N. (eds) (2006) *Enhancing Everyday Communication for Children with Disabilities*, Baltimore, MD, Brookes Publishing Co.

Smith, B. (2004) 'Boy's Business: an unusual North Australia music programme for boys in the middle years of schooling', *International Journal of Music Education*, vol. 22, no. 3, pp. 230–236.

Strickland-Clark, L., Campbell, D. and Dallos, R. (2000) 'Children's and adolescents' views of family therapy', *Journal of Family Therapy*, vol. 22, no. 3, pp. 324–341.

Sunderland, M. (2000) *Using Story Telling as a Therapeutic Tool with Children*, Bicester, Winslow Press.

Tammet, D. (2007) *Born on a Blue Day*, London, Free Press.

Turner, C. (2003) *'Are You Listening?' What Disabled Children and Young People in Wales Think About the Services They Use*, Cardiff, Welsh Assembly.

Turner, M. (1996) *The Literary Mind*, Buckingham, Open University Press.

Vygotsky, L.S. (1962) *Thought and Language*, Cambridge, MA, MIT Press.

Weare, K. (2004) *Developing the Emotionally Literate School*, London, Sage.

Chapter 2

Developing positive relationships

Janet Collins

> Young children experience their world as an environment of
> relationships, and these relationships affect virtually all aspects of
> their development – intellectual, social, emotional, physical,
> behavioral and moral. The quality and stability of a child's human
> relationships in the early years lay the foundation for a wide
> range of later developmental outcomes that really matter –
> self-confidence and sound mental health, motivation to learn,
> achievement in school and later in life, the ability to control
> aggressive impulses and resolve conflicts in nonviolent ways,
> knowing the difference between right and wrong, having the
> capacity to develop and sustain casual friendships and intimate
> relationships, and ultimately to be a successful parent oneself.
>
> (National Scientific Council on the Developing Child, 2004, p. 1)

Introduction

As adults we may feel instinctively that positive relationships are a crucial
part of children's lives. Nevertheless, we need evidence from research and
practice to identify what kinds of relationships help to support children's
development. We might also reflect on experience and question the
assertions implied above, that relationships alone directly influence
personal development and success in later life. There are, undoubtedly,
individuals who become successful and respected citizens despite poor
relationships in childhood. Not all children who experience maltreatment
later become aggressive, anxious or depressed (Sroufe et al., 2005).
Moreover, some individuals become aggressive, anxious or depressed
despite apparently happy childhoods.

However, research suggests that the major factors which enable individuals
to 'break the cycle' of poor relationships are: experiences of relationships
with significant others; 'having an alternative responsive caregiver in
childhood, a long-term therapy relationship in childhood, and, a current
supportive relationship with a partner' (Egeland et al., 1988, cited in
Sroufe et al., 2005, p. 50).

Researchers, no doubt reflecting the interest of society as a whole, seem intrigued to understand how babies engage with the highly complex task of establishing their first relationships with those who care for them. Historically a child's primary carer was assumed to be the mother (Bowlby, 1958). However, the potential role of fathers, grandparents, other family members and adults from outside the family is now fully acknowledged (Aldgate and Jones, 2006). Throughout this chapter we will use the terms 'parents' and 'carers' as shorthand for the large and varied group of people who may act as care givers to individual children or groups of children.

In order for adults to support children and improve their quality of life, an understanding of the nature and value of relationships with 'significant others', including parents, other adults, siblings, peers and other children, is important. The previous chapter in this book focused on communicating with children. This chapter builds on this understanding to examine aspects of children's development of, and through, positive relationships with significant others. The first section focuses on children's relationships within families or with people who are most significant in their lives. The second section focuses on children's relationships with friends and peers. These two sections look at the positive and negative aspects of relationships among and between children. The third section discusses strategies to reduce the incidence and effects of bullying, which many children tell us is an important aspect of their relationships.

Core questions

- What is the meaning of positive relationships in children's lives?
- What happens when relationships are not 'good enough'?
- What is the role of friendships in children's lives?
- How might children be helped to deal with bullying?
- How might people who work with children recognise, and work to prevent, bullying?

1 Children's relationships within families

The following quotations are from informal interviews with children in 2006 by Janet Collins:

> because my mum's a bit boring most of the time, she sends me to my grandma's, but I like staying at home ... My mum's moving and I might be staying with grandma 'cos I'm not staying with my mum. She's moving to another city so I'm staying with grandma not moving. (Child A)
>
> My dad says I'm the bestest daughter of our family ... My dad always gives me money when I want some. My mum is kind to me; she lets me do whatever I want. (Child B)
>
> My dad he's like a mum and a dad. And he helps my sister. He copes well. Like you'd think a one parent family would struggle but he don't like he takes things easy. My dad helps me a lot now my mum's left. (Child C)
>
> (From informal interviews with Janet Collins, 2006)

These three girls were in the same class in primary school when they were interviewed about their families and friends. Their reflections on their parents reveal a range of family circumstances. According to Child A she is about to move in with her Grandma rather than move house with her mother. As she also says that she prefers staying at home to spending time with Grandma this doesn't appear to be her preferred choice. Child C reflects on her father's ability to cope with his role as a single parent, whilst Child B clearly has contact with both birth parents who appear to indulge her with money and freedom to do as she wishes. But what do we know about the nature and quality of children's relationships with significant adults? How would we begin to identify what made a relationship positive or, in Winnicott's words, 'good enough' (Winnicott, 1965)? What qualities do we value when establishing positive relationships of our own?

Thinking point 2.1   What kind of information about relationships with primary carers would you need if you were a practitioner working with any of these girls?

Defining or investigating relationships is no easy task. This is because we do not directly observe a relationship – we *infer* it. What we observe are interactions between people as they participate in a joint activity or spend time together in a shared place. Our understanding of relationships formed between children and their carers arises from an observation of their shared interactions and our inferences based on those observations.

Moreover, what we observe and infer is influenced by prior experience, expectations and cultural norms.

Cultural norms have a substantial impact on the way in which adults behave towards the children in their care and the way in which they think about being a parent.

> Parental belief systems are likely to play a major part in determining parental practices, which in turn influence children's behavioural development as well as the belief systems which children themselves come to develop.
>
> (Schaffer, 1996, p. 223)

For example, Woolfson (1994) reported how cultures vary in their attitudes to the expression of aggression. Inuit communities believe that aggression can, and should, be controlled, and the Great Whale River Inuit of northern Canada forbid acts of hostility towards another person. By contrast, the Kwoma tribe of New Guinea value aggression as a useful way of releasing tension: the Kwoma positively reward children who retaliate aggressively when attacked. Each community would certainly respond differently to a child exhibiting aggressive behaviour. Moreover, it is unlikely that every member of any given community would react in exactly the same way.

Relieving tension or out of control?

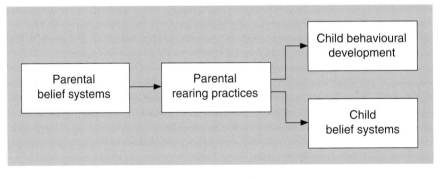

The relationship of parents' beliefs to rearing practices and child development

Thinking point 2.2   How might you respond to the child in the photograph? How might the child's age or gender influence your response?

1.1 Children's first relationships with care givers

Reciprocal communication

Before children learn to talk, relationships with parents, prime carers and significant others are based on reciprocal communication. This turn-taking is apparent even in very young babies during feeding. The infant's sucking response can occur in bursts with pauses during which the mother interacts with the baby by jiggling, stroking or talking. Moreover, each

Baby's noises are accepted as contributions to the conversation

adult–child pair tends to develop its own distinctive interaction pattern (Schaffer, 1996, p. 109). As babies gets older, adults talk to them in a conversational manner which implies that the child is responding even though they have not yet learned how to speak.

Even within the first six months or so children are able:

> to sustain attention and to switch readily from one focus to another on their own initiative rather than being dependent on and merely reactive to the mother's (or carer's) actions.
>
> (Schaffer, 1996, p. 107)

Thus children become more active in their communication with adults.

Once again, the interpretations of behaviour and relationships have to take account of cultural expectations and norms, for example that parents themselves have regular habits of eating and sleeping into which they want to coordinate the baby.

Babies born prematurely have been described as:

> behaviourally disorganised, less predictable, less adaptable and over reactive to some forms of stimulation and under reactive to other forms
>
> (Schaffer, 1996, p. 111)

All of this can have a profound impact on interactions between adults and premature babies.

Thinking point 2.3   How important is facial communication, and why?

As far back as the 1970s Fraiberg's research on interaction between mothers and their blind babies showed how their forming good relationships was threatened (Fraiberg, 1977). When babies could not see and respond to their mothers' facial gestures, the mothers grew increasingly frustrated and depressed. Fraiberg helped the mothers to understand that their infants were indeed responding to them – just not through facial expressions. The infants' responses were centred in the hands and their hand gestures were contingent upon, and in perfect synchronicity with, the mothers' communicative overtures. This discovery enabled the mothers to redefine their communication with their children. This work also raises a lot of issues for everyone working with children with communication difficulties or a wide range of physical disabilities.

Reciprocal communication, in terms of being heard and understood, is important to children of all ages.

> Everyone likes to be listened to. You can't really have a relationship if they don't listen to you. That's friends and parents. Everyone really.
>
> (Child in informal interview with Janet Collins, 2006)

Knowing that they are heard and accepted is part of what makes children feel secure and reassured.

Security and reassurance

Sroufe et al. (2005, p. 51) identify three aspects of positive parent–child relationships which they relate to Bowlby's theories of attachment. According to their research, parents provide 'a haven of safety' or a secure base from which the growing child can move away to 'explore' the wider environment, and 'a source of reassurance when the child is distressed'. Longitudinal research completed in the late twentieth century suggests that early 'insecure' attachment is strongly related to individual differences in dependency throughout children's lives (Sroufe et al., 1983; Urban et al., 1991). Attachment theory has often been criticised but these findings appear to support it. Other researchers have argued that other 'types' of attachment are also significant predictors. 'Anxious resilient' attachment in infancy was the best predictor of anxiety problems in late adolescence whilst 'avoidant and disorganised' attachment predicted conduct problems and dissociation respectively (Carlson, 1998; Warren et al., 1997).

Knowledge of attachment and separation behaviours can be useful in supporting children who show unusual signs of stress in unfamiliar social situations, such as the transition to school. According to Barrett and Trevitt (1991), children with positive relationships at home are more likely to appear confident and can relate positively to adults and peers outside the family environment. Such children expect others to respond positively towards them, they are able to wait for attention, and are not overwhelmed by apparent rejection. They are also self-reliant, can be observed finding solutions to problems independently or in cooperation with their peers, and show a responsive interest and a lively curiosity in a school environment that is initially unfamiliar to them. By comparison, children who do not have positive relationships within the family or who are neglected or over-protected by parents and carers often find the transition to school more problematic. Similarly, children who are coping with trauma or distress at home may come to their teachers' attention not only because of their potentially slow academic progress, but also because of their behaviour, which can range from disruptive 'acting out' to total withdrawal.

However, child development is complex and subject to a myriad of ecological influences. Consequently, even exponents of attachment theory recognise that attachment history is only partially useful in predicting some outcomes for children. Research (for example, Sroufe et al., 2005) suggests a number of other factors which appear to impact on the development of the child. These include the quality of the parental relationship, the comings and goings of men in the home, the amount of general stress being experienced by primary parents and relationships with siblings (Pianta et al., 1990). In addition there are important influences on development that lie outside the family. Notable among these are relationships with peers (Sroufe et al., 2005, p. 52).

Children's relationships with siblings and peers will be discussed in detail later in this chapter. The focus of this section is the quality of parent–child relationships, and we have already established some of the characteristics of positive relationships as those in which parents, carers, grandparents, and other adults offer:

- provision of a secure base from which the child can explore
- provision of a safe haven at times of distress
- continuity of relationships (with the minimum of coming and going)
- low general stress being experienced by primary carers.

Thinking point 2.4   What might be the impact of inadequate housing provision, acute poverty or substance abuse on parent–child relationships? What are the specific issues which might occur during a family break-up?

At the time of writing, between a half and a third of young people in the UK are likely to experience life in a single parent family at some stage. Their views are important.

> Kids should have their say about whether they want their parents to split up or not. They might want to live with their Mum and Dad like a normal child and not have to see their father just on the weekend. It takes up all your spare time having to go and see another parent over the weekend.
>
> (Child quoted on Headliners, 2001, webpage)

In fact most children report that no-one talked to them about their parents' separation at the time. The extent to which children are involved in post-separation arrangements also has an influence on how positively they feel about moving between different households (Dunn and Deater-Deckard, 2001). This highlights the importance of understanding children's perspectives on their own families – children as young as four have been shown to be able to give coherent accounts of relationships with other family members (Pike et al., 2006).

Other important features of positive relationships

Apart from the features already mentioned, Sroufe et al. state that, in positive relationships, parents and/or prime carers also:

- Provide stimulation for the child

- Provide guidance and limits

- Provide interactive support for problem-solving

- Support the child's competence in the broader world by making possible and supporting social contacts outside the home

- Promote the child's relationships with peers.

(Sroufe et al., 2005, p. 51)

This is not an exhaustive list. Judging from the volumes of parenting books, magazines and television programmes, what contributes to positive relationships is an issue of concern to a lot of new and would-be parents.

Advice to adults who foster or adopt children is to maintain the child's stress at manageable levels through relationships which are 'secure', 'attentive', 'friendly' and 'empathetic' or, to use the mnemonic, SAFE (Cairns, 2002, p. 73).

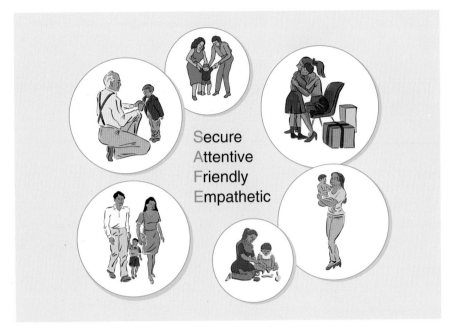

Secure
Attentive
Friendly
Empathetic

However, as previously identified, the quality of the relationship between adult and child is determined with reference to social norms and expectations.

> We now know that from the moment of birth, indeed it may be argued from the moment of conception, the growing individual is in a complex interaction with their environment. Through this process of mutual attunement and adaptation each changes the other forever.
>
> (Cairns, 2002, p. 46)

To gain some insights into the influences on individual interactions and relationships, Hinde (1992) proposed the following model in which the study of interactions is seen as separate from the study of relationships, the latter suggesting continuity over time and more than individual interactions.

Hinde's model suggests that in order to understand relationships one must take into account the group, or family, in which the relationship is embedded, the interactions which occur and the individuality of each of the participants – as well as the socio-cultural context and the physical environment in which the relationship occurs.

An understanding of the factors which impact on relationships within the family begins to explain why siblings brought up in the same family exhibit such different characteristics, and have such different relationships with parents or carers. Sibling relationships will be the focus of the next section of this chapter.

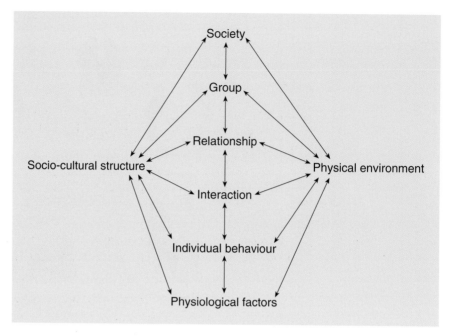

Relations between
successive levels of
social complexity

1.2 Relationships with siblings

> By the time they are adults, adoptive siblings who were reared
> in the same home will, on average, bear no resemblance to each
> other in personality. Biological siblings who were reared in the
> same home will be somewhat more alike, but still not very
> similar. Even identical (monozygotic) twins reared in the same
> home will not be identical in personality. They will not be
> noticeably more alike than identical twins reared in separate homes.
>
> (Harris, 1995, p. 458)

Thus Harris sums up some of the findings of developmental genetics which
reveal that the similarity between individuals from the same family is more
attributable to shared genetics than to the nature of the environment in
which they grow up. Each individual's genetic code is unique (unless they
are a monozygotic twin) so it is not surprising that every child exhibits
unique characteristics in terms of behaviour, appearance and personality.
Moreover, these individual differences may lead to different responses from
parents, potentially accentuating the original differences. This has been
termed a 'reactive' or 'evocative' effect (Scarr and McCartney, quoted in
Harris, 1995, p. 459).

Thinking point 2.5 How might you respond to a parent who tells you that their oldest child is very bright compared to the youngest, who prefers sport to learning? What would you say to a child who claims to be bad at music, unlike their sibling who plays the steel pans at school?

Sulloway (1996) suggests a reason why siblings find a niche which accentuates the differences which might exist between them rather than the similarities which might unite them:

> Siblings become different for the same reason that species do over time: divergence minimises competition for scarce resources.

> (Sulloway, 1996, p. xv)

According to this view the function of sibling diversity is to increase parental investment and time in the individuals concerned.

Harris' (1995) controversial, but thought-provoking, research suggests that genetics and peer group relationships may be more important than parental relationships in supporting individual child development. Sanders (2004, pp. 1–2) sees this as one reason why sibling relationships are important and worthy of research and understanding.

The second reason that sibling relationships are significant, according to Sanders, is that, in most families, siblings spend more time together than they do with anyone else in the family – especially their father. Moreover, interactions between siblings are different in style and nature to those between parents and children. Analysis of interactions between adults and children reveal that these often focus on caretaking activities. By comparison, sibling interactions are often 'playful and humorous situations where children share jokes or tease each other' (Schaffer, 1996, p. 265). This might be related to a more equitable relationship between siblings of a similar age.

Close sibling relationships, such as the one between the Williams sisters, can be significant for some children

The closeness of some siblings is highlighted by Edwards et al.:

> I'm never really alone. But one of my friends, she doesn't have a brother or a sister or a – she doesn't have anybody at all, so she misses out ... Because [my sister] kind of lives with me and she shares – cos she knows more about me so I'm kind of closer to her than I would be to [friends] ...
>
> (Child quoted in Edwards et al., 2005, p. 12)

Siblings can be agents of social support in situations of stress or of parental difficulties, for example tempering the impact of living with domestic violence and devising coping strategies (Cleaver, 2006).

Of course not all children report feeling close to their siblings.

> I don't really like them ... I spend most of the time by myself.
>
> (Child talking about his younger siblings, Edwards et al., 2005, p. 13)

Spending time alone may not be possible for families in small houses and may be further discouraged in a society which values harmony within families and encourages signs of affection between siblings. The situation may be further complicated by the fact that, for many individuals, sibling relationships are the most long-lived relationships they experience and have the potential to continue long after the death of parents. However, we have to acknowledge that siblings can become voluntarily, or forcibly, separated or estranged. Alternatively, siblings can find themselves spending a lot of time together as the elder child acts as carer or second parent to the younger children. This may be a particular issue where the younger child has a disability (Burke, 2004). The network of family relationships can therefore be complex. All children have to learn to exist within a relationship with their adult carers but then adjust to new relationships as additional children join the family.

Sanders argues that sibling relationships are pervasive in society, however, this is not true in all cultures or, increasingly, in the changing demographics of many western societies. Nevertheless, Sanders' view may be justified by the fact that sibling relationships are part of the collective psyche in the stories, legends and literature of many cultures (Sanders, 2004).

Other reasons for justifying research into, and understanding of, sibling relationships relate to the links between the family and wider society. Siblings provide opportunities for individual children to refine their social skills and test out what is acceptable in a wide range of situations.

Squabbling, bickering, rivalry, hostility and conflict are commonly reported aspects of sibling relationships. Older siblings often report that their younger brothers and sisters ignore or fail to understand unspoken rules about space, privacy and possessions in and outside the home. Siblings who behave in this way are likely to be described as 'annoying' and accused of 'winding me up'.

> Sometimes I try and read and he just keeps on talking.
>
> (Child talking about his younger brother, Edwards et al., 2005, p. 46)

> Like when I am watching TV ... best programmes he screams more, shouts and runs round the room.
>
> (Child talking about his younger half-brother, Edwards et al., 2005, p. 46)

Severe or protracted rivalry between and among siblings is likely to come to the attention of any professional working with a family. Moreover, knowledge of the theory and research with regard to sibling relationships is of primary importance to social workers in the placing of siblings and also in understanding the potential impact on children in the receiving fostering or adoptive family (Sinclair, 2005).

Birth order is important both to individuals and as an aspect of sibling relationships. Younger siblings can feel powerless when compared with their older siblings.

> It's kind of ... I like it in some ways [being the youngest], cos some people say the youngest can do no wrong, but cos you're younger you can get picked on a lot easier. The youngest seem to be not able to argue back easily.
>
> (Child talking about her older sisters, Edwards et al., 2005, p. 49)

However, there is a growing literature associated with the impact of being the first-born, youngest and middle child – some even refer to the 'syndromes' associated with birth order. What is less acknowledged and, as yet, under researched, is the impact of the changing birth order status of individual children as they move between family groups.

Being a sibling has come to mean more than simply children born of the same parents.

> Considering the biological, emotional and social connections between siblings, and the child's and siblings' residential arrangements, there is potentially a range of different types of sibling arrangements. Treffers et al. (1990) identified ... 26 types of siblings a child can have.
>
> (Kosonen, 2004, quoted in Sanders, 2004, p. 2)

Thinking point 2.6   How many different sibling relationships can you identify? How could you ensure that your practice is as inclusive as possible?

Children sharing both parents in common might be described as 'full siblings', 'half-siblings' have one parent in common, 'step-siblings' have no parent in common. However, defining relationships outside of marriage is difficult and subject to societal norms and expectations. There is a wealth of information and self-help materials available to all families, including step-families, as well as those involved in adoption and fostering. However, whilst all variations might be described as a 'family', each social group is in fact unique with its own set of relationships and interrelationships. The shifting nature of family relationships can also make it more complex for practitioners to engage them; this issue is discussed further in Chapter 3.

Thinking point 2.7   What issues might there be for a child who had been the eldest in their first family and who becomes the youngest in a second, reconstituted, family? How might this relate to the transition from being the oldest pupil in a primary school to the youngest in a secondary school?

Key points

1   Reciprocal communication and establishing security and reassurance are key elements of relationships forming between children and their carers.

2   Attachment theory can be useful in understanding family relationships.

3   Interpretations of behaviour and relationships need to take account of wider family, social and cultural contexts.

4   Sibling relationships are important and unique relationships in children's lives.

5   Sibling relationships can be a source of support and provide the opportunity to test out social skills, although the patterns of relationships within families are very diverse.

2 Children's relationships with peers

> I still felt left out because like in the playground right, some of my friends weren't outside, they were all together inside practising or something and I just felt left out.

> I had two friends on my table and they were always arguing to one another and going 'I'm not your friend now', right 'I'm not your friend now' and they ... and they were always like putting me off my work.

> (Comments from two Year 6 girls, from informal interviews, Janet Collins, 2006)

The centrality of peer relationships, outside the family, to children's lives is evident from research such as that conducted in three primary schools in the Republic of Ireland (Devine, 2003). In this research, involving 133 children between the ages of 7 to 11, the majority (72 per cent) identified a child, rather than an adult, as having the most power in school. From a child's perspective, having power implied being big and strong, a member of a gang, clever or knowledgeable or a teacher's pet. Children seen as physically weak were perceived to have least power.

> Anthony is the most powerful cos he has a gang ... everybody is afraid of them and they are not afraid of anybody.

> (Grade 5 boy, Devine, 2003, p. 26)

This research indicated that power in children's minds was also linked to popularity and the ability to influence others. For these children popularity and status appeared to stem from the degree to which peers were prepared to challenge adult norms and expectations. Some commentators argue that:

> An important rule in child culture is not 'telling tales' and this ensures that much of children's behaviour that would be frowned upon by adults remains hidden from them.

> (Devine, 2003, p. 27)

This is a culture that adults sometimes have to try to change if they are to protect children from harm such as bullying or abuse. Moreover, adults have to acknowledge and be sensitive to the fact that children may not want to talk about their own problems, for fear of either not being heard or stirring up something powerful that they cannot control.

Other children hold powerful positions in children's lives – and the pleasures, betrayals, jealousies and intrigues which make friendships key to the quality of children's lives begin long before school (Dunn, 2004).

To help children to make friends and understand how relationships work we need to understand the nature of children's peer relationships: what makes them successful and why they break down. The next section looks specifically at the nature of children's friendships. Section 3 focuses on an example of relationship breakdown, namely, bullying.

2.1 The nature of friendship

Friendships among and between children are based on a completely different set of structural relationships to those with parents and other adults. Friendships are far more egalitarian than relationships with adults. They are more symmetrically or horizontally structured, in contrast to adult–child relationships which are more asymmetrically or vertically structured. Friends are often similar to each other in developmental status, engaging each other mostly in play and socialising. Thus interaction between friends rests on a more equal power base than the interaction between children and adults, although, as noted above, there still remains a power dynamic to some degree in peer relationships.

Another essential of friendship is reciprocity or mutuality of affection. Reciprocity distinguishes friendship from one child's desire to be liked by another when that child does not return the preference (Dunn, 2004, p. 3). Reciprocity also distinguishes friendship from mere acceptance or tolerance by an individual or group. Acceptance is a one-way construct, while friendship is defined by mutual reciprocity and can be observed in toddlers as young as twenty months old. In their observational studies of thirty-two children, Ross and Lollis (1989) witnessed children making 'friendly initiations specifically towards those who had been friendly towards them earlier' (quoted in Dunn, 2004, p. 19). Moreover, these 'relationship effects' increased in prominence over the time that the children spent together. Some writers regard friendships as 'affiliative relations' rather than attachments; nonetheless, children can make a large emotional investment in their friends, and their relationships can be relatively enduring.

Friendship is a voluntary relationship, not one that is prescribed or obligatory. Thus whilst children may be encouraged to play with, and be friendly towards, other children, this does not constitute a friendship unless, and until, the participants volunteer to become friends. According to Dunn (2004) those who study friendship in middle childhood (between approximately eight and twelve years old) commonly describe friendship as a relationship which includes companionship, intimacy and affection. Traits of loyalty and commitment, seen as key features of adult relationships, are often assumed to be achieved only from adolescence onwards.

Children establish
powerful relationships
with other children

Friendships are important to young children but there is a change at the beginning of adolescence ... a move to intimacy that includes the development of a more exclusive focus, a willingness to talk about oneself and to share problems and advice. Friends tell one another just about everything that is going on in each other's lives ... Friends literally reason together in order to organise experience and to define themselves as persons.

(Shucksmith et al., 1993, webpage)

Thinking point 2.8   Think about a friend from your childhood or schooldays. What were the characteristics of your relationship which made you describe this other person as your friend? How is this relationship sustained today or what caused you to stop being friends?

Whilst the characteristics of friendships may be constant throughout childhood, into adolescence, and beyond, the way in which friends behave towards each other changes with maturity. However, we have to acknowledge the effect of individual developmental differences. Some children develop faster than their chronological age would suggest. Others develop more slowly and exhibit what children of the same age regard as childish behaviour. This discrepancy in developmental rates can, of itself, provide difficulties for children educated in classes of children their own chronological age. Issues of both culture and ethnicity also complicate simple age-related developmental stages. Nevertheless, an outline of these changes such as that by Goodman and Gurian (1999) can help to shed light on the changing nature of friendships.

Friendships through the ages

Although infants respond to each other, social play becomes prominent during the second year. Two- and three-year-olds generally have playmates they know from the neighbourhood or nursery school.

During the school years, the child's circle of friends widens and increases. Compared to younger children, school-aged children interact more with each other and participate more in social activities, most of which are task-oriented, such as working in teams and on projects together. Because they can now communicate better and they are able to understand another person's point of view, cooperation and sharing increase, while aggression and fighting decrease.

Between ten and fourteen years, children's groups become more structured and may have membership requirements and rituals. Social pressures intensify and cliques may form, often around shared interests like sports and music. At this time formal organisations such as athletic teams and scouts become more important. At about age twelve, friendships are judged on the basis of understanding and sharing inner thoughts.

Preadolescents and adolescents help each other with psychological problems such as fear, loneliness and sadness. By adolescence, the time spent with peers is greater than the time spent with adults, including parents.

The meanings of friendship

- Three- and four-year-olds are tuned in to the here and now. They define a friend as someone who happens to be near them or whose toys they like.

  'My friend gives me bubble gum and she never punches me. Bobbie is my friend 'cause he's my size.'

- Five- and six-year-olds focus on their own needs. They're beginning to realise that someone else may have a different point of view, but they don't realise that friendship is an ongoing process. They have a short-term view of friendship; it applies to episodes of being together.

  'Alice can't be my friend any more; she won't come to my house. Graham plays what I want; he's my friend.'

- By seven, eight and nine, children realise that friendships are personal and they may like or dislike a person because of certain traits.

  'A friend is somebody you need bad, and sometimes he is very busy but he helps you anyway. A friend is somebody who likes me and I like them back. You could be friends for a long time, like twenty weeks.'

- At age ten, children see friendships as an ongoing collaboration; they are able to take another person's point of view, share feelings, help each other and show interest in each other's activities, but they may exclude others. In the middle years of childhood children emerge as more independent social beings. Less reliant on the security of the family, they form ties with their peers.

  'A friend is somebody you can depend on. My best friend and I like to see horror movies together. We trust each other and we hate the same kids. A friend listens to your troubles and keeps your secrets.'

- From twelve years on, children recognise and value the complexity of human relationships.

  'We understand that we're both individuals and have different feelings about things. No matter how stupid my ideas are, like when I'm working on a project, my friend still listens and she doesn't tease me about it. You take a chance with a good friend; you can't be mad at her when she goes out with other friends too.'

  (Adapted from Goodman and Gurian, 1999, webpage)

Thinking point 2.9   How might an understanding of the importance of children's friendships affect your work with children?

2.2 The importance of friendship

Peer relations contribute substantially to both social and cognitive development and to the effectiveness with which we function as individuals. Indeed, the single best childhood predictor of adult adaptation is not school grades nor classroom behaviour but how well the child gets along with other children (Shucksmith et al., 1993). Children who are generally disliked, who are aggressive and disruptive, who are unable to sustain close relationships with other children, and who cannot establish a place for themselves in the peer culture, are seriously at risk. This may be particularly true for children who have a transient life style where there is little opportunity to develop and sustain friendships before the next move becomes imminent. Consider, for example, the particular needs of traveller children, recent immigrants, or Looked After children where settled domestic arrangements may not be possible.

Children's friendships are important in four key respects. At their best they provide children with:

- emotional resources, both for having fun and adapting to stress
- cognitive resources for problem-solving and knowledge acquisition

Friendships can help to sustain children at times of separation and change

- contexts in which basic social skills (for example, social communication, cooperation, and group entry skills) are acquired or elaborated

- forerunners of subsequent relationships

These aspects of friendship are discussed below.

Supportive friends

As emotional resources, friendships furnish children with the security to strike out into new territory, meet new people, and tackle new problems. Friends set the emotional stage for exploring one's surroundings, not unlike the manner in which carers serve as secure bases for the young child. These relationships also support the processes involved with having fun. Researchers have found that the duration and frequency of laughing, smiling, looking and talking are greater between friends than between strangers, and that friends mimic one another more extensively than strangers (Schaffer, 1996). Mannarino (quoted in Hartup, 1996) also established that stable friendships are linked with higher measures of altruism and self-concept.

Friendships may buffer children and adolescents from the adverse effects of negative events, such as family conflict, terminal illness, parents' unemployment, and school failure. Parker and Asher (1987), for example, found consistent links between low peer acceptance and likelihood of dropping out of school and a consistent link between aggressiveness to peers and crime. By comparison, friendships can ease stress, for example, the stress associated with divorce, though in different ways for boys and girls. Strong gender differences occur. Girls care more about who they play with – boys about what they play. 'Unless they are in the older age range in secondary education, it would appear that most boys start some type of informal game or activity with whoever is interested and competent ... the girls sought their closest friends' (Besag, 2006, p. 25). Female friendships might be close but they are also volatile, with constant changes in who is best friends with whom.

Learning through friendship

In all societies children learn by imitating others. They learn by imitating their parents or significant others, but they learn by imitating many other people as well: siblings, non-family adults and children.

Children are generally effective teachers for each other, in a wide range of situations. Damon and Phelps (cited in Schaffer, 1996), identify three main varieties of peer teaching:

- **Peer tutoring** is the didactic transmission of information from one child to another, ordinarily from an expert to a novice.

- **Cooperative learning** requires children to combine problem-solving contributions and share rewards.

- **Peer collaboration** occurs when novices work together on tasks that neither can do separately.

Topping (2001, p. 3) identifies six examples of peer-assisted learning (or PAL):

- **Peer tutoring**, characterised as structured and focused on curriculum content.

- **Peer modelling**, referring to information transferred by imitation.

- **Peer monitoring**, when peers observe, check and comment on the behaviour of others.

- **Peer assessment**, when peers evaluate the products or outcomes of others.

- **Peer education.**

- **Peer counselling.**

Although PAL was developed in schools it could have relevance in a number of out-of-school settings. It has yet to be determined whether friends are better tutors than non-friends or how friendship affects cooperative learning and modelling. Peer collaboration among both friends and non-friends has been studied more extensively than other forms of PAL. One would expect friends to share motives and develop verbal and motor scripts that enable them to combine their talents in achieving their goals. And indeed, recent studies show that collaboration between friends results in more mastery of certain tasks than collaboration between non-friends. Friends talk more, take more time to work out differences in their understanding of game rules, and compromise more readily than non-friends do. This evidence suggests that friendships are unique contexts for transmitting information from one child to another.

2.3 Learning about friendship

Both cooperation and conflict occur more readily in friendships than in other contexts. Preschool children engage in more frequent cooperative exchanges with their friends than with neutral associates or children they do not like. Conflicts occur more often between friends than non-friends, but friends emphasise disengagement and equity in conflict management to a greater extent than non-friends do. Research corroborates the notion that children's relationships with their friends support cooperation and reciprocity and effective conflict management (Hartup, 1992).

Children's relationships with other children also provide important opportunities for them to demonstrate and develop what some psychologists call a 'theory of mind'. According to Bentham (2004), theory of mind involves a growing awareness that:

- As you have thoughts, emotions and feelings, so do other people.
- As your beliefs about the world influence your behaviour, other people's behaviour will be influenced by their beliefs.
- Different people will have different beliefs.
- By watching what a person does you can to some extent guess what they are thinking and feeling.

(Bentham, 2004, p. 27)

Children, like adults, differ considerably in terms of having, and using, an awareness of the needs and views of others. Some children find it very difficult indeed to read other people's behaviour and to understand what is going on around them. Other children are acutely aware of even subtle changes in the mood and behaviour of others.

Developing an understanding of other people's thoughts and feelings is an important precursor to the development of empathy. Hoffman (1987) defined empathy as experiencing or understanding an emotion experienced by another person and hypothesised that this heightened emotion would lead to an increased desire to help. For Hoffman, empathy develops in stages: from the 'global' empathy demonstrated by a baby (for example, matching the emotions of another person); through to children understanding how others feel in certain situations.

Children's friendships are thought to be templates for subsequent relationships. However, relatively few investigators have actually sought to verify the developmental significance of friendship. The issue is certainly complicated. Close relationships may support good adjustment and its development but, alternatively, well-adjusted children may simply be better at establishing friendships than poorly adjusted ones. Nevertheless, studies suggest that friendships forecast good adjustment during the early weeks of nursery, and that making new friends changes children's adjustment in positive directions during the school year (Sroufe et al., 2005).

Outcomes, however, may depend on the nature of the relationship. Friendships are not all alike. Some are secure and smooth-sailing; others are rocky with disagreement and contention. New evidence shows that these differences spill over into school adjustment. Students whose friendships are marked by conflict and rivalry become progressively disruptive and disengaged.

However, the effects of friendships are difficult to disentangle from other factors which influence child development. Having friends, making friends and keeping them, forecasts good developmental outcomes but it is unlikely that these results can be attributed exclusively to friendships. Moreover, friendship may contribute more to certain adaptations, such as positive self-attitudes or self-regard, than to the development of social skills more generally. Friendship may also contribute more to relationship-functioning (for example, with siblings, other friends, or romantic partners) than to being generally well-liked. Friendship networks may also, by creating a social support system, contribute toward the development of **social capital** (Morrow, 2005).

Social capital is a core concept in sociology, defined as the advantage created by a person's location in a structure of relationships. The main implication of social capital theory is that social networks have benefits.

Whether friends are necessities in child and adolescent development remains uncertain. Should friends not be available, other relationships may be elastic enough to serve the friendship functions enumerated earlier. Children with friends are better off than children without friends but, if necessary, other relationships may be substituted for friendships. Consequently, friendships are best viewed as developmental advantages rather than developmental necessities, and the evidence that friendships contribute to educational progress should be read in this light (Hartup, 1992).

Making friends

To help children to learn how to make and sustain friendships it is important to know the skills exhibited by children who make friends easily. These might include:

- They know how to get in touch and how to break the ice. They offer a greeting and invite participation.

  'Hi. What's your name? Would you like to play? Where do you live? Do you want to come to my house?'

- They know how to stay in touch. Once the ice has been broken, the child maintains the contact, sometimes by what she says, sometimes by what she does. Friendly children express their interest by nodding, looking at the other child, talking, expressing thanks or affection. They offer help and comfort. How they do it is important; for example, too much hugging is unpleasant for some children.

- They have fights but stay in touch. Socially adept children manage conflict well. They've been able to assert their rights without being rejected.

  'I'm playing with this right now. Stop pushing me. I don't like to be pushed.'

- They listen to another child and acknowledge the other child's feelings. They know how to work out a compromise.

  'I'm sorry you're crying. I'll use this for a little while and then you can have it.'

- They stand up against aggression and/or unreasonable demands.

  'This is mine and I won't let you take it away from me.'

Less socially successful children are apt to be aggressive, impatient, critical, demanding, or pleading in their strategies. They may interrupt, grab things, act bossy, and whine. They may talk too much or not at all. Then, when they sense rejection, they don't have the resources or the flexibility to change to another approach. Thus the cycle of rejection perpetuates itself.

'You better be my friend or I'll tell on you. I can so get in your game and I can beat you anytime.'

(Adapted from Goodman and Gurian, 1999, webpage)

Key points

1   The nature and meaning of friendships in children's lives changes as the children develop.

2   Friendships are important in children's lives, in terms of learning and a range of aspects of social and emotional development.

3   A child's ability to form positive relationships can be a key indicator of positive outcomes.

3 Bullying and how to prevent it

Building positive peer relationships is important to children and their development. By contrast, the aspect of their relationships most commonly identified by children as negative is bullying. Bullying is a long-standing and widespread problem occurring in the workplace, homes, prisons and nursing homes as well as schools. Evidence suggests that bullying is also a worldwide phenomenon (Sanders and Phye, 2004, p. 2). Since the late 1980s the World Health Organisation (WHO) has included bullying as an aspect of its cross-national studies into the health and behaviour of school-aged children. Yet, despite this wealth of research, a number of key questions remain relevant to those working with children today, namely;

- How should adults and children define bullying?
- What do we know about the levels of bullying for children?
- What are the causes and effects of bullying behaviour?
- How can the effects of bullying be reduced if not eliminated?

Each of these questions will be discussed in the remaining section of this chapter.

Thinking point 2.10   What is your experience of bullying? What are your feelings towards potential bullies and victims?

3.1 Defining bullying

Over time, bullying has been defined in a number of different ways:

> Bullying happens when one person or a group of people tries to upset another person by saying nasty or hurtful things to him or her again and again. Sometimes bullies hit or kick people or force them to hand over money; sometimes they tease them again and again. The person who is being bullied finds it difficult to stop this happening and is worried that it will happen again. It may not be bullying when two people of roughly the same strength have a fight or disagreement.
>
> (Mellor, 1990, webpage)

In the context of this definition, bullying occurs over time and involves an element of power and the inability of the bullied individual to defend or protect themselves from the effects of the bullying. For many commentators 'intentionality' is a major factor in defining an action as bullying. The Durham Anti-Bullying Policy defines bullying as:

> the intentional abuse of power by an individual or a group with the intent and motivation to cause distress to another individual or group.
>
> (Quoted in Katz et al., 2001, p. 7)

The American Psychological Association (APA) lists many different forms of bullying, including

> physical violence, teasing and name-calling, intimidation, and social exclusion. It can be related to hostile acts perpetrated against

racial and ethnic minorities, gay, lesbian, and bi-sexual youth, and persons with disabilities.

(American Psychological Association, 2005, webpage)

These definitions, however, do not, in themselves, clarify what makes an action negative or aggressive rather than neutral or passive. Nor do they explain how often or with what frequency an action has to take place before it becomes bullying rather than a different kind of nuisance or irritation. The difference between teasing by friends and inconsiderate behaviour by potential bullies is clear for one young person:

> A bully – they can probe for weak points. Some people will make fun of me and tease, it might seem as if we are picking on each other, but if you understand each other you can have a laugh and a banter. There are times when you are not in the mood. A good friend can identify with that – a bully goes over the top.
>
> (Katz et al., 2001, p. 7)

Thus the intention of a particular act is socially constructed by the bully, the victim and possible bystanders depending on a range of factors which might include:

- the nature of the reported behaviour – some actions might be more likely to be thought of as bullying than others
- the incidence of the behaviour – the number and frequency of events over time
- the intention of the person initiating the behaviour
- the mood or attitude of the recipient of the behaviour.

All of these can be difficult for a third party to determine, especially as the power relationships between, and among, the participants also need to be taken into account. Moreover, bullying might be reported between former or future friends, especially in the case of bullying among girls (Besag, 2006). There are also incidents of children being bullied by adults, and vice versa.

On a children's news website, children have described bullying as:

- being called names
- being teased
- being pushed or pulled about
- being hit or attacked
- having your bag and other possessions taken and thrown around
- having rumours spread about you
- being ignored and left out
- being forced to hand over money or possessions

- being attacked or teased or called names because of your religion or colour
- being attacked or teased or called names because of your sexuality

(ChildLine, 2007a, webpage)

'Direct' bullying occurs where a victim is more or less openly attacked by the perpetrator. This includes verbal, physical, gestural, extortion and e-bullying.

'Indirect' bullying is more covert and usually involves the deliberate manipulation of social relationships in order to isolate someone or to make others dislike them. Being physically hit or threatened are, after name-calling, the second most frequent forms of bullying reported in school. Girls are less likely to be physically hit or threatened than boys. Traditionally, girls are more likely to engage in indirect bullying involving the social isolation or ostracisation of victims. However, some commentators suggest incidents of physical violence involving girls may be on the increase (Prothrow-Smith and Spivak, 2005; Jackson, 2006).

The popularity and widespread use of mobile, internet and wireless technologies provides increasing opportunities for 'cyberbullying' – defined, in research for the Anti-Bullying Alliance, as:

> an aggressive, intentional act carried out by a group or individual, using electronic forms of contact, repeatedly over time against a victim who cannot easily defend him or herself.

(Smith et al., 2006, webpage)

The advent of cyberbullying adds new dimensions to the problem of bullying. Unlike other forms of bullying, cyberbullying can follow children and young people home, into their private spaces outside school hours; there is no safe haven for those being bullied. Cyberbullies can communicate their messages to a wide audience with remarkable speed, and can often remain unidentifiable. Since cyberbullying is virtual, and occurs in private communications, it is inherently difficult for adults to identify, monitor and counteract it without feeling that they are invading the child's right to privacy.

Smith et al. (2006) identified seven categories of cyberbullying in their research for the Anti-Bullying Alliance:

- **Text message bullying** which involves sending unwelcome texts that are threatening or cause discomfort.

- **Picture/video-clip bullying** via mobile phone cameras, which is used to make the person being bullied feel threatened or embarrassed, with images usually sent to other people. 'Happy slapping' has involved filming and sharing physical attacks.

- **Phone call bullying** via mobile phone which uses silent calls or abusive messages. Sometimes the bullied person's phone is stolen and used to harass others, who then think the phone owner is responsible. As with all mobile phone bullying, the perpetrators often disguise their numbers, sometimes using someone else's phone to avoid being identified.

- **Email bullying** which uses email to send bullying or threatening messages, often using a pseudonym for anonymity or using someone else's name to pin the blame on them.

- **Chat room bullying** which involves sending menacing or upsetting responses to children or young people when they are in a web-based chat room.

- **Bullying through instant messaging** (IM), an internet-based form of bullying where children and young people are sent unpleasant messages as they conduct real-time conversations online.

- **Bullying via websites** which includes the use of defamatory blogs (web logs), personal websites and online personal polling sites. There has also been a significant increase in social networking sites for young people, which can provide new opportunities.

Whatever form the bullying takes, its effects can be devastating, as discussed later in this chapter.

3.2 The extent of the problem

From January to July 2006 Bullying Online (now Bullying UK, http://www.bullying.co.uk) carried out the largest survey ever in the UK into the extent of school bullying. In total, 8574 surveys were completed by children (4772), parents (2160), teachers (323) and other adults (1323).

- 69 per cent (3293) of the children complained that they had been bullied.

- Name-calling was the biggest problem: 56 per cent of abusive remarks referred to weight and appearance.

- 50 per cent (2386) of bullied pupils said they were physically hurt and 34 per cent of those needed to see a doctor or go to hospital.

- 3 per cent (143) of attacks involved a weapon.

These figures confirm that bullying still occurs in schools. However, statistics as to whether bullying is increasing or decreasing are inconclusive.

One issue in determining levels of bullying centres around the way in which bullying is defined and reported. Completion of a survey, such as that carried out by Bullying UK, may appeal more to those who suffer directly or indirectly from the effects of bullying than to individuals for whom bullying has never been an issue. Moreover schools and other organisations with a strong anti-bullying strategy may be at some pains to 'prove' that their strategies are having the desired effect. In all cases both what 'counts as bullying' and how bullying is defined and reported, are likely to have an effect on the levels of reporting.

In general, schools take reports of bullying extremely seriously, and try to ensure zero tolerance of violent and abusive behaviour. This is not to say that schools are havens of peace. They are a continuation of the communities that they serve, and it would be naïve to suggest that pupils, teachers, parents and other adults are transformed as they walk through the school gates.

The view of world politics and global issues we get through the media often seems to implicitly sanction the use of power and force by world leaders against those less able to protect themselves. The depiction of violence and bullying in films, on television and in computer games may also have a part to play in a general desensitisation. So does the climate of the education system itself. Schools have to respond to children's social and emotional needs as well as their academic achievement. Yet teachers remain under severe pressure to raise standards irrespective of the needs of individual children. Ironically, the pressure on raising academic achievement can be at its most acute for those who work in areas where social, emotional and material needs are most acute.

3.3 The causes and effects of bullying behaviour

> Bullying hurts. It makes you scared and upset. It can make you so
> worried that you can't work well at school. Some children have told
> us they have skipped school to get away from it. It can make you
> feel that you are no good, that there is something wrong with you.
> Bullies can make you feel that it's your fault.
>
> (ChildLine, 2007a, webpage)

The victims of bullying often suffer from low self-esteem, high levels of
stress or fear and feelings of loneliness. However, the extent to which these
factors are the cause or the effect of bullying is not clear. For example,
children who are lonely and find it difficult to make friends are more likely
to be bullied than more popular peers. Moreover, bullying can accentuate
feelings of loneliness. Similarly, depression, anxiety, and sometimes
suicidal thoughts can be brought on or accentuated as a result of bullying.
Cases of bullying-related suicides or 'bullycides' are rare but devastating.

> In January 2000 Danielle Goss is the first bullycide of the New
> Millennium after a campaign of bullying which included abusive
> messages on her mobile phone.
>
> (Bully OnLine, 2007, webpage)

Children who are bullied also often have a higher rate of school absences.
'It is a challenge to be fearful in school and focus on one's school work',
reports Daniel (2006, webpage). 'There is not enough room in the brain for
both.'

Some children and adolescents develop real, or psychosomatic, physical
complaints in order to avoid situations where they have been bullied, such as
school. Victims of bullying may exhibit signs of anxiety and changes in their
behaviour, including those listed below:

Be frightened of walking to and from school

Be unwilling to go to school and make continual excuses to avoid
going

Beg to be driven to school

Change their route to school every day

Begin doing poorly in their schoolwork

Regularly have clothes or books or schoolwork torn or destroyed

Come home starving (because dinner money was taken)

Become withdrawn

Start stammering

Start acting out or hitting other children (as a reaction to being bullied by those children or others)

Stop eating or become obsessively clean (as a reaction to being called 'fatty' or 'dirty')

Develop stomach and headaches due to stress

Attempt suicide

Cry themselves to sleep

Begin wetting the bed

Have nightmares and call out things like, 'leave me alone'

Have unexplained bruises, scratches, cuts

Have their possessions go 'missing'

Ask for money or begin stealing money (to pay the bully)

Continually 'lose' their pocket money

Refuse to say what's wrong

Give improbable excuses to explain any of the above

(Katz et al., 2001, p. 62)

Whilst none of these behaviours confirm bullying (reluctance to attend school, for example, can be the result of many other factors), they should lead to further investigation by a concerned parent or carer.

Causes

Research focusing on what makes potential bullies behave the way they do is inconclusive. Where research assumes that bullying is a dyadic process involving individual bullies and a lone victim it tends to focus on the distinct personal characteristics or home circumstances of the bully and the victim (Sanders and Phye, 2004). However, as we have already established, bullying implies an imbalance of power, and the deliberate attempt to cause harm. In the jostling for power, status and control that takes place in any group setting (child or adult) bullies are not a clearly identifiable group which can be 'dealt with'. A child who has more power at one moment, and who uses it to bully a less powerful child, may find themselves in a relatively powerless position shortly afterwards, and become a victim themselves.

Relationships in groups are rarely stable, and it is the fluid and dynamic nature of peer relations which makes tackling bullying so difficult. Teachers and other adults can only really be effective if they educate young people in how to deal with both the positive and negative aspects of group behaviour. Hilary Cremin's (2002) work investigating peer mediation as a strategy for reducing bullying is an example of this approach.

Some researchers feel that bullying should be viewed as a group phenomenon involving a wider circle of children, either directly or indirectly. Pepler and Craig (1999) found that peers were present in eighty-five per cent of bullying situations and thus the impact of the bullying was felt by more than the individuals directly involved. Older children often try to take some responsibility for their younger siblings or peers.

> 'It's OK for us in year 8 – we have to think about the younger children when they first come into the school. It is in year 7 with the 12-year-olds that bullying can start. We have to have a way to help them cope.'
>
> (Boy speaking at an anti-bullying forum in Birmingham, 2006)

Working in Scotland, Karatzias et al. (2002) identified four participant categories: 'bully', 'victim', 'bully-victim' and 'uninvolved'. Menesini et al. (2002), working in Italy, divided individuals into 'bullies', 'victims', outsiders' and 'defenders'. The social phenomenon approach was also emphasised by Salmivalli et al. (1996) who distinguished between 'ringleader bully', 'assistant of the bully', 'reinforcer of the bully', 'defender of the victim', 'outsider' and 'victim'. Sutton and Smith (1999) found that children in their study tended to downplay their role in supporting the bully and play up their role in supporting the victim.

Physical characteristics can be exploited by potential bullies who will pick on and victimise individuals who are weaker or who exhibit greater physical disadvantages than themselves (Besag, 2006). Children with special educational needs are substantially more at risk of being involved in bully/victim situations. In one study, Whitney et al. (1994) matched children with special needs to mainstream children of the same school year group, age, ethnicity and gender. Children with special needs were two to three times more at risk of being bullied; they were also more at risk of taking part in bullying others. Gender also plays a role: boys are usually victimised by other boys while girls may be bullied by either boys or girls.

3.4 Reducing bullying

There is a wealth of material about bullying and how to prevent and deal with bullying situations (see, for example, the work of Kidscape, ChildLine and the Anti-Bullying Campaign, and the Scottish Schools Ethos Network). ChildLine reports that bullying is the single most common reason for children and young people to call their organisation, with over seventy per cent of children saying that the bullying takes place in school (Macleod and Morris, 2002). These organisations also provide a lot of accessible online material. Their advice to children is straightforward, if not always easy to implement. The successful implementation of anti-bullying strategies will depend on adults and children working together to define, recognise and reduce bullying in schools, homes and public spaces.

If you are being bullied, you can do something about it. You can make a difference!

- TELL, TELL, TELL
- Practise what you want to say
- Keep a note or diary of what is happening
- Don't give up
- Ask your parents to visit the school
- Talk over what to do with a friend, a teacher, your mum or dad or someone you trust

Remember that teachers have to listen carefully when a child tells them about being bullied.

Remember – it's right to tell an adult that you are being bullied and to ask for their help. But you don't have to let them take over. You can talk with them about what you would like to happen.

(ChildLine, 2007b, webpage)

This advice recognises that talking openly about bullying and enabling victims and bystanders to report bullying incidents is an important step in empowering potential victims. Children need to know how an adult will react if they decide to speak out against a bully. They must be confident that their concerns will be heard and dealt with in a way which respects confidentiality and is sensitive to the possibility of retaliations or recriminations. Teachers and other adults can help by ensuring appropriate supervision. However vigilant an adult is, it is impossible to prevent all bullying by relying on supervision alone. The presence of friends and supporters is also likely to reduce bullying, which reinforces the need for children to be socially aware and appear socially confident.

Advice to schools from the Anti-Bullying Network is likely to be relevant to all who work with children in terms of having clear anti-bullying policies, procedures which are applied consistently and useful strategies to reduce and deal with bullying. In addition, levels of accountability to children, parents, carers and the wider society are emphasised. Strategies which have been developed in schools, but have a much wider application, are identified below.

Practice box 2.3

Which strategies can schools use?

The single most effective thing that a school can do to tackle bullying is to develop a policy outlining how the issue is raised within the curriculum, and how incidents are dealt with after they have happened; i.e. the policy must acknowledge the need for both proactive and reactive strategies. Such a policy must involve all members of a school community including pupils, parents, teachers and non-teaching staff.

Examples of the proactive strategies which schools have used to prevent bullying include:

- Questionnaire surveys which have helped reveal the scale and nature of the problem
- Short awareness-raising poster campaigns
- Improved supervision in known problem areas
- Using drama, role-play, novels etc. within the formal curriculum to help pupils understand the feelings of bullied children and practise the skills they need to avoid bullying
- Developing the playground as a learning environment
- Circle time
- Improving links with parents and the community through meetings and other activities
- Peer support and buddy schemes
- Assertiveness training
- Featuring bullying at school assemblies
- Asking the student council to agree an anti-bullying code

Examples of the reactive strategies which schools have used to deal with bullying once it has happened include:

- Bully courts and councils, where pupils decide what should happen to people accused of bullying
- Bully boxes, in which pupils can post notes about their worries
- Telephone help lines, run by pupils in the school
- Shared Concern Method and the No Blame approach – these are similar strategies for dealing with group bullying which allow something to be done even when circumstances are not clear
- Counselling for victims
- Peer counselling, where older pupils are trained to help younger ones
- Mediation, as a non-violent way of resolving disputes

- Safe rooms for victims
- Punishment, an option if bullying is serious and proven

N.B. It is vital that practitioners assess the true nature of an incident before applying any of these strategies. Many different types of behaviour are classed as bullying and each requires an appropriate response.

(Adapted from Anti-Bullying Network, 2007, webpage)

Thinking point 2.11   What could you do to help the children you know to eradicate bullying in their lives?

Schools, homes and public spaces need to be places where children are safe from bullying. The ethos of a place, and any necessary rules, need to be agreed between adults and children and then applied in ways that are consistent and fair. This, however, is only the beginning. More needs to be done to empower adults to work proactively to develop the pro-social skills of the children in their care. In school this needs curriculum time and proper training and support for teachers and other staff. The introduction of Social and Emotional Aspects of Learning (SEAL) in English primary schools is a positive sign, as are many of the ideas enshrined in *Every Child Matters* (Department for Education and Skills, 2003), and the opening up of the curriculum in 2020 Vision. It is to be hoped that all who work with children will increasingly be enabled to respond to the needs of the whole child, and to actively work towards non-violent, ethical and moral communities.

Key points

1 Bullying in relationships between children can have a powerfully negative effect on their wellbeing.

2 There are uncertainties about the exact nature, causes and extent of bullying.

3 There are many anti-bullying strategies available and it is vital that all adults working with children are clear about implementing them.

Conclusion

Relationships are of vital importance in children's lives. Early relationships within the family are highly influential in supporting children's development and underpinning their ability to form subsequent connections. Peer relationships and friends also provide resources for children's learning, social and emotional development and an understanding of these dynamics is important for practitioners to be able to support the formation of friendships in their work settings. The extent and negative impact of bullying underlines just how important it is to support positive relationships in children's lives.

References

Aldgate, J. and Jones, D. (2006) 'The place of attachment in children's development' in Aldgate, J., Jones, D., Rose, W. and Jeffrey, C. (eds) *The Developing World of the Child*, London, Jessica Kingsley.

American Psychological Association (APA) (2005) *Bullying*, available online at <http://www.apa.org/ppo/issues/bullying.html>, accessed 20 July 2007.

Anti-Bullying Network (2007) *Information for teachers and school managers about whole school anti-bullying policies*, available online at <http://www.antibullying.net/staffwhole.htm>, accessed 20 July 2007.

Barrett, M. and Trevitt, J. (1991) *Attachment Behaviour and the Schoolchild: An Introduction to Educational Therapy*, London, Routledge.

Bentham, S. (2004) *Psychology and Education*, London, Routledge.

Besag, V. (2006) *Understanding Girls' Friendships, Fights and Feuds: A Practical Approach to Girls' Bullying*, Maidenhead, Open University Press.

Bowlby, J. (1958) 'The nature of a child's tie to its mother', *International Journal of Psychoanalysis,* no. 39, pp. 350–373.

Bully OnLine (2007) *Bullycide memorial page*, available online at <http://www.bullyonline.org/schoolbully/cases.htm#UK>, accessed 20 July 2007.

Burke, P. (2004) *Brothers and Sisters of Disabled Children*, Gateshead, Athenaeum Press.

Cairns, K. (2002) *Attachment, Trauma and Resilience: Therapeutic Caring for Children*, London, British Association for Adoption & Fostering (BAAF).

Carlson, EA. (1998) 'A prospective longitudinal study of disorganised/disorientated attachment', *Child Development*, no. 69, pp. 1107–1128.

ChildLine (2007a) *Bullying Help and Advice page*, available online at <http://www.childline.org.uk/Bullying.asp>, accessed 20 July 2007.

ChildLine (2007b) *How to stop the bullying Help and Advice page*, available online at <http://www.childline.org.uk/Howtostopthebullying.asp>, accessed 20 July 2007.

Cleaver, H. (2006) 'The influence of parenting and other family relationships' in Aldgate, J., Jones, D., Rose, W. and Jeffrey, C. (eds) *The Developing World of the Child*, London, Jessica Kingsley.

Collins, J. (2006) *The Quiet Child*, London, Cassell.

Cremin, H. (2002) 'Pupils resolving disputes: successful peer mediation schemes share their secrets', *Support for Learning*, vol. 17, no. 3, pp. 138–143.

Daniel, J.H. (2006) 'What makes a bully?', *Pediatric Views*, Children's Hospital Boston, available online at <http://www.childrenshospital.org/views/august06/what_makes_a_bully.html>, accessed 22 July 2007.

Department for Education and Skills (DfES) (2003) *Every Child Matters*, London, DfES.

Devine, D. (2003) *Children, Power and Schooling: How Childhood is Structured in the Primary School*, Stoke-on-Trent, Trentham.

Dunn, J. (2004) *Children's Friendships: The Beginnings of Intimacy*, Oxford, Blackwell.

Dunn, J. and Deater-Deckard, K. (2001) *Children's Views of their Changing Families*, York, Joseph Rowntree Foundation.

Edwards, R., Hadfield, L. and Mauthner, M. (2005) *Children's Understandings of their Sibling Relationships*, London, National Children's Bureau.

Egeland et al. (1988) in Sroufe, A., Egeland, B., Carlson, E.A. and Collins, W. (2005) *The Development of the Person*, New York, The Guilford Press, p. 50.

Fraiberg, S. (1977) *Insights from the Blind; Comparative Studies of Blind and Sighted Infants*, New York, Basic Books.

Goodman, R.F. and Gurian, A. (1999) *Friends and Friendships*, NYU Child Study Center, New York University School of Medicine, available online at <http://www.aboutourkids.org/aboutour/articles/friends.html>, accessed 20 July 2007.

Hantler, A-M. (1994) 'Children's views of bullying', *Health Education*, no. 5, November, pp. 8–14.

Harris, J.R. (1995) 'Where is the child's environment? A group socialization theory of development', *Psychological Review*, vol. 102, no. 3, pp. 458–489.

Hartup, W.W. (1992) 'Friendships and their developmental significance' in McGurk, H., *Childhood Social Development: Contemporary Perspectives*, East Sussex, L. Erlbaum Associates.

Hartup, W.W. (1996) 'The company they keep: friendships and their developmental significance', *American Psychologist*, vol. 45, pp. 513–520.

Headliners (2001) *Answer back: children's views on family breakdown*, available online at <http://www.headliners.org/storylibrary/stories/2001/answerbackchildrensviewsonfamilybreakdown.htm>, accessed 20 July 2007.

Hinde, R.A. (1992) 'Human social development: an ethological/relationship perspective' in McGurk, H., *Childhood Social Development: Contemporary Perspectives*, East Sussex, L. Erlbaum Associates.

Hoffman, M. (1987) 'The contribution of empathy to justice and moral judgement' in Eisenberg, N. and Strayer, J. (eds) *Empathy and its Development*, Cambridge, Cambridge University Press.

Jackson, C. (2006) *Lads and Ladettes in School: Gender and a Fear of Failure*, Buckingham, Open University Press.

Karatzias, A., Power, K.G., Flemming, J., Lennon, F. and Swanson, V. (2002) 'The role of demographics, personality variables and school stress on predicting school satisfaction/dissatisfaction: review of the literature and research findings', *Educational Psychology*, vol. 22, no. 1, pp. 33–50.

Katz, A., Buchanan, A. and Bream, V. (2001) *Bullying in Britain: Testimonies from Teenagers*, East Molesey, Surrey, Young Voice.

Kosonen, K.J. (2004) in Sanders, R. (2004) *Sibling Relationships: Theory and Issues for Practice*, Basingstoke, Palgrave Macmillan, p. 2.

Macleod, M. and Morris, S. (2002) *Why Me? Children Talking to ChildLine about Bullying*, London, ChildLine.

Mannarino, A.P. (1980) *Evaluation of Social Competence Training in the Schools*, paper presented at the 52nd Annual Meeting of the Midwestern Psychological Association (St Louis, MO, 1–3 May 1980).

Mellor, A. (1990) *Spotlight 23 – Bullying in Scottish Secondary Schools*, Scottish Council for Research in Education (SCRE), available online at <http://www.scre.ac.uk/spotlight/spotlight23.html>, accessed 20 July 2007.

Menesini, V., Sanchez, A., Fonzi, R. and Ortega, A. (2002) 'Moral emotions and bullying: a cross-national comparison of differences between bullies, victims and outsiders', *Aggressive Behavior*, vol. 29, no. 6, pp. 515–530.

Morrow, V. (2005) 'Conceptualising social capital in relation to the well being of children and young people: a critical review' in Hendrick, H., *Child Welfare and Social Policy*, Bristol, The Policy Press.

National Scientific Council on the Developing Child (2004) *Young children develop in an environment of relationships*, working paper no. 1, available online at <http://www.developingchild.net/pubs/wp/Young_Children_Environment_Relationships.pdf>, accessed 20 July 2007.

Parker, J. and Asher, S. (1987) 'Peer relations and later social adjustment: are low-accepted children at risk?', *Psychological Bulletin*, no. 102, pp. 357–389.

Pepler, D. and Craig, W. (1999) 'Peer involvement in bullying: insights and challenges for intervention', *Journal of Adolescence*, vol. 22, no. 4, pp. 437–452.

Pianta, R., Egeland, B. and Sroufe, L.A. (1990) 'Maternal stress and children's development: prediction of school outcomes and identification of protective factors' in Rolf, J., Masten, A., Cicchetti, D., Neuchterlein, K. and Weintraub, S. (eds) *Risk and Protective Factors in the Development of Psychopathology*, New York, Cambridge University Press, pp. 215–235.

Pike, A., Coldwell, J. and Dunn, J. (2006) *Family Relationships in Middle Childhood*, York, National Children's Bureau and Joseph Rowntree Foundation.

Prothrow-Smith, D. and Spivak, H.R. (2005) *Sugar and Spice and No Longer Nice: How We Can Stop Girls' Violence*, San Francisco, Jossey-Bass.

Ross, H.S. and Lollis, S.P. (1989) 'A social relations analysis of toddler peer relationships', *Child Development*, no. 60, pp. 1082–1091.

Salmivalli, C., Lagerspetz, K., Björkqvist, K., Sterman, K. and Kaukiainen, A. (1996) 'Bullying as a group process: participant roles and their relations to social status within the group', *Aggressive Behavior*, vol. 22, pp. 1–15.

Sanders, R. (2004) *Sibling Relationships: Theory and Issues for Practice*, Basingstoke, Palgrave Macmillan.

Schaffer, H. (1996) *Social Development*, Oxford, Blackwell.

Shucksmith, J., Hendry, L., Love, J. and Glendinning, T. (1993) 'The importance of friendship', *Research in Education*, no. 52, Spring, available online at <http://www.scre.ac.uk/newsold.html>, accessed 20 July 2007..

Sinclair, I. (2005) *Fostering Now; Messages from Research*, London, Jessica Kingsley.

Smith, P., Mahdavi, J., Carvalho, M. and Tippett, N. (2006) *An investigation into cyberbullying, its forms, awareness and impact, and the relationship between age and gender in cyberbullying*, report to the Anti-Bullying Alliance, available online at <http://www.anti-bullyingalliance.org.uk/downloads/pdf/cyberbullyingreportfinal230106_000.pdf>, accessed 20 July 2007.

Sroufe, A., Egeland, B., Carlson, E.A. and Collins, W. (2005) 'Placing early attachment experiences in developmental context: the Minnesota longitudinal study' in Grossmann, K.E., Grossmann, K. and Waters, E., *The Development of the Person*, New York, The Guilford Press.

Sroufe, L.A., Fox, N. and Pancake, U. (1983) 'Attachment and dependency in developmental perspective', *Child Development*, no. 54, pp. 1615–1627.

Sulloway, F.J. (1996) *Born to Rebel: Birth Order Family Dynamics and Creative Lives*, New York, Vintage Books.

Sutton, J. and Smith, P.K. (1999) 'Bullying as a group process: an adaptation of the Participant Role Scale approach', *Aggressive Behavior*, vol. 25, no. 2, pp. 97–111.

Topping, K. (2001) *Peer Assisted Learning: A Practical Guide for Teachers*, Newton, Brookline Books.

Urban, J., Carlson, E., Egeland, B. and Sroufe, L.A. (1991) 'Patterns of individual adaptation across childhood', *Development and Psychopathology*, vol. 3, pp. 445–460.

Warren, S.L., Husten, L., Egeland, B. and Sroufe, L.A. (1997) 'Child and adolescent anxiety disorders and early attachment', *Journal of the American Academy of Child and Adolescent Psychiatry*, no. 36, pp. 637–644.

Whitney, I., Smith, P.K. and Thompson, D. (1994) 'Bullying and children with special needs' in Smith, P.K. and Sharp, S. (eds) *School Bullying: Insights and Perspectives*, London, Routledge, pp. 213–240.

Winnicott, D.W. (1965) *The Family and Individual Development*, London, Routledge.

Woolfson, R. (1994) *Understanding Children. A Guide for Parents and Carers*, Glasgow, Faber and Faber.

Chapter 3

Positive practice relationships

Andy Rixon

Introduction

In the previous chapter we identified some of the perspectives of children on relationships with their families, friends and peers and the importance of these relationships in their lives. As children's social networks gradually expand, they come into contact with other adults and models of adult relationships. Drawing on their earlier experiences, children will contribute to, and make judgements on, these relationships, including those with the practitioners who provide care and services for them. It is these relationships that are the focus of this chapter.

The ability to form positive working relationships is fundamental to all those involved in practice with children and their families. It is perhaps the most essential skill required and is closely interlinked with the communication skills discussed in chapter 1. Positive relationships are a pre-requisite if practitioners are to connect with children, understand their perspectives, promote their rights, and contribute to safeguarding and promoting their wellbeing.

The importance of forming relationships features in many professional standards and codes of practice – and the view that it involves skills that should be common to all practitioners has also been confirmed in government policy. For example, stressing the importance of practitioners' ability to:

> Establish rapport and respectful, trusting relationships with children, young people, their families and carers ...

> Build open and honest relationships by respecting children, young people, parents and carers and making them feel valued partners.
>
> (DfES, 2005a, p. 7)

However, in spite of the many statements about the importance of relationship-building, it is an issue that is not always paid sufficient attention.

Increasingly children's views are being sought on a whole range of topics, in line with changing perspectives on rights, on policy, and on children themselves. What can be learnt about the important elements of relationships from research with children will be our starting point for this chapter. We will then explore how common, clear and consistent messages from children are translated into practice settings.

Most practitioners' relationships with children are closely linked to relationships with their parents, carers, or wider family. Even settings such as schools, which have more traditionally focused exclusively on work with children, have experienced a shift towards involvement with children's wider social and familial networks. The second section of this chapter focuses on practitioner/family relationships, exploring the complexity of the 'family' and debates about the roles that different workers can play.

Forming and sustaining relationships in the working environment can be demanding for practitioners; this chapter concludes by looking at some different perspectives on relationships in practice and considering how the focus on the central importance of relationships can be supported.

Core questions

- What does listening to children tell us about the importance of positive relationships with practitioners in children's lives?
- How might connecting with children be enhanced by listening to the views of children?
- How can practitioners develop working relationships with parents and carers in diverse family forms?
- What different perspectives are there on the place of 'relationship' in practice?

1   Learning from listening to children

'My perfect worker would keep my problems to herself and help me out more'

(Child quoted on Headliners, 2007, webpage)

'Just their friendly nature, being on first name terms was a lot better than, it made it seem like a friend instead of a teacher.'

(Ahmad et al., 2003, p. 65)

My perfect social worker would be happy, easy to talk to, and really helpful.

(Child quoted on Headliners, 2007, webpage)

Research findings about what children value in terms of relationships with practitioners have been fairly consistent. As these quotes suggest, this includes being friendly, helpful, and easy to talk to but also being prepared to listen:

'They're nice, they try to help you, but they don't listen. They just do things to you. I would like them to listen to me a bit more.'

(Child quoted in Butler and Williamson, 1994, p. 93)

Being reliable and accessible is also important:

'E always came to see me ... She was reliable and helped me, and explained what to do and what not to do'

(Child quoted in Bell, 2002, p. 5)

Children and young people also frequently report other characteristics, such as relationships that are supportive, non-judgemental and based on trust and respect, as being important (Turner, 2003; Morgan, 2005; Ahmad et al., 2003).

For practitioners committed to forming more positive relationships with children, the meaning of these qualities may need more exploration. For example, Rose (2006) cites work with children and young people by the Children's Rights Alliance that discussed in more detail the idea of 'trust' and what characteristics would make an adult trustworthy. They identified four key groups of characteristics which illustrate how meanings can be complex and overlap with other qualities:

- Being there – children and young people having the general feeling that an adult is there for them.
- Proving yourself – an adult taking the time to listen; asking appropriately; and keeping promises.

- Having the right attitude – not losing temper or trying to take over.

- Knowing what you're talking about – sharing relevant experience, and not acting as if they know more than they do. (Older teenagers particularly cited this as important.)

(Children's Rights Alliance for England, 2003, quoted in Rose, 2006, p. 307)

The meaning of these concepts for older children will also be different, perhaps more sophisticated, than for young children. In addition, any conclusions about forming positive relationships need to be appropriately translated to fit the level of understanding of individual children. Practitioners need to beware of over-generalising.

Thinking point 3.1   What particular qualities in relationships might be important to children in a setting with which you are familiar?

While these universal views can be valuable in informing practice across all disciplines, more specific attributes can be key depending on the context of the child–practitioner encounter. Some disabled children, for example, have particularly frequent contact with health workers who can potentially become an important part of their lives. Claire Turner, in research commissioned by the Welsh Assembly to ascertain the views of disabled children and young people, found some important common messages:

> Throughout all the personal stories about health services, routine and reliability, being treated as an individual, and being treated the same as any other child or young person were key themes that cut across all ages and abilities.

(Turner, 2003, p. 31)

The continuity of relationships seemed particularly important:

> 'Being able to see the same person every time is important because people get used to you and they know what they are doing and don't have to look at your notes all the time ...'

(Child quoted in Turner, 2003, p. 33)

This continuity also lessens the frustration for children caused by new staff over- or under-estimating a child's capabilities. The value placed on continuity in relationships is a theme echoed in the voices of children, both in the UK and internationally, who are looked after by the local authority (Petrie et al., 2006). Yet, in many agencies, the structures and staff turnover work against providing children with this stability.

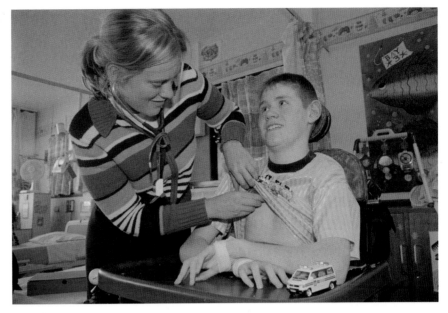

Disabled children would like practitioners to be reliable, to treat them as individuals and to involve them in decisions about their treatment

Turner's research also found that across services from all agencies, disabled children and young people valued practitioners who did not just listen but also enabled them to be 'involved in making decisions and choices about their own care and treatment' (Turner, 2003, p. 27). In practice, experience of such participation was, however, found to be very variable – especially in school and hospital settings.

In schools, recurring themes inevitably focus on relationships in the classroom – children seem to respect teachers who 'don't shout', and who are consistent, flexible, fair and fun (Pollard, 2002). At the same time children want to learn in a classroom environment that is organised and under control. Pollard suggests that 'strict/soft' are two common constructs that children use in relation to teachers: 'softness' is seen not as an advantage but as a sign of weakness while 'strict but fair' is often positively valued (Pollard, 2002, p. 123).

A closer reading of children's voices reveals other important dimensions, such as those of gender, ethnicity and age. Morrow (2006) emphasises that gender is of major importance in all areas of children's lives, from family relationships and friendships, to their experiences in more 'institutional' settings such as pre-school and after-school clubs. In an overview of research in out-of-school care Morrow stresses that practitioners in a range of settings can implicitly reinforce traditional gender identities (even though policies will encourage workers to question this).

A study of out-of-school care in Wales and England, illustrated the potential impact of this: 'They treat girls differently, and they treat boys like they are things that don't belong here' (girl quoted in Smith and Barker, 2000, p. 326). This example – in response to the limiting of space used by boys to play football – was complicated by the fact that most of the workers were women. The issue was not whether restricting the space given for football was reasonable or not (indeed, it might have been an important issue in relation to work with the girls), but that it was interpreted in terms of gender.

Gender can also play a part in the choice of people with whom children prefer to form relationships in the first place. Help-seeking about issues of concern is highly gendered: girls and young women in particular often report a preference for talking to other females within the family, in friendship groups and among practitioners (Featherstone and Evans, 2004; Hallett et al., 2003). Boys are significantly less likely to ask for help at all – ChildLine has reported that they speak to four times as many girls as boys and their analysis suggests that this is often for reasons related to gender expectations (ChildLine, 2003). In response they try to offer a choice of gender of worker and also a slightly different emphasis in their approach to developing working relationships:

> Because boys tend to approach things from a practical problem solving standpoint, we don't talk too much about 'feelings'. We ask boys to tell us what they think about their situation and what they have already tried to do about it.

> (ChildLine, 2003, p. 12)

Boys may be less likely to talk about feelings or ask for help

Smith and Barker's research also found that children believed that the staff in their clubs should reflect the ethnic mix of the children they looked after (Smith and Barker, 2000). Age too can be a relevant factor. None of these factors are prescriptive in terms of forming relationships – children will have their own individual preferences – but they can raise issues for practitioners to consider both individually and in terms of the structure of their organisations. At both levels, how are the views of children taken into consideration?

Arguably the feedback from children of the importance of these abilities and attributes should be central to all staff training, qualifications and job descriptions. It has been suggested that, if these characteristics are not easily taught, then child welfare agencies should employ only those who already have these characteristics and interpersonal skills (de Boer and Coady, 2007). Involving children in selection and interviewing processes has been seen as a step in this direction in some settings.

While the requirement that practitioners need to learn from listening to children's views on relationships is uncontroversial, the realities of different practice settings inevitably give rise to complexities. The quotes at the start of this section emphasise how being friendly and helpful are valued by the children concerned. However, they also hint at potential tensions for practitioners. For example, one child's perfect practitioner would 'keep my problems to herself'. There is no doubt from sources such as ChildLine (MacLeod, 2000) and research into children's help-seeking behaviour (Hallett et al., 2003) that concern about losing control of information is a big disincentive to children when discussing issues of concern with practitioners. Children and young people clearly value an opportunity to talk in a confidential way. Yet, in reality, there are often difficult issues around the exercise of confidentiality which, dependent on the setting, limit the extent to which 'keeping things to yourself' is an option. The ground rules about confidentiality in any setting should be clear to practitioners and children alike – but there will still be fine judgements about what should, for example, be passed on to parents or other agencies. Government increasingly advocates confidential services and independent advice for children and young people while, at the same time, promoting increased information-sharing between agencies as a crucial part of improving safeguarding. Against this background of potentially conflicting priorities a substantial amount of work may need to be done to establish or negotiate parameters about confidentiality.

A further potential dilemma is raised by the child who values a 'friendly nature'. Being more like a 'friend' than a teacher may be valued by this particular child but what then of setting 'boundaries' and maintaining 'distance' – the focus of much practitioner training? What sorts of relationships are right or appropriate, and how is this shaped by the practice context? That children want friendly relations with practitioners does not necessarily mean that they want them as friends – children still also want them to have the necessary expertise, to be 'really helpful' and to resolve their problems.

The subsequent sections will explore some of these complex issues for practitioners as they take forward these messages from children into the reality of different practice settings.

Thinking point 3.2   What are some ways in which the views expressed by children about relationships can be taken forward by practitioners? How might this differ in different settings?

The Children Act Now: Messages from Research distilled some key points from twelve research studies on different aspects of the implementation of the Children Act 1989.

It was clear from the research studies that children are well able to turn appropriately to individuals from a variety of agencies – teachers, doctors, youth workers, the police – as well as to social workers and residential and foster carers. There were five qualities in professionals that were important to children:

- Reliability – keeping promises;

- Practical help;

- The ability to give support;

- Time to listen and respond; and

- Seeing children's lives in the round – not just the problems.

(Department of Health, 2001, p. 93)

1.1 Strict but fair – relationships in the classroom

One of the most common experiences for children of relationships with adults in a 'professional' role will be that with teachers.

The recognition of the importance of relationships is emphasised in the training of teachers, who are expected to: 'Have high expectations of children and young people including a commitment to ensuring that they can achieve their full educational potential and to establishing fair, respectful, trusting, supportive and constructive relationships with them' (Training and Development Agency for Schools, 2007).

However, as Andrew Pollard points out: 'despite its importance the issue of classroom relationships often seems to defy analysis. Perhaps this is so because relationships are the product of such very particular, complex and subtle interactions between teachers and children' (Pollard, 2002, p. 114).

In exploring this issue Pollard draws on the work of Carl Rogers and his highly influential ideas on 'person-centred' relationships. From a counselling perspective, Rogers argued that such relationships could only be achieved through acceptance, genuineness, empathy and, ultimately, an 'unconditional positive regard' for the other person (Rogers, 1980). However, while these principles can be a valuable starting point for teachers to draw on, there are clearly complexities in transferring this to the classroom situation where other factors, such as managing many children and power relationships between pupil and teacher, come into play. Relationship-forming is therefore not straightforward but 'a finely judged balance' between a range of different elements (Pollard, 2002, p. 117).

Pollard puts forward the concept of the 'Working Consensus' as one possible way of achieving this balance. This recognises that the classroom environment, and relationships within it, are to some extent mutually created – children are active participants in relationship formation – while still being in the context of this power dynamic. He emphasises that such a consensus will not emerge spontaneously but must be created by different teachers as they begin to establish the rules in their classroom. Pupils will respond (particularly to the perceived fairness of the rules) and it is how these responses are understood and acted upon that is key. To achieve this, teachers need to develop ways of monitoring children's reactions and perspectives.

Thinking point 3.3   From your own experience as a pupil or a practitioner, how do you think teachers can begin to assess children's responses to classroom rules?

Careful observation and recording is advocated as a general approach for achieving an understanding of children's responses. Pollard suggests that one way of gaining more specific feedback is having a whole-class discussion about what makes a good teacher, perhaps by asking questions such as 'what advice would the class give to a trainee teacher?' Through this process children can subtly influence the nature of classroom relationships and rules. A key point here is that such receptiveness to the views of children, and acceptance of the collaborative nature of relationships, can only be achieved through teachers being prepared to work in a 'reflective' way. We will return to this reflective style of working later in the chapter.

The recognition of power relationships in this model is particularly important, as a power dynamic to a greater or lesser extent permeates all relationships between children and the variety of practitioners they encounter. Children are acutely aware of how this power is exercised. They are also aware of power dynamics between practitioners. Interviews with primary school children about the roles of teachers and the growing number of other adults in classrooms, reflected a clear understanding of this hierarchy. Teachers were seen as having a higher status than teaching assistants even though children did not find the differences in their roles easy to explain (Eyres et al., 2004).

Within the development of overall relationships in the classroom environment, the formation of individual relationships may also be highly influential. One American study suggested that, as early as kindergarten:

> [T]he association between the quality of early teacher–child relationships and later school performance can be both strong and persistent. The association is apparent in both academic and social spheres of school performance.
>
> (Hamre and Pianta, 2001, p. 636)

From the teacher's perspective, a positive relationship can mean that more time and energy is devoted to that child's learning needs than to the learning needs of children with whom there is a negative or conflictual relationship. From the child's perspective, a positive relationship with a teacher can be a protection against poor school performance and 'may operate as a protective factor against risks for a range of problem outcomes' (Hamre and Pianta, 2001, p. 636). This is not a matter of teachers being more positive about well-behaved children. The study concluded that even children with significant behavioural problems, if they were able to form positive relationships with kindergarten teachers, were more likely to avoid future difficulties than similar children with poor relationships.

Clearly one implication of this evidence is that teachers, and other early years practitioners, need to be aware of the vital importance of these early relationships. It also suggests that if children are actively involved in relationship-building then they too need to be equipped with the skills to do so successfully.

The challenge of creating positive child–adult relationships within the classroom

The importance of children developing relationships with other children and adults was recognised in the development of the Social and Emotional Aspects of Learning (SEAL) materials for primary schools in England. Relationships were one of seven key themes the programme addressed to promote children's social, emotional and behavioural skills – below is an extract illustrating the approach with Year 1 and 2 children (aged five to seven):

Practice box 3.1

Learning opportunities: dealing with our hurt feelings without hurting others

Intended learning outcomes

I understand that being unkind and hurting someone doesn't make me feel better.

I can think of ways to make me feel better when I feel hurt without hurting others.

Read the following story:

Pam was playing in the playground. She was feeling sad because her mum was in hospital. She missed her mum. She was feeling so sad that she didn't look where she was going. She trod on Marcus's toe.

Marcus called Pam stupid.

Pam said she wasn't as thick as he was. At least she didn't get 1 out of 10 for her spelling.

Marcus sat in class. He knew he wasn't very good at learning his spellings. He was worrying about spelling. He forgot to do his work.

At playtime he still hadn't finished. Miss Johnson said he would have to stay in. She had to stay in to look after him. She didn't have time to have a cup of tea. This put her in a bad mood.

When the children came in Miss Johnson was thirsty and cross. She was going to ask Sebastian to read his story but she forgot. Sebastian had been excited about reading his story – he was very proud of it. He felt disappointed.

At home time Sebastian ran out to see his mother and little sister. He had promised his little sister that they would play together when they got home. Sebastian sat and watched television. His sister came to ask him to play with her but he was cross and he pushed her.

Explain that sometimes our feelings get out of hand and we do things that hurt others when it is not their fault. Ask the children for ideas about what they should do if the following things happen:

- You are feeling sad because your mum is in hospital.

- You are feeling cross because someone was nasty to you at playtime.

- You feel hurt because someone treads on your toe.

- Your teacher forgets to let you read out your story.

- You are worried about your work.

These are some ideas the children might come up with:

- Stop and think.

- Explain how you are feeling.

- Talk to your teacher.

- Ask someone to help you sort things out.

- Tell the person involved how you are feeling.

Write the best ideas on the board in a general format and add some of your own if appropriate. The children should volunteer to say what the character might do to stop things getting worse.

Read the story again. This time the children can put up their hands to stop you with an idea as you go through.

(DfES, 2005c, pp. 10–11)

There may be particular challenges for teachers as they work with children in large groups, although the core issue is one shared by most practitioners. Children seen as 'difficult' or even 'withdrawn' may require a different approach, or more time, in what may be time-pressured working environments.

Reflective practitioners will question why relationships with some children are harder to initiate and sustain, including whether this is influenced by their own personal views and experiences as well as by work-related pressures.

Assumptions based on gender, ethnicity or class can subtly affect relationships. Lloyd and Stead (2001), for example, noted responses to the children of travelling communities in a number of Scottish schools. Some disruptive behaviour by these children appeared to be linked to bullying and name-calling in school, however this was often not recognised by the staff and anti-bullying policies were not always implemented. Where name-calling was acknowledged, some teachers appeared to view this as normal or inevitable believing that the traveller pupils were 'quite capable of standing up for themselves' and 'tend to tough it out' (Lloyd and Stead, 2001, p. 368).

While schools increasingly attempt to be inclusive of all cultures, this study highlights the potential pitfalls of stereotypical views. The lack of a broader cultural awareness can prevent the building of positive social relationships. This might be particularly difficult where agency norms, such as school attendance, are being challenged.

1.2 Child-centred assessments?

Successive frameworks designed to enable multi-agency assessments have emphasised the importance of seeing and involving children, ensuring they are not 'lost' in the assessment process, and making assessments 'child-centred' (DH, 2000; DfES, 2005b; Scottish Executive, 2007). An evaluation of the impact of the 'Framework for the Assessment of Children in Need and their Families' concluded that practice in relation to involving children and young people in their assessments had 'not kept pace' with developments in involving parents and carers (Cleaver et al., 2004, p. 95).

Research into assessments by Holland (2004) suggested that the 'child-centeredness' of assessments can, on closer observation, be more rhetoric than reality. In practice, assessments tend to be dominated by information from verbal dialogue with adults which is easier to ascertain. Her review of assessment reports revealed children as 'objects rather than the subjects' (Holland, 2004, p. 71), often containing plenty of observations about the children's stage of development but little evidence of their perceptions of issues in their lives. In addition, the reports reflected some uncertainty on the part of practitioners as to how much weight to place on the child's views when they were ascertained. Holland points out that this is not an issue restricted to the UK context but that research from Australia and Scandinavia underlines the widespread nature of this problem (Holland, 2004).

Thinking point 3.4   How can practitioners try to ensure that the assessments they are involved in are 'child-centred'?

Holland identified one positive example of an assessment that was detailed, substantial in length, and non-judgemental about the weight to be placed on the child's views. This report was more in-depth because it had been the product of a number of individual play sessions with the child. Enabling children to participate in decisions about their lives will be explored in more detail in Chapter 5 – but a key point that emerges here is the emphasis needed on:

> the individuality of children, and the need for careful observation and *relationship building* before beginning to explore in-depth issues with children.
>
> (Holland, 2004, p. 81, author's emphasis)

Children should, of course, be routinely asked their views. It is a requirement that they be asked to contribute to their assessments, and they can have significantly different perspectives from adults, which need to be understood for plans to be successful. However, just asking is unlikely to be enough. In order to obtain a meaningful reply, time and skills need to be invested in the relationship between child and practitioner. Margaret Bell, writing about promoting children's rights, states that:

> It is only within the context and security of a trusting relationship that children can assimilate information, make informed choices as to what their views are and how they are best represented and be enabled to exercise their rights to participation and service provision.
>
> (Bell, 2002, p. 3)

For some practitioners this will be a daily part of their work – for others possibly a daily frustration because their working environment does not allow the time required to achieve this level of relationship. Yet, arguably, Bell's conclusions summarise what is ideally required for assessments to be truly 'child-centred'.

One other important issue raised in the discussion above was the uncertainty of some practitioners about how to weigh the views of children when compared to other (adult) perspectives. Weighting is important in analysing information, but the mindset of workers on this issue could also influence the extent of their investment in relationship-building.

It is likely that most practitioners working with children support the principles of children's rights, and the idea that children should participate in decisions affecting their lives. Changing perspectives on children have led to an increasing recognition that children can be 'active agents' (Prout, 2002) and make a contribution to decisions, not just at the individual level but also in wider society. This can be contrasted in this context with constructions of children that place them purely as the objects of protective adult interventions on their behalf. In practice there are 'inherent tensions and dilemmas in giving due consideration to children's views and acting upon them, when in the judgement of adults, the children's wishes and feelings may not be compatible with their welfare' (DH, 2001, p. 84). However, the extent to which individual workers believe that children have a genuine perspective that should be given considerable weight might be vital to their 'going the extra mile' in developing positive relationships.

Children need to be enabled to contribute their views to decisions that affect their lives

Building (and indeed appropriately ending) relationships is not dependent on specific 'therapeutic' sessions. There are many techniques available for direct work that can be embedded in everyday practice. It is a matter of finding methods of creative communication that enable children to express what they feel.

Practitioners need to develop skills and techniques in direct work with children. In the example above, a practitioner is involved because a child is having problems at school. The practitioner has drawn a cartoon strip, as well as talking, as a way of engaging the child and explaining their role.

All practitioners working with children need to reflect on, and improve, their level of knowledge and skills – and some children will need a more specific therapeutic intervention. In the context of exploring therapeutic approaches, Bannister and Huntington (2002) suggest the following principles for developing child-centred practice:

Following, rather than always thinking we can or should lead; actively listening rather than always talking; engaging with children on their terms not just ours; being respectful of what they can do rather than largely focussing on what they cannot do (applying the deficit model of child development); or bringing our creativity and knowledge to the interactions we have with them, are all examples of routes to child-centred interactions.

(Bannister and Huntington, 2002, p. 12)

Key points

1   Listening to children reveals some clear messages about the qualities that they value in relationships with practitioners. The challenge for practitioners is to translate these messages into developing relationships in different and complex practice settings.

2   Children are not passive but are active participants in relationship formation.

3   The nature of a 'positive' relationship needs to acknowledge power relationships and the role of factors such as disability, gender, age and ethnicity.

4   The ability to develop relationships is vital for children, and some children may need positive strategies to help them achieve these skills.

5   Skilled relationship-building is an important element in ensuring that practice remains child-focused.

6   Forming positive relationships with children can be influenced by practitioners' views on children's rights and constructions of childhood.

2 Positive relationships with, and within, the 'family'

> The majority of parents want to do the best for their children.
> Whatever their circumstances or difficulties, the concept of
> partnership between the State and the family in situations where
> families are in need of assistance in bringing up their children, lies
> at the heart of child care legislation.
>
> (DH, 2000, p. 12)

> The clearest message is that what is 'good' for the family cannot
> necessarily be assumed to be 'good' for the child.
>
> (MacLeod, 2000, p. 140, commenting on messages from ChildLine)

These quotes emphasise the centrality of the family in all work with
children but also hint at the tension that there can be between the needs of
the family and the children and adults within it. To what extent can their
interests be seen as the same? In section 1, we have stressed that children's
voices should be given weight in decisions about their lives – yet children
live in an ecological network of family (and wider) relationships and this
whole 'system' may need to be the target for any successful intervention or
support. We also know that help specifically for children is most successful
when fully supported by the adults in the child's life.

The extent to which individual practitioners work with the whole family
will vary but, increasingly, links with the family have been stressed even
where practitioners have seen their roles as primarily working with
children. Extended services based around schools and children's centres,
for example, have increasingly involved parents and carers; while
transitions to school are often supported by home visits from teaching staff.
Connecting with children and promoting their wellbeing is therefore often
dependent on the ability of practitioners to form positive working
relationships with their parents and carers.

Perhaps not surprisingly, the qualities that adults seek in relationships with
practitioners do not differ substantially from those identified by children.
Research into the views of parents and carers, in the UK and
internationally, repeatedly shows that they value workers who are warm,
empathetic, respectful, friendly, honest, caring, and good listeners (de Boer
and Coady, 2007; DH, 2001). Acknowledging that parenting can be
difficult and stressful, especially in situations of multiple adversity, is
particularly important. One example is the recognition of the particular
issues experienced by parents from minority ethnic groups which highlight
the need for culturally sensitive practice (Seale and Mkandla, 2000). Even
in situations that are potentially highly conflictual, such as child protection
investigations, parents and carers can still appreciate practitioners who

demonstrate warmth and concern (Thoburn et al., 1995), and do not make them feel like 'bad parents' (McCurdy and Jones, 2000).

Relationships with parents are often cast in the language of 'partnership'. The term is used in different ways (for example, increasingly in relation to involving parents in service developments) but for many years has been advanced as the ideal shared working relationship at the individual level. The Children Act 1989 (and subsequently the Children (Scotland) Act 1995), in particular, advocated this principle.

The meaning of partnership has often been debated in relation to power imbalances in relationships between practitioners and parents and carers. These imbalances may be quite acute in certain contexts and can be further overlaid by issues of gender, ethnicity and class. However parents do not necessarily expect 'partnership' to mean equality, in fact attempts to deny this power dimension by workers can be seen as patronising (DH, 2001). They do, however, expect a level of involvement and engagement, and a lessening of power differences can still be aspired to – through practitioners being prepared to let go of power and their 'expert' status and seeking to empower family members to participate.

Practice box 3.2

Successful features of partnership with parents

Aldgate and Statham (DH, 2001, p. 67) suggest the following as successful features of partnership with parents:

- A shared commitment to negotiation and actions about how best to safeguard and promote children's welfare
- Mutual respect for the other's point of view
- Recognising the unequal nature of power between parents and professionals
- Recognising that parents have their own needs which should be addressed
- Good communication skills by professionals
- The establishment of trust between all parties
- Integrity and accountability on the part of both parents and professionals
- Shared decision making
- Joint recognition of constraints on services offered
- Recognition that partnership is not an end in itself.

There is evidence that good outcomes for some children are associated with practitioners gaining a shared agreement with the family about the nature of a need or problem – a high value is placed on cooperation. This illustrates the importance of forming positive relationships. However, the danger that a positive relationship has developed just because practitioners and parents happen to share belief systems needs to be borne in mind as this could exclude those with a different worldview (Holland, 2004).

2.1 Who is the family?

Exploring the issue of practitioners working with the family raises the question of who we see as the family, and how relationships within families are constituted and defined. The label 'family' has increasingly come to represent a diverse, complex and fluid concept. It is important not to exaggerate the extent to which family relationships were 'fixed' in the past – anxieties about the family and its fragmentation are long-standing. However, significant economic, social and cultural changes affect family structures and give rise to concern about their impact on children's wellbeing, including:

- Changes in marriage patterns, partnering and single parenthood
- Changing social relations and gender roles
- Changing employment patterns for men, women and young people
- Widening economic differentials
- The broader impact of social change, migration, globalisation, and consumerism.

Some of these will be explored further in Chapter 4.

Thinking point 3.5   Reflect on your own views about whether family structures have changed. What do you think is the impact of these changes on children's welfare?

Brid Featherstone (2004), summarising research on family life, suggests that while the meaning of family, as described by both adults and children, increasingly stretches beyond marital and blood ties, core features of what families 'do' may remain the same, e.g. 'sharing resources, caring, responsibilities, and obligations' (Featherstone, 2004, p. 24).

Children's views seem to reinforce this idea that consistent love and care are more important than the details of family structure. Relationships with birth parents, however, remain very important for most children even as they increasingly broaden their definitions of family to include a range of diverse forms, including lone parenting and step-parenting.

Dunn and Deater-Deckard (2001) researched the views of children aged five to sixteen on their changing family structures through the use of family 'maps'.

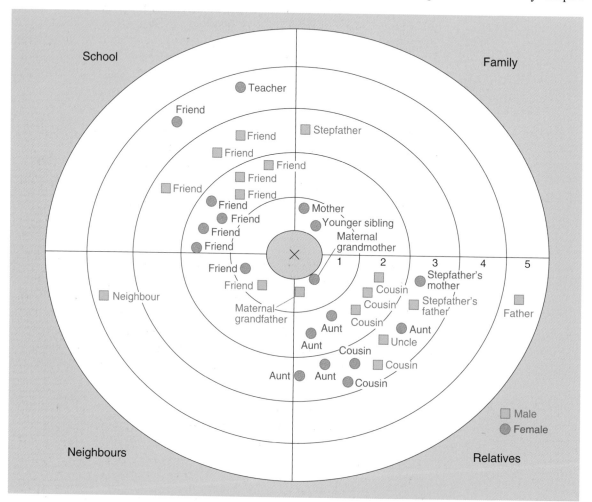

Four field maps are a tool with which children can show how close they feel to family members and other people in their lives. (Dunn and Deater-Deckard, 2001.)

They found that there was a high degree of confusion and distress as a result of parental separation, especially where there had been little explanation of the reasons. Children's experience of post-separation family structures depended, in particular, on levels of conflict and the extent to which they had a say in subsequent contact arrangements. In some cases relationships with grandparents (especially maternal grandparents) became more significant while children's perceptions of the role of step-parents were very varied;

'They should be a parent and care about you, and look after you, and give you treats and that.'

'He wasn't anything to do with me so why should he tell me what to do?'

(Dunn and Deater-Deckard, 2001, p. 22)

Children's views of family post-divorce revealed a rethinking of what 'family' meant in other ways. For example, some children questioned assumptions about bonds with parents. These sometimes taken-for-granted relationships were, in fact, often influenced by ideas of 'respect' and 'liking', criteria more usually associated with the assessment of non-family members (Smart, cited in Featherstone, 2004, p. 37).

Thinking point 3.6   What implications might changing family structures have for practitioners?

What are the implications of this complexity and diversity for practitioners and their attempts to form positive working relationships? Featherstone suggests that practitioners often feel ill-equipped to work with the complications of reconstituted family relationships, particularly when these relationships themselves might be in a state of negotiation – for example between children and a new partner – where there is no specific template to draw on.

Given the variety of family forms, it is vital that practitioners start by understanding the self-definitions of individuals, including the children, rather than by imposing a top-down view of the family. In order to form positive relationships based on 'partnership', practitioners may also need to question the 'deficit-comparison' model. This model uses the nuclear family as the ideal and therefore inevitably portrays single parent and step-families as inferior (Batchelor, 2003). It is more productive for practice to be informed by 'difference' than 'deficiency'.

Jane Batchelor (2003) provides insights for practitioners into a number of areas where step-families (the term used here to describe a range of re-partnering arrangements) frequently do differ from nuclear families. One example is their more common experiences of loss and change as a result of separation, death, or loss of contact. Children may become part of two separate households. Gender relations may be changing in all families but they can be particularly acute in reconstituted families, in terms, for example, of the expectation that women will always 'mother' the children in their care. Similarly, step-families are more likely to experience being at different stages in individual and family life cycles as a result of new partners having children (Batchelor, 2003).

Using a life cycle perspective can help families to understand the stages they are going through, be more realistic about the time involved and develop new strategies for coping with family life. These perspectives can translate into simple developments in practice – antenatal classes, for example, can 'specifically look at the impact of the impending birth on step- and half-siblings and the contrasting experiences of the couple if it is a first child for one and not the other' (Batchelor, 2003, p. 162).

Engaging fathers and father figures to involve them in the lives of their children

The perspective of the family as a system where all relationships influence each other implies that, in developing effective working relationships with the adults in a family, practitioners may need to recognise and engage with their general concerns, rather than only those impacting directly on the children. Featherstone (2004) argues that a key issue emerging from her research is that the relationships between fathers and children are often mediated by relationships with the mothers in the family. To influence the position of the child, workers also need to engage in the negotiations between men and women.

2.2 Positive relationships – men and boys

Just as we often believe that we are developing relationships with children when, in fact, we are really working with adults, so the same can be true of other family members. The day-to-day work of supporting families is often centred on relationships between a predominantly female workforce and mothers/women. Many settings that aim to offer 'family' support, in practice do very little work with men.

The national evaluation of Sure Start programmes, for example, found that in spite of an explicit intention of working with men there were only 'low levels' of father involvement (Lloyd et al., 2003).

Thinking point 3.7   Think about a setting with which you are familiar – are there barriers to practitioners forming working relationships with men?

One explanation may lie within changing family patterns. Mothers can be the most constant figure in children's lives when other relationships are shifting. Some fathers may not be engaged in the fathering role or appear to avoid involvement with formal agencies. Agencies, too, can merely reinforce stereotypes of gender roles, believing fathers not to be involved and making little effort to ensure that services are delivered in an accessible way. There can of course be circumstances in which it is important to work exclusively with women. Family problems can be related to domestic violence perpetrated by men, which raises problems for worker engagement. However, changing family structures have also brought with them a more diverse range of 'fathering' (and perhaps 'grand-fathering') practices with which workers can potentially engage (Featherstone, 2004).

The Sure Start programmes that succeeded in engaging men were those which had decided early in the planning stage that involving fathers would be central to their work. The schemes that worked best were the ones that had a dedicated worker (Lloyd et al., 2003).

'There's quite a lot of support in terms of dad's work in this city, but it's fragile. It's not knitted into the fabric of early years work.

Dad's work tends to happen if there's a male that's interested in developing it.'

(Father Development Worker in Chawla-Duggan, 2006, p. 94)

Practitioners whose specific task it is to engage with fathers need not necessarily be men, but it is interesting to briefly consider our topic of 'relationships' in the intersection between boys, their fathers/father figures, and male workers.

Men and masculinity are frequently seen as objects of concern in policy terms and boys, too, have been increasingly positioned as 'problematic'. Concerns about boys related to educational performance, crime and health seem more closely associated with adolescence, yet the idea that they are objects of concern appears in some cases to be well established by age eleven (Featherstone, 2004).

The government has argued strongly that practitioners working with families must engage with fathers, and father figures in children's lives, based on evidence that: 'Positive father involvement in their children's learning is associated with better educational, social and emotional outcomes for children ...' (DfES, 2004, p. 5). This conclusion draws on studies illustrating a link between the interest, involvement and expectations of fathers and academic and behavioural outcomes in school (Goldman, 2005). The research on the impact of fathers' involvement demonstrates benefits to both girls and boys, although there has been a particular interest in the connection between boys' educational and social development and relationships with fathers.

Poorer levels of educational achievement, and higher rates of school exclusion and truancy, amongst boys from some black and minority ethnic groups is even more marked (Connolly, 2004) and has also led to a particular interest in involving fathers and father figures, amongst other strategies (Goldman, 2005; Lindsay and Muijs, 2006).

Again, the work done in this area emphasises the development of individual relationships. The DfES (2004) document stresses the importance of developing one-to-one relationships in the playground and reports better success rates being achieved when schools 'reach out' to fathers. A small-scale study of the work that male Father Development Workers (FDW) undertook in Sure Start, Early Excellence Centres and family centre settings similarly found relationship-building to be key (Chawla-Duggan, 2006). It explored groups that were run to both raise confidence and responsibility and improve children's learning. The theme of trust featured strongly. An example is given by one worker of starting their work with a group of fathers with a building project and DIY until 'trust' was established – enabling more personal discussions and work aimed at building self-esteem and confidence. '[A]s you start to build up the trust and relationships they begin to open up' (Father Development Worker quoted in Chawla-Duggan, 2006, p. 100).

Interviews with the development workers revealed another dimension in the relationships between them and the fathers (or father figures) with whom they were working – that of 'modelling'. This idea of social learning was often very explicit:

> 'All children need adult directed play, I sort of model it and will talk to the little boy, engage with him, like we hope the parent will take on. I was talking to the dad about it.'
>
> (Father Development Worker quoted in Chawla-Duggan, 2006, p. 104)

This idea will be familiar to many practitioners working with children. It is, however, often alluded to in relation to men working with younger children: that they can be role models both to fathers in encouraging their participation in childcare, and to the children with whom they are working. This idea has been used explicitly as an argument for involving more men in children's services – compensating for absent father figures, or modelling a style of 'masculinity' to boys.

Cameron (2001), reviewing the literature on men in early childhood services, questions some of these assumptions. The presence of men in early childcare can be equally likely to reinforce gender roles, particularly if men frequently move to more senior posts. Even if role modelling is desirable, men, in fact, present a wide diversity of masculine roles, and their presence is sometimes viewed with suspicion by parents as a potential source of risk of sexual abuse. It seems therefore that we should be cautious about automatically assuming what men in such roles will achieve. Male workers are themselves 'actively constructing their identities as men and as workers, drawing on a range of often contradictory discourses about gender and the care of children' (Robb, 2001, p. 238).

However, if fathers are key to improving outcomes for children, then male practitioners forming positive working relationships with men to encourage them into playing a greater role with their children may be one useful strand of a strategy to promote children's wellbeing.

2.3 Children don't come with an instruction manual

'Parenting education' is one area where practitioners explicitly work on relationships within families. It is a topic that is also on the agenda of practitioners from a wide variety of disciplines.

Concerns about parenting have increasingly been a topic of political debate. 'Poor parenting' has become linked with a range of problems in society, and interest in prevention and early intervention has emphasised the potential of educating parents in how to bring up children. 'Parenting can be seen to be a public activity open to the scrutiny of parents and professionals alike', the idea of parenting as common sense can be made to appear 'hopelessly naïve and amateurish ...' (Miller and Sambell, 2003, p. 32). How to parent properly has even been dissected on popular television programmes.

The idea of targeting parenting is not new but became a central feature of a number of government strategies, such as the Sure Start programme and the 'Respect' agenda (where good parenting is clearly linked with reducing later anti-social behaviour). Government websites are also full of tips for good parenting and links to other sources of information on parenting skills.

Several government websites offer guidance on parenting. Here the emphasis on good parenting preventing later anti-social behaviour is explicit.

Other elements of the focus on parenting have been more controversial. *Every Child Matters* (Chief Secretary to the Treasury, 2003) summarised the government's position in England, advocating supportive universal and specialist programmes – but also emphasising the value of compulsory parenting orders for parents who are seen to be condoning persistent offending or anti-social behaviour. Pronouncing on the right way to parent is fraught with issues related to class and culture.

Many programmes focus particularly on behavioural issues, as well as aiming to strengthen children's social competence. Systematic reviews tend to support the use of behaviourally oriented programmes and find those delivered in groups to be most effective, and cost-effective (Bunting, 2004). However a key element is often parent–child communication, underpinned by a focus on the quality of relationships.

> The quality of the parent–child relationships is fundamental to effective parenting support of all kinds: without good

communication and warm relations between parent and child, even the most promising programmes may fail to deliver good outcomes.

(Moran et al., 2004, p. 86)

Scott et al. (2006) looked at a small-scale study of parenting programmes (in this instance, a well-researched behavioural programme) in a disadvantaged, ethnically diverse area. The study argued that the programme, despite a wide variety of cultural beliefs about child-rearing practices, could be equally effective in this environment. Here too the 'gold standard' was sensitive responding within parent–child relationships (Scott et al., 2006).

Reviews of parenting work also reveal the extent to which it has involved all agencies and disciplines, with health visitors, psychologists, social workers and a diverse range of family support workers being involved in facilitation. While much parenting education or support is offered via these regular, structured, time-limited programmes, a wide spectrum of work can fall under this heading. Although all practitioners can draw on a common body of theoretical methods and evidence-based programmes for work with parents, the discipline of the 'lead' worker or agency can still influence the approach to practice.

Ranson and Rutledge (2005) looked at three family centres that had been established by what were, at the time, different local government departments (Community Development, Education, and Social Services). Each centre also had a differing partnership arrangement with the voluntary sector. In exploring the nature of their work on 'family learning' some distinct differences in approach were apparent. Where Social Services (with National Children's Homes) were the lead agency, 'modelling' was the main approach to practice – sitting on the floor showing how to play and communicate with children and encouraging parents to try out their skills and increase their confidence. The Education 'approach' was distinctly different, emphasising the value of parents developing their ability to reflect and, for staff, the value of respectful relationships:

> You don't come up to somebody and say 'you've got a problem here and we can do this about it.' Rather, it's like saying 'What do you think of the situation? Are there some changes that can be suggested? What is the implication of working in that way? What can we do to move forward on that?

(Family worker quoted in Ranson and Rutledge, 2005, p. 41)

Paradigm
In its simplest sense, a paradigm is a pattern or model. However, within academic and practice-related discussions it can be used to describe a distinct view of the world composed of a range of concepts, theories, values and ways of interacting. Thus the practice of parenting education will differ markedly depending on the paradigm underpinning it.

The different **paradigms** stemming from the philosophies of the main agencies led to the services offered to parents and children being distinctly different. However, the research still identified a 'unity of purpose' – one of 'learning in the family: enriched communication as the medium of enriched understanding' and 'capability to cope with the pressures of social and economic change' (Ranson and Rutledge, 2005, p. 44).

Parental perspectives on parenting programmes suggest that they value a mixture of models being available. Miller and Sambell (2003) are critical of what they see as a 'dispensing model' whereby a professional, such as a health visitor, gives 'expert' advice on how to tackle 'problems' parents are experiencing. Yet parents reported that they valued exactly this sort of direct practical information from someone they perceived as an expert. However, parents also appreciated more reflective discussions which relied on the facilitator being able to create a supportive and non-judgemental environment.

This raises issues for practitioners both about the range of skills and expertise needed and about what changes they are trying to achieve. Is it to equip parents with information, or with the skills to understand and find their own solutions to parenting situations? The findings also reinforce the idea that while the focus of parenting education is on the parent–child relationship, this is linked to the need to change patterns of relationships and gender arrangements amongst the adults in the family.

The views of parents highlighted again the role played by individual practitioners in being able to create the right environment and forge working relationships. The individual qualities of the group leader were reported as being important, as were issues such as whether they had children of their own – suggesting the significance of how we use ourselves and our experiences, an issue which we will explore in the next section.

Thinking point 3.8   What personal qualities or experiences could you bring to forming relationships with families?

Key points

1   Parents and carers value relationships with practitioners that are based on values similar to those described by children, for example, honesty, empathy and respect – even in situations of difficulty or conflict.

2   Practitioners need to adapt their knowledge and skills to work with increasingly complex families.

3   The experience of involving men in family work highlights the value of exploring issues such as gender in more detail in relation to forming positive relationships.

4   Parenting has increasingly become the focus of policy and an area of practice for practitioners from all disciplines.

3 Putting the 'relationship' into positive relationships

3.1 Relationship-based practice

The central importance of practitioners having 'relationship skills' in their work with children and their families may seem obvious but professional training and practice has not always placed a strong emphasis on developing and analysing these skills (Howe, 1998). In some areas, practitioners may even feel that the skills they have acquired in forming relationships have been undermined or marginalised. In 1998, Schofield, writing in a social work context, identified something of a crisis in the profession's beliefs about the importance of relationships:

> Many social workers have lost confidence in the value of their relationships with children and families and in their capacity to understand and help them.
>
> (Schofield, 1998, p. 57)

In reasserting the importance of relationship, Schofield, borrowing from the work of Winnicott, uses the idea of 'outer worlds' – those of external events and relationships – and 'inner worlds' – the emotional life. This reflects the reality for practitioners who might have to enable someone to deal with problems in their lives related to finance or housing (the outer world) while being aware of their issues of self-esteem and anger (the inner world).

Clearly the two worlds have a dynamic connection – a worker should be able 'to understand the two different worlds' and 'act as a bridge between them' (Schofield, 1998, p. 58). Only through understanding both will the specific perspective of an individual be ascertained. In this model, developing a relationship and understanding the complex interactions within it is key. It is acknowledged that the type of (longer-term) work implied by this approach 'may be dismissed as a luxury' in the modern working environment although the model is still applicable to everyday practice – 'even a single interview can draw on sophisticated relationship skills' (Schofield, 1998, p. 63).

A renewed interest in 'relationship-based practice' is often presented as a counterweight to increasingly bureaucratic approaches to practice. However, this is precisely why it is in danger of being seen as the 'luxury' referred to above. Practitioners in a range of agencies often describe experiencing the modern working environment as one dominated by a growth in procedures, regulation, bureaucracy and accountability, usually linked to specific outcomes:

> 'More than ever before ... it seems like accountability is very hot on the agenda – demonstrating out-comes and having to have almost number-crunching-type pieces of information you can give'
>
> (Social work manager quoted in Banks, 2004, p. 151)

It is an environment, too, where practitioners experience pressure on time and budgets, factors that can undermine their efforts to demonstrate some of the key characteristics of establishing positive relationships that we have explored.

QUARTER 2 2005/06 Name of project	Monitoring on time & complete	Target met	Quarterly report on regular support		Spending to budget
			Target	Achieved	
Play Day	🙂	🙂	7	14	🙂
Kids are Kool	😐	🙂	10	12	🙁
The Parenting Project	🙂	🙁	36 families	9 families	🙂
The Early Intervention Project	🙂	🙂	10	14	🙁
SPLASH	🙂	🙂	20	20	🙂
The Big Helpline	🙂	🙂	50 calls	72 calls	😐
Education for Life	🙁	🙂	8	9	🙂
Have a say (participation)	😐	🙁	18	12	🙂

Targets, and regular target-focused reports, are increasingly common in the modern practice environment. In the adapted example above, a report on projects funded by the Children's Fund uses a 'traffic light' system to indicate whether targets and budgets are being met.

This 'modern' environment is not just a UK phenomenon. A survey of early years professionals in Australia on the impact of regulation found that, while regulation underpinned some aspects of quality of care, it also worked against building effective partnerships with children and parents. Regulation was also seen as undermining the autonomy of workers (Fenech et al., 2007). It is important to note here that regulation, procedures and targets can be seen by practitioners as having an important role in improving outcomes for children while, simultaneously, reducing the time to work with them.

Voluntary organisations can equally feel the effects of targets and budgetary expectations on their work. As a more mixed economy of care has developed, so many voluntary sector organisations have become increasingly dependent on central and local government funding, often tied to specific outcomes (Hayes, 2004; Ivory, 2007). These changes have enabled a valuable expansion of the sector and clear focusing of their work but can also result in challenges to the core aims and values of individual projects and the practitioners within them. It is possible that 'relationship-forming' with children can suffer when projects are required to focus on time-limited work to achieve specific outcomes, for example, those related to social exclusion.

There are, however, other reasons why practitioners can appear to be tied up with forms and procedures. When the issues being worked with are complex, practitioners have to manage their own responses to difficult subjects. Children's distress can 'propel workers into devoting their energies to working around rather than with children', while falling back on procedures and forms 'facilitates the sidestepping of messy, distressing emotional issues' (Charles and Butler, 2004, p. 194).

While, arguably, all work with children and their families is conducted through a relationship, Gillian Ruch argues that the idea of relationship-based practice is more explicit, drawing on a psycho-social model of practice that aims to engage with the complexity of individuals (Ruch, 2005). This is not just interpersonal skill, in terms of being able to actively listen, although such skills are clearly vital, but places a value on the 'use of self' and the quality of the relationship.

> What the idea of 'use of self' conveys is that the individual is, in a sense, a resource for practice: you draw on your own experience, feelings, perceptions to make sense of the world and to frame your understanding of others.
>
> (Turney, 2007, p. 66)

In fact social work, for example, does have a history of relationship-based work but this early psycho-dynamic model came to be criticised as individualistic and pathologising, locating the problem in the individual and setting up the worker as expert. New versions of this model of practice have attempted to address this by recognising the impact of the broader social and political context in which people live and the value of anti-oppressive practice and empowerment.

The importance of practitioner relationships can be interpreted as significant in children's lives in other ways too. Margaret Bell (2002), for example, suggests that the idea of 'secondary attachment' is a useful concept in working with children. The previous chapters have explored the theory of attachment and debates about the extent to which attachments subsequent to the primary one can, over the life course, play a positive role in modifying a child's 'internal working model'. Usually this discussion is in relation to significant others in their lives: family and friends. However, it is possible that other adults in a 'practitioner' role can play a part – the encouraging teacher, or the leader in the Brownies who boosts self-esteem, for example.

The value placed on practitioner relationships also fits with the concept of resilience (see Chapter 7). This suggests that a significant supportive relationship outside the family can be a valuable resource to offset the impact of adverse experiences on children. Practitioners can help enable the development of these relationships but may also contribute directly to a child's sense of self-esteem through their own relationship.

3.2 Constructing relationships

Another perspective on developing relationships between practitioners and children and families is provided by ideas drawn from social constructionism. This suggests that social worlds are created, not given, each of us constructing our own realities through interaction with other people. Equally what constitutes a 'problem' within the social world, for example, is a problem because a particular issue has been described, or constructed, as such (Parton and O'Byrne, 2000).

The idea of issues being 'described' is important, as it is the use of language and narratives in this process that is seen as particularly significant. The ideas of social constructionism take the practitioner beyond just 'listening': someone talking is not just describing the reality of their life but is actively constructing it. Talking is also the medium through which the relationship is constructed and shared views (or differences of opinion) discovered.

> In order to understand a human situation we must go to the actors themselves and the act of telling their stories not only becomes the focus of the work but a central way in which their situation can be improved.
>
> (Parton and O'Byrne, 2000, p. 184)

Parton and O'Byrne argue that adopting this perspective leads to an approach to working with people distinct from that drawing on psycho-dynamic models and including the following elements:

- What is important is what people actually say rather than seeking the hidden meanings behind it.

- Workers are not positioned as experts; the service user has some expertise of their own. Both perspectives are then shared.

- An emphasis on solutions rather than hypotheses about causes and explanations. This also means an approach that focuses on strengths rather than deficits.

This approach still emphasises the importance of the relationship-building skills we have discussed in this chapter. There also remains a power dynamic, as with all other practitioner interactions, but, arguably, this approach can enable a working relationship – the co-construction of conversations and solutions – based more firmly on partnership and participation.

Butler and Green (1998) illustrate in more detail how this approach can apply to work with children. Children too, they argue, have 'constructs' that define the ways in which they interact with the world and which shape their behaviour. Again children are seen as the experts on themselves and the practitioner's role is to understand the world through their eyes – perhaps a bigger challenge than understanding an adult perspective.

Practitioners need to gain an understanding of children's views of themselves and their world

Achieving this understanding requires the ability to communicate with children and the skills to enable them to, for example, describe themselves (perhaps in writing, drawing or self-portraits), or describe how they think others see them. Practitioners must also be able to create a trusting relationship within which it is safe for children to express themselves. A sense of being non-judgemental is crucial, stressing that individual views will be respected and that there are no right or wrong answers (Butler and Green, 1998).

Thinking point 3.9   What other ways could practitioners use to try to understand a child's 'worldview'?

3.3 Reflecting on the boundaries

Many of the approaches mentioned in this chapter require practitioners in all settings and disciplines to be prepared to think about and develop their practice around relationships with children and their families. What implications do the views of children have for my practice? How have I taken into account the issues of gender, ethnicity or disability? How would I assess my own relationship-building skills with children? 'Reflecting' can help new skills develop and new strategies for practice to emerge.

The value of 'reflection' has long been advocated in many areas of professional training – nursing, teaching and social work – as a mechanism for developing practice. But it is equally valued in the emergence of more recent qualifications, for example, for early years workers and teaching assistants, and is applicable to any role where connecting with children is important. The broad principle that all practitioners should 'know how to reflect and improve' was also confirmed in the 'common core' of skills and knowledge for the whole children's workforce in England (DfES, 2005a).

On one level, reflection is simply a process of learning by reviewing previous experiences. However, the concept of reflection has been developed much further, requiring a more critical questioning not just of practice but of ourselves and our assumptions. Our notions of what families should be like, for example, may be particularly strongly held, perhaps depending on our own experiences. But what is the impact of these beliefs on our practice? Are we more or less likely to be able to form effective working relationships with stepfathers, for example? Why do we find certain families particularly 'hard to reach'? Reflective practice is seen as even more central to approaches that emphasise the 'use of self':

> Reflective practice is the key determinant in the effective and successful application of relationship-based practice
>
> (Ruch, 2005, p. 115)

There is now a substantial and complex literature on reflection, exploring how reflection can occur both when looking back on an incident (reflection-on-action) and when 'thinking on your feet' (reflection-in-action) (Schon, 1987). Given that practitioners do not always see theory as related to real-life experience, reflection can also provide the opportunity to integrate theory into practice.

Reflective practice can also help with issues of drawing the boundaries round the role of individual workers. There are many potential models of relationships with children and families – friend, adviser, advocate, for example. Which model is most appropriate for which role? The demand for practitioners to form relationships with children and families by drawing on personal qualities, or the 'use of self', inevitably raises the issue of where the 'professional' boundary should lie.

Gray (2002) provides one illustration of this in relation to a small-scale study of family support workers in east London. The role of the workers in the family support service was specifically to 'befriend' families, develop close relationships and engage with them at an emotional level. The service also specifically attempted to recruit, from the same community, people with similar backgrounds to those with whom they were working. This recruitment strategy was evaluated by families as being particularly helpful in promoting culturally sensitive practice in an ethnically diverse area. It also seemed to enable family support workers to act as intermediaries between the family and other practitioners, such as social workers, who by implication were not able to create such close, trusting, relationships.

A Canadian study of social worker–'client' relationships found two significant categories emerged from their analysis that were central to building good relationships:

> Soft, mindful and judicious use of power ...

> Humanistic attitude and style that stretches traditional professional ways-of-being.

> (de Boer and Coady, 2007, p. 35)

The first of these is a reminder of how, for parents and carers, the issue of power runs through all relationships with practitioners to some degree. The second underlines the difficulty of drawing the boundaries of working relationships. Clients, for example, appreciated the disclosure of personal information:

> 'I think [the worker] had the most influence on me by letting me know little tidbits of information about her own life. Knowing that she had been through things was really helpful to know. She may be the worker but she has had a couple of knocks too.'

> (de Boer and Coady, 2007, p. 38)

Informality, 'small-talk', going 'the extra mile', were all qualities reported positively arguing as one client did that '... the roles need to be bent a bit (de Boer and Coady, 2007, p. 39).

Similar issues can arise in relationships with children and young people. Turney (2007), for example, considers the challenge of whether practice can be underpinned by authentic relationships and 'loving care' and yet be contained within clear and appropriate boundaries.

The family support service discussed above recognised the dangers of over-identification, and the dilemma inherent in setting out to establish 'close relationships, verging on peer relationships, but maintaining some professional distance' (Gray, 2002, p. 19). Working in a reflective way can enable difficult boundary issues to be managed but also requires the recognition of an emotional dimension that needs supporting.

Key points

1 Practitioners can experience situations in which the skill of relationship formation has to take a lower priority than the demands of procedures and targets.

2 'Relationship-based practice' provides one alternative view of the nature of professional relationships.

3 Relationships can be viewed as being co-constructed through the medium of language by practitioners in partnership with children and adults. This approach emphasises reaching shared understandings and solutions.

4 Enhancing skills in developing positive relationships with children and families needs to be underpinned by reflective practice.

Conclusion

For all those working with children and their families, the ability to form positive relationships is both a basic requirement and a complex skill. There are clear and simple messages from children and adults about the qualities that they seek in relationships with practitioners but they have to be translated into a variety of practice settings. Relationships are overlaid by issues of power, gender, ethnicity and class, and the nature of what constitutes 'good' and 'positive' relationships, and their boundaries, is also an area for debate and discussion. Practitioners need to be able to question and reflect on these issues to start the process of connecting with children and their worlds.

References

Ahmad, Y., Dalrymple, J., Daum, M., Griffiths, N., Hockridge, T. and Ryan, E. (2003) *Listening to Children and Young People*, Bristol, University of the West of England.

Banks, S. (2004) *Ethics, Accountability and the Social Professions*, Basingstoke, Palgrave Macmillan.

Bannister, A. and Huntington, A. (2002) *Communicating with Children and Adolescents: Action for Change*, London, Jessica Kingsley.

Batchelor, J. (2003) 'Working with family change: repartnering and stepfamily life' in Bell, M. and Wilson, W., *The Practitioner's Guide to Working with Families*, London, Palgrave Macmillan.

Bell, M. (2002) 'Promoting children's rights through the use of relationship', *Child & Family Social Work*, vol. 7, pp. 1–11.

Bunting, L. (2004) 'Parenting programmes: the best available evidence', *Child Care in Practice*, vol. 10, no. 4, pp. 327–343.

Butler, I. and Williamson, H. (1994) *Children Speak: Trauma and Social Work*, Harlow, Longman.

Butler, R. and Green, D. (1998) *The Child Within: The Exploration of Personal Construct Theory with Young People*, Oxford, Butterworth Heinemann.

Cameron, C. (2001) 'Promise or problem? A review of the literature on men working in early childhood services', *Gender, Work and Organisation*, vol. 8, no. 4, pp. 430–453.

Charles, M. and Butler, S. (2004) 'Social workers' management of organisational change' in Lymbery, M. and Butler, S. (eds) *Social Work Ideals and Practice Realities*, Basingstoke, Palgrave Macmillan, p. 194.

Chawla-Duggan, R. (2006) 'Explaining the role of father development workers in supporting early years learning', *Early Years*, vol. 26, no. 1, pp. 93–109.

Chief Secretary to the Treasury (2003) *Every Child Matters*, London, The Stationery Office.

ChildLine (2003) *Boys Allowed – What Boys and Young Men tell ChildLine About Their Lives*, London, ChildLine.

Cleaver, H., Walker, S. and Meadows, P. (2004) *Assessing Children's Needs and Circumstances*, London, Jessica Kingsley.

Connolly, P. (2004) *Boys and Schooling in the Early Years*, London, Routledge Falmer.

de Boer, C. and Coady, N. (2007) 'Good helping relationships in child welfare: learning from stories of success', *Child & Family Social Work*, vol. 2, no. 1, pp. 32–42.

Department for Education and Skills (DfES) (2004) *Engaging Fathers – Involving Parents, Raising Achievement*, London, DfES.

Department for Education and Skills (DfES) (2005a) *Common Core of Skills and Knowledge for the Children's Workforce*, London, DfES.

Department for Education and Skills (DfES) (2005b) *The Common Assessment Framework*, London, The Stationery Office.

Department for Education and Skills (DfES) (2005c) *Excellence and Enjoyment: Social and Emotional Aspects of Learning. Relationships Years 1 and 2*, London, DfES.

Department of Health (DoH) (2000) *Assessing Children in Need and Their Families*, London, HMSO.

Department of Health (DH) (2000) *Assessing Children in Need and Their Families*, London, HMSO.

Dunn, J. and Deater-Deckard, K. (2001) *Children's Views of their Changing Families*, York, Joseph Rowntree Foundation.

Eyres, I., Cable, C., Hancock, R. and Turner, J. (2004) '"Whoops, I forgot David": children's perceptions of the adults who work in their classrooms', *Early Years*, vol. 24, no. 2, pp. 149–162.

Featherstone, B. (2004) *Family Life and Family Support: A Feminist Analysis*, London, Palgrave.

Featherstone, B. and Evans, H. (2004) *Children Experiencing Maltreatment: Who Do They Turn To?*, London, NSPCC.

Fenech, M., Robertson, G., Sumsion, J. and Goodfellow, J. (2007) 'Working by the rules: early childhood professionals' perceptions of regulatory requirements', *Early Child Development and Care*, vol. 177, no. 1, pp. 93–106.

Goldman, R. (2005) *Fathers' Involvement in their Children's Education*, London, National Family and Parenting Institute.

Gray, B. (2002) 'Emotional labour and befriending in family support and child protection in Tower Hamlets', *Child & Family Social Work*, vol. 7, pp. 13–22.

Hallett, C., Murray, C. and Punch, S. (2003) 'Young people and welfare: negotiating pathways' in Hallett, C. and Prout, A. (eds) *Hearing the Voices of Children: Social Policy for a New Century*, London, Routledge Falmer.

Hamre, B. and Pianta, R. (2001) 'Early teacher-child relationships and the trajectory of children's school outcomes through eighth grade', *Child Development*, vol. 72, no. 2, pp. 625–638.

Hayes, D. (2004) 'Government bodies could swamp community sector, LSPs fear', available online at <http://www.communitycare.co.uk/Articles/2004/07/16/45546/government-bodies-could-swamp-community-sector-lsps.html?key=TARGETS>, accessed 30 August 2007.

Headliners (2007) *Children's professionals: what I really think of my ...* , available online at <http://www.headliners.org/storylibrary/stories/2005/childrensprofessionalswhatireallythinkofmy.htm?id=6787184094961558887>, accessed 8 August 2007.

Holland, S. (2004) *Child and Family Assessment in Social Work Practice*, London, Sage.

Howe, D. (1998) 'Relationship-based thinking and practice in social work', *Journal of Social Work Practice*, vol. 16, no. 2, pp. 45–56.

Ivory, M. (2007) 'The moral and ethical debate over the voluntary sector's acceptance of public money for services' available online at <http://www.communitycare.co.uk/Articles/2007/04/12/104128/the-moral-and-ethical-debate-over-the-voluntary-sectors-acceptance-of-public-money-for-services.html?key=RELATIONSHIP>, accessed 30 August 2007.

Lindsay, G. and Muijs, D. (2006) 'Challenging underachievement in boys', *Educational Research*, vol. 48, no. 3, pp. 313–332.

Lloyd, D., O'Brien, M. and Lewis, C. (2003) *National Evaluation Summary: Fathers in Sure Start Local Programmes*, London, DfES.

Lloyd, G. and Stead, J. (2001) 'The boys and girls not calling me names and the teachers to believe me', *Children & Society*, vol. 15, pp. 361–374.

MacLeod, M. (2000) 'What do children need by way of protection? Who is to decide?' in Baldwin, N. (ed.) *Protecting Children: Promoting Their Rights*, London, Whiting & Birch.

McCurdy, K. and Jones, E. (2000) *Supporting Families: Lessons from the Field*, Thousand Oaks, CA, Sage.

Miller, S. and Sambell, K. (2003) 'What do parents feel they need? Implications of parents' perspectives for the facilitation of parenting programmes', *Children & Society*, vol. 17, pp. 32–44.

Moran, P., Ghate, D. and van der Merwe, A. (2004) *What Works in Parenting Support? A Review of the International Evidence*, Research Report 574, London, DfES.

Morgan, R. (2005) 'Finding what children say they want: messages from children', *Representing Children*, vol. 17, no. 3, pp. 180–188.

Morrow, V. (2006) 'Understanding gender differences in context: implications for young children's everyday lives', *Children & Society*, vol. 20, pp. 92–104.

Parton, N. and O'Byrne, P. (2000) *Constructive Social Work: Towards a New Practice*, Basingstoke, Palgrave.

Petrie, P., Boddy, J., Cameron, C., Wigfall, V. and Simon, A. (2006) *Working with Children in Care – European Perspectives*, London, Open University Press.

Pollard, A. (2002) *Reflective Teaching: Effective and Evidence Informed Professional Practice*, London, Continuum.

Prout, A. (2002) 'Researching children as social actors: an introduction to the children 5–16 programme', *Children & Society*, vol. 3, pp. 67–76.

Ranson, S. and Rutledge, H. (2005) *Including Families in the Learning Community: Family Centres and the Expansion of Learning*, York, Joseph Rowntree Foundation.

Robb, M. (2001) 'Men working in childcare' in Foley, P., Roche, J. and Tucker, S. (eds) *Children in Society: Contemporary Theory, Policy and Practice*, Milton Keynes, Palgrave/Open University Press.

Rogers, C. (1980) *A Way of Being*, Boston, Houghton Mifflin.

Rose, W. (2006) 'The developing world of the child: children's perspectives' in Aldgate, J., Jones, D., Rose, W. and Jeffery, C. (eds) *The Developing World of the Child*, London, Jessica Kingsley.

Ruch, G. (2005) 'Relationship-based practice and reflective practice: holistic approaches to contemporary child care social work', *Child & Family Social Work*, vol. 10, pp. 111–123.

Schofield, G. (1998) 'Inner and outer worlds: a psychosocial framework for child and family social work', *Child & Family Social Work*, vol. 3, pp. 57–67.

Schon, D. (1987) *Educating the Reflective Practitioner*, San Francisco, Jossey-Bass.

Scott, S., O'Connor, T. and Futh, A. (2006) *What Makes Parenting Programmes Work in Disadvantaged Areas? The PALS Trial*, York, Joseph Rowntree Foundation.

Scottish Executive (2007) *Getting it Right for Every Child: Guidance on the Child's or Young Person's Plan*, Edinburgh, Scottish Executive.

Seale, A. and Mkandla, M. (2000) 'Work partnerships with Black Communities: issues and principles for social work education, training and service delivery' in Baldwin, N. (ed.) (2000) *Protecting Children: Promoting Their Rights*, London, Whiting & Birch.

Smith, F. and Barker, J. (2000) 'Contested spaces: children's experiences of out of school care in England and Wales', *Childhood*, vol. 7, no. 3, pp. 315–333.

Thoburn J., Lewis A. and Shemmings, D. (1995) *Paternalism or Partnership? Family Involvement in the Child Protection Process*, London, HMSO.

Training and Development Agency for Schools (TDA) (2007) *Professional Standards for Teachers: Qualified Teacher Status*, London, TDA.

Turner, C. (2003) *'Are You Listening?' What Disabled Children and Young People in Wales Think About the Services They Use*, Cardiff, Welsh Assembly.

Turney, D. (2007) 'Practice' in Robb, M., *Youth in Context: Frameworks, Settings and Encounters*, London, Sage/The Open University.

Chapter 4

Listening across generations

Pam Foley

Introduction

The varying views of childhood provided by politics, literature, law, education, and health and welfare agencies have one thing in common: they raise anxious questions rather than providing confident answers. Many of these questions focus on changes experienced by different generations.

Expressions such as 'future generations', 'the next generation', 'the *i*generation' (the *internet* generation), 'the generational gap', figure frequently in everyday interactions – as do questions about how adults can relate to the next generation. How should adults define themselves in relation to children and what does this mean for children's lives? How can adults connect with and listen to children, and vice versa? How do children listen and talk to each other? These are among the central, and often disturbing, questions of any society.

This chapter begins with a principally sociological discussion of adulthood and childhood and how they are constructed in relation to each other. It goes on to examine some of the ways in which adulthood and childhood are played out in life, focusing on some key dimensions including 'human becomings', dependency and care, children in public spaces and children's voices and choices.

Core questions

- Is generation an important dimension of children's lives?
- How is care and dependency a fundamental dimension of child–adult relations?
- What is children's agency?
- How do listening to children, providing choice, and supporting decision making, relate to the ways age relations between adults and children are played out, and why is this fundamental to children's wellbeing?

1 Generations

In the early years of the twenty-first century, ways of understanding what childhood is and what children are, need and aspire to, continue to draw upon some very old, as well as some relatively new, ways of thinking. Within a couple of post-war generations, the relationships between children and adults have undergone some highly significant changes. However, traditional approaches to the care and upbringing of children may be latent in modern families, and certain institutions still hold back or attenuate ideas which could change the ways we relate to and provide for today's children.

Thinking point 4.1   Think about the fundamental social changes during the decades between your generation and your parents' generation. What change has affected your family life most significantly?

Contemporary adults and children live with considerable instability and diversity in their personal familial and social lives. Profound changes in family forms, structures and functions can be seen as having directly affected contemporary adults' and children's lives. Families are no longer so inflexibly built around power differentials centred on particular divisions of labour, and gender no longer restricts opportunities in life as much as before. The family continues to decrease in size and Western European families exist in diverse forms rare in previous generations (Office for National Statistics (ONS), 2006). Demographic changes mean that populations are ageing with relatively fewer children; fewer and fewer adults in Britain live with children (ONS, 2006).

With higher standards of living, children have become significant consumers of goods, toys and leisure services. Consumerism, the internet and mass entertainment have created a shared culture for more affluent children and contribute to a generation gap perhaps more significant than the gaps between children of different classes, genders or ethnicities – even perhaps some nations.

The family is located at a crucial position at the intersection of generational lines. Below the collective and above the individual level, the economic and social dimensions of families have long been recognised as capable of profoundly shaping the lives of individuals. In much of the political rhetoric of the UK, the family is still portrayed as a private and autonomous institution providing materially, culturally, emotionally and socially for its various members and which can be relied upon to work hand in hand with the state.

Yet some early twenty-first century demographic and social changes involving the British family are so marked that they have fuelled deep-seated disquiet about the ability and necessity of 'the family' to care for dependent members, to form the cornerstone of society and instil particular collective values. Changes over recent decades have undoubtedly opened out some families and enabled some individuals to breach boundaries to aspiration; such changes around and inside families present a complex and fast-changing arena for political and social debate, policy and practice formation. These kinds of changes have been referred to as the 'democratisation of the family' by Giddens (1998):

> All is not well with marriage, the family and the care of children, but the question is what effective political strategies could improve them and what ideal state of the family we should strive for. First and most fundamentally we must start from the principle of equality between the sexes, from which there can be no going back. There is only one story to tell about the family today, and that is of democracy. The family is becoming democratized, in ways which track processes of public democracy; and such democratization suggests how family life might combine individual choice and social solidarity ... Democracy in the public sphere involves formal equality, individual rights, public discussion of issues free from violence, and authority which is negotiated rather than given by tradition. The democratized family shares these characteristics, some of which are already protected in national and international law.
>
> (Giddens, 1998, p. 93)

Of course these kinds of changes have been seen by some as family breakdown rather than family democratisation – and it would seem that any democratisation of a family is likely to reflect, among other things, class, ethnicity, religion and gender. Children differentiate, and then absorb into their own identity construction, understandings of differences and social divisions. Gender and childhood, for example, is constructed and mediated through family relationships, friendships and peers, use of public spaces, popular culture and consumption (which is itself highly gendered), and children's own accounts of gender differences (Morrow, 2006). Furthermore, within the same society, families will have widely different attitudes to children's gender identity, autonomy and responsibility, that may reflect their social, cultural, ethnic and religious backgrounds (Aapola et al., 2005).

But it would seem that, if Giddens (1998) is right, this generation of adults may be one of the first to wrestle with becoming part of a democratised family and to face the implications of this for child–adult relations. How might the spread of democratic families, with individuals who have rights and who discuss and negotiate ideas, issues and authority, be affecting this generation's relationship with the next?

Uncertainty certainly seems to be a characteristic of adult–child relations as they are played out in institutions, agencies, services and practices for children and young people. Judgements seem to regularly be made simply on the basis of the child's age rather than an assessment of individual experience and circumstances. The transition from childhood to adulthood has perhaps become more complex and less linear. The erosion of many traditional family forms and communities and the growth in individualisation may have contributed to adults' greater emotional investment in children in what is seen as an increasingly unsafe world (Parton, 2006).

Parents, politicians and social commentators can be heard to express a pervasive anxiety that, if children are not allowed a 'proper' childhood, something largely modelled on perceptions of childhoods of the past, they will become warped, possibly distressed or troublesome adults. But there is little consensus about what such a 'proper childhood' actually is.

Choices made by adults with regard to their family lives, including choices previously seen as unorthodox, have been increasingly backed by law, policy and rights; mothers as full-time workers or homosexual couples as parents, for example. Some phenomena, such as young people who are primary carers for others in their families (Aldridge and Becker, 2003), or the many children who live with horrifying levels of domestic violence while effective preventative measures remain unused (Mullender et al., 2003), challenge ideas about the family in other ways. The majority of mothers with dependent children are now employed outside the home (Office for National Statistics, 2006) and the demise of the distant, authoritarian, father is an equally significant change. For many in previous generations male authority was absolute and children usually encountered the same male authority across all of society: in their families, their schools and their neighbourhoods.

Lee suggests that modern adulthood is a time of particular instability:

> as we enter the twenty-first century the experience of adult life is a lot less stable than it used to be. With regard to being 'grown up' we have entered an age of uncertainty, an age in which adult life is newly unpredictable and in which whatever stabilities we manage to produce cannot be expected to last our whole lives.
>
> (Lee, 2001a, p. 7)

Thinking point 4.2   Is there considerable instability in the current generation of adults about adulthood itself? And, if adults are increasingly unsure about what it means to be an adult, what might this mean for what adults think about childhood, and what being a child means?

Lee (2001a) suggests there will be major implications for children if adulthood is unstable:

> This change in the experience of adulthood is of central importance to the social study of childhood because after some decades of adult stability, we had grown used to making sense of childhood *through* adulthood ... in terms of what it might tell us about how far a given child has travelled ... A sense of certainty about adulthood and its stability has been the rock on which social scientific knowledge of childhood is built.
>
> (Lee, 2001a, p. 8)

You may or may not agree either that families have become democratised or that generations are experiencing an unprecedented level of instability. But, if either or both are true, an effect may be that adults are more likely to draw upon the more familiar and common concepts of childhood, such as children being innocent, vulnerable and inept. At times when considerable change and instability are being experienced, adults may be less likely to engage with new ideas about children and childhood concerning competence, participation and rights. It is to these notions and conceptions of the child, children and childhood that we turn next.

1.1 The 'otherness' of children

In everyday language, we have a tendency to think and talk in dualisms and among these are some that can be particularly important for any analysis of child–adult relations. Some of these dualisms are among the fundamental concepts which can shape children's lives: children are dependent and pre-rational, adults autonomous and rational; adults are competent and children incompetent; children play while adults work; children are innocent and vulnerable, adults invulnerable; adults know things, children are only learning things; adults have rights but children acquire rights as they grow up. Decisions are frequently made using these kinds of conceptual frameworks about what children want and need, about children's ability to form and express opinions or make decisions about, for example, their own medical treatment. So where have these ideas about ignorance, innocence and dependence (Hendrick, 1997) come from? We need to take a brief look back in time.

Throughout the twentieth century the expansion of, first, education and, subsequently, childcare, saw education gradually replacing work and wage-earning as the principal focus and occupation of children and young people. Simultaneously, childcare became something which was increasingly carried out outside the home. The expansion of the education system has meant that young people are now dependent on their parents for longer although, paradoxically, the same period has seen a fall in the ages at which children reach physical maturity. Schools, particularly, forming their own ethos, behaviours and processes, made several highly significant contributions to the construction of a twentieth-century childhood. Hendrick (1997) observed:

> It is worth noting that by compulsorily keeping children within the classroom, schooling lengthened the years of 'childhood', while simultaneously reinforcing notions of the characteristics that were said to constitute *proper* childhood, namely ignorance, innocence and dependence. In this way, the *concept* of childhood (especially for working class children) was altered.
>
> (Hendrick, 1997, p. 64)

Once children occupied separate, designated spaces apart from adults, they were no longer seen by adults as 'rural children' or 'working class children' but as a single homogenous group to which concepts such as 'childhood innocence' could more readily be applied. And once children became a less differentiated group, it was easier to construct and record the 'natural' or normal child, and the normal childhood (Hendrick, 1997). The separation of children led to the development of educational, psychological and political theories that made the definition of a 'normal' child and a 'normal' family possible. The public health movement was also crucially positioned to make a significant contribution to the normalisation of children and childhood (Armstrong, 1983):

> The clinic was one of the most significant ways in which 'society' (in the form of psychiatrists, social workers, psychologists, educators, magistrates and penal administrators) came to 'know' children and to seek to 'adjust' them to what was regarded as normal behaviour.
>
> (Hendrick, 1997, p. 53)

The twentieth century also saw a proliferation of advice on parenting, and on childhood as a critical developmental phase, which continues unabated. From evolutionary theorists at the beginning of the century, this interest in childhood spread through a whole range of behaviourists and psychologists. The child was no longer seen as an empty vessel to be filled with knowledge, shaped and disciplined, but as an impressionable and vulnerable creature whose entire future hopes and happiness hung to a disturbing extent on infantile experience. The emerging sciences of psychology and psychoanalysis repeatedly 'problematised' the early stages of life. While treating only a small number of children, child psychologists offered explanations of physical, emotional and mental growth and development that fed directly into guidance to parents, the nursery school movement, educational psychology, psychoanalysis, and child guidance within education (Foley, 2001).

More recent theories have successfully challenged some of those ideas, which portray children as progressing through a series of essential, sequential, critical events, or which specify particular damaging family structures and circumstances. An ecological approach, with its emphasis on social context, has now been widely adopted. The rethinking of childhood services of the past few years owes much to the critical movement in psychology of the 1970s and the analysis of child development theory as a primarily social construct in the 1990s (Burman, 1994). The life course is undergoing a process of re-interpretation in terms of both its phases and the linearity of its progress. It is now recognised that people 'time shift', may choose to change the apparently prescribed ordering of life events or maybe omit or return to particular life stages.

There is growing acceptance of the idea that psychologically healthy personalities can develop in a variety of social groupings and family structures, and that a variety of adults and settings contributes to a child's quality of life. Traditional developmental psychology has been criticised for dissecting childhood into sequential, immutable levels or stages that all children must pass through on a path to adulthood (James and Prout, 1997). The assumption of a linear path of development, through age-graded educational institutions towards abstract rational adulthood, has been criticised as depicting children (as opposed to adults) as incomplete, and moving in a preordained narrow direction (Burman, 1994). The critique of this aspect of child development had much in common with those who stress learning through cultural frameworks, and developmental psychology has now become more contextualised. But child development theories and psychotherapeutic understandings of children and families remain deeply rooted in the ways we think about, and respond to, children and childhood.

The institutionalisation and reproduction of particular family forms and structures was consolidated throughout the twentieth century and became embedded in state and legal policies and processes (Donzelot, 1979). Each family, with limited support from health, social care and educational systems, is expected to instil in children values essential to operating successfully beyond the family. At the same time there have been some radical criticisms of the family. Sociologists have problematised the concepts of private and public worlds, particularly for women and children, and have challenged the notion of the family as a uniformly supportive haven. The family has been deconstructed to focus on its positioning of individuals according to gender and generation (Aapola et al., 2005).

Disquiet about children's, young people's and families' behaviour that transgresses certain rules has long been a cyclical feature of societies. Tactics to deal with what is now referred to as anti-social behaviour, use the language of respect and responsibilities to draw on those semi-mythical days when all children are remembered as respecting all adults. Policies with an emphasis on inclusivity and social justice are conditional on a 'no more excuses' approach; younger and younger children have been locked in institutions even as concerns grow regarding the treatment of children in custodial care (Goldson et al., 2002). Media representations of children, with their sense of panic about behaviour and lack of (self) control, have little trouble connecting with the public's anxieties. There is a sense of adult unease and fear for the collective future, with which children are naturally connected, that has resulted in an increasingly anxious tone to some government policies. In a world with complex economic, social and moral problems, policy responses can seem an ineffectual way to change the present; controlling the future through controlling children may seem a more feasible option for politicians, and others (Prout, 2005).

Separation anxieties

However much some adults need or wish to separate themselves from children, separation itself also figures largely in adult anxieties about children. Children's first experiences of personal relationships, notably their 'attachment', is widely seen as essential for both healthy psychological 'adjustment' and successful socialisation. Yet too much family care can be criticised as preventing children from developing independence and self-sufficiency. While, on the other hand, too many care providers or too little care from parents is also thought to exceed a child's capacity to cope, producing bewilderment, distress and inability to form strong relationships in adulthood. Ideas about what is needed for healthy emotional and social development have become less definitive; the notion that certain things must happen at particular times is now thought to be erroneous. Child development is understood as related to a wide range of influences and not as a staged series of predictable events. But a significant level of unease remains around these questions which seem crucial to children's development and wellbeing.

Children still need to be able to make claims upon adults, and upon adults' organisations, to protect them as individuals and to shield them as a group from the most pernicious aspects of social and economic change. The welfare of children, with and apart from their parents, is one of the central issues in a long-running debate about the division of responsibilities between the individual and the state; whose responsibility is it that children grow up safeguarded from harm, physically, emotionally and mentally healthy and happy, and how can this be measured? Children are believed to be surrounded by many concentric layers of adult protection, first parents and the home, then health and welfare workers, then the state itself. But economic and environmental deprivation remain powerfully negative circumstances in which it is difficult to effectively and kindly parent, or to fulfil potential and perhaps be happy as a child. Inequalities and discrimination further exacerbate economic differentials.

Many parents remain profoundly anxious about their ability (or the state's ability) to effectively protect their children, and this is reflected in children's access to and use of spaces outside the home. Better-quality housing and more indoor space and comfort mean that children spend less time outdoors and are consequently less visible in shared public places, such as the street. Smaller families have also contributed to the erosion of the street-orientated lives of children, based on families and neighbourhoods. Many parents, grandparents and other carers feel different, but very real, anxieties about children and public spaces:

> parental fears for children's safety in public space are constructed and mobilised through the media, vicarious experiences, 'community' and educational campaigns ... global and national reporting of violent crimes against children may distort local fears by heightening parents' awareness of extreme and rare events in public space causing them to restrict their children's use of space excessively, while also obscuring the extent to which children are at risk in 'private' space and from people they know. This false geography of fear potentially makes it more difficult for children to recognise or speak up about unsafe experiences in domestic contexts.
>
> (Valentine, 2004, p. 29)

Past norms of child-rearing saw children's ownership of their neighbourhoods as an essential aspect of childhood but this has been subsumed by the demands of traffic. So, although children of all classes now travel further afield than ever before (including abroad for holidays), their independent movement is ever more curtailed. Debates about space for children have become arguments about which is more dangerous, the local park or the local streets, the play scheme or the beach.

Concerns about safety and the risk of abuse or violence have severely limited the amount of time that children use the outdoors and public spaces alone. Far fewer play outside or travel alone before they are teenagers or are allowed to attend groups, clubs and entertainment without adults. The status of British childhood has meant that children are increasingly confined to special institutions, to safe contacts, fixed times and preserved spaces (Prout, 2005). Children's play spaces, particularly for urban and suburban children, are becoming more privatised and are frequently confined, controlled, and essentially artificial, spaces designed by adults.

Thinking point 4.3   Are children and adults spending less time together in communal intergenerational spaces? Do children spend less time together not being watched by adults? What effects might this have on child–adult relations?

Twenty-first-century children spend much less time playing outside than their parents and grandparents

It seems important to examine how changes to connections between children and adults have an impact on day-to-day child–adult relations. For example, Valentine (2004) identified how this is particularly difficult for men who may now feel unable to respond to children in public spaces – as this man, interviewed for her research, describes:

> Father: We went to this show ... and this little kiddie came wandering up ... and he's crying 'Where's my mummy?' And my immediate reaction was God, you know, keep the kid here where he's safe, don't let him go wandering round, but at the same time it was God, I hope nobody thinks I'm taking this kid. And I was terrified to actually hold on to the child in case somebody thought I was taking him.
>
> (Valentine, 2004, p. 28)

If British children are increasingly living their lives within designated spaces over which they have little influence, their dependence on adults will also increase. They become dependent on adults to supply places for them to meet and play and to transport them to these particular environments. For some children their day-to-day movements are located in places so disparate, and at times so specified, that they are totally dependent on parents for timing and transportation. So adults can be essential to make children's spaces accessible to children. Adults take on those roles because of a perceived necessity to protect children but perhaps also from the perception that other adults should be protected from disturbance by children and relieved of having to take children's needs into account. Many children are thereby doubly dependent on adults, both to provide spaces for them as children and as a bridge to those extra-familial environments thought suitable for children. This highly dependent situation is a distinct change for this generation of parents and children.

Inevitably, when restricted to certain times and spaces, child-to-child contact is briefer and more segmented. A child is now less likely to meet another child as a whole person but as a possessor of a certain interest or characteristic they share. Playing football, for example, is now more likely to entail a footballing coaching session stratified into age groups at a designated place, to which the child is taken and picked up at specified times, than an improvised activity in the street or park with like-minded children of widely differing ages. Such an over-structured family and school life, it has been suggested, can suffocate children who are never in control of their own times and spaces (Ennew, 1994). Children today may therefore have fewer 'inclusive places' than previous generations; an 'inclusive space' may be understood as space that has been, and is, produced and reproduced to reflect the interests of all those who might wish to use that space (Gallagher, 2006). Local streets are still inclusive places for some children but, as Mayall suggests, streets as public spaces can be problematic:

> We should note initially that children at home and school are generally thought to be in the right place, whereas children anywhere else offer challenges to many adults' assumptions ... it is especially common for children outside the home to be ascribed low moral status; they find themselves regarded as unreliable, feckless, lying, opportunistic and even dangerous.
>
> (Mayall, 2006, p. 208)

Reports focusing on the emotional and mental health and wellbeing of children repeatedly highlight that, if children are able to play outside and get around on their own, they will develop more resilience and be healthier. As Valentine writes:

> This decline in children's independent mobility and use of space in contemporary western societies matters because play is a means through which children's physical, mental and creative capabilities are developed. ... Outdoor play in particular is crucial because it is the primary mechanism through which children become acquainted with their environment.
>
> (Valentine, 2004, p. 74)

Of course, for many adults certain spaces are also inaccessible; but it is through aspects of modern life, such as the provision and use of space, that a modern childhood is shaped and realised.

Human beings, human becomings

Perhaps the most profound division in the perception of adulthood and childhood is that of 'human being' and 'human becoming'. This has been identified by sociologists such as Qvortrup:

> Children are human beings, not only "human becomings", they have not only needs, a fact which is recognized, they have also interests, that may or may not be compatible with interests of other social groups or categories, and they are exposed to societal forces like other groups, layers, and classes. At the same time children and childhood are influenced by external social forces in particular ways, exactly as other groups in our society are influenced in accordance with their status, their activities and how they are valued.
>
> (Qvortrup, 1994, p. 18)

To Lee (2001a) the concept of children as 'human becomings' is one of the crucial ways they figure within adult concepts and concerns; socialisation, for example, could be considered the answer to adult concerns with the social order, while developmentalism provides an answer to the conception that children need different things at different ages.

Thinking point 4.4   What is another example of thinking of children as 'human becomings' rather than as 'human beings'?

One example of 'human becomings' might be the rights discourse, as it relates to children. Children have human rights on the same basis as everybody else – but children also seem to need 'children's rights' because children have been excluded from what is understood as universal (Leach, 1994). The United Nations Convention on the Rights of the Child (UNCRC) (United Nations, 1989) was considered necessary despite the existence of the Universal Declaration of Human Rights since 1948 (Lee, 2001a). The UNCRC has stimulated work for children all over the world as it supports children to make claims on adults to respond to and uphold their rights. The rights approach does not obscure what children require for a decent quality of life – education, healthcare, a family, a home, a safe environment – but places greater emphasis on the strengths and capacities of children, and on their entitlement to equal consideration while they are still children.

The mainstreaming of a rights discourse in relation to children and children's services has led to a new focus on self-determination and participation as well as provision and protection (Osler and Starkey, 2005). The rights discourse has value not least because it is among the concepts of differentiation between adulthood and childhood that children readily grasp and effectively use, as these children make clear:

> 'Child rights means that children can't just be bossed about by older people. I don't think children's rights are heard and taken seriously. I think that children should be heard in parliament. A teenager, someone who is eighteen, could represent them. Adult and child rights are both as important because they are the same, it's just their age that's the difference. I don't think children all over the world have the same rights because in some places women and children have got to be married by the time they are twelve.'
>
> (Child, Headliners, 2001, webpage)

> 'Child rights are something that you are entitled to. All children should have the right to have a life, the right to live somewhere and the right to have education. The right to have choice would be my own child right. Children's rights are more important than adults because they have a future ahead of them.'
>
> (Child, Headliners, 2001, webpage)

> 'A Child right means what children want and what children need. The government makes decisions on what children want. I would stop child abuse if I could bring out my own child rights. Children's rights are more important than adults because adults can defend themselves. In some countries children don't have schools.'
>
> (Child, Headliners, 2001, webpage)

As these quotes illustrate, talking about children in terms of their rights means focusing on children as they are now, rather than what they are becoming. For example, the UNCRC states that children have a right to physical integrity which is absolute irrespective of culture, religion or tradition. Bodily integrity, a person's right to autonomous control over their own body, cannot be overestimated. It is this right that informs, for example, judgements about how the competence of children is assessed to make medical decisions. So the status of children and adults as 'human becomings' as opposed to 'human beings' is, as Lee pointed out, of fundamental importance:

> This being/becoming division underlies and informs relationships between adults and children. It provides adults both with powers over children and with the right and obligation to mediate for them and to protect them. The relationship between being and becoming is clearly a very important issue for students of childhood because, in the case of adults and children, power follows being.
>
> (Lee, 2001a, p. 105)

1.2 Generation gap or generation congestion?

Are we experiencing a time when the gap between generations is unusually wide, unusually narrow or similar to that between previous generations? Are the current generations bumping up against each other in 'generation congestion'? Perhaps it is in the material world that adults and children appear most obviously to be coming closer together.

New technology may close or widen the generation gap

The consumerism of the twentieth century quickly breached the supposed sanctuary of childhood. A brief struggle to protect children and childhood from the market was wholly abandoned in the post-war affluence of most western societies; homes and childhood, far from proving to be havens, now generate their own consumer culture. Some parents, if they can afford to, choose to express their love through gifts and amusements, seeing childhood as a brief period of life to be wholly indulged. The huge market in nursery goods, play equipment, toys, food, sportswear and clothing is now a powerful incentive for parents to earn and spend (Leach, 1994). The visibility of child poverty among contemporary children's levels of consumption can be particularly difficult for children who feel constrained to conform to expectations, and whose failure to do this can make a difference to how they both see themselves and feel about themselves (Ridge, 2006). In Western Europe and North America, children, long ago banished from the workplace, have been repositioned not as producers or workers but as consumers. Many children seem to have become committed and enthusiastic consumers, with elements of 'childhood' being locked into a vast interconnected industry of movies, TV, toys and clothing.

For twenty-first-century children and young people particularly, consumer goods seem to contribute to a blurring of the boundary between adulthood and childhood, as music and leisure entertainment seeks to appeal simultaneously to children as well as to young people and adults. While children's consumption of, for example, films, alcohol, drugs and tobacco is controlled, British governments and parents remain reluctant to interfere in the intensive marketing to children of toys, clothes, food and confectionery. But there is a significant amount of concern expressed about children's involvement with computers and the internet, perhaps reflecting a mixture of emotions and concerns among adults (Hutchby and Moran Ellis, 2001).

Lee (2001a) has suggested that it will become more credible for children to be viewed as 'beings' rather than 'becomings' in a society in which people define themselves through what they own.

Children already, he argues, play an active part in the economy, not as producers, but as people who express and define themselves through what they (albeit indirectly) buy, and this contributes significantly to the de-differentiation of adults and children (Lee, 2001b). At other times children were significant producers, as well as consumers, and this is still the case in much of the world. But a childhood in Western Europe today can be something expressed through material goods and their consumption.

Childhood can be defined and expressed through what is bought and owned

Thinking point 4.5   It can be argued both that the generation gap is expanding and that the generations are becoming more congested. Which argument is the stronger, in your opinion? Or is this a paradox of modern childhood?

Negotiating a childhood

Increasing numbers of children now experience childhoods that are characterised by significant amounts of time away from their parents in day care, schools and after-school clubs, for example. Across and between these settings they encounter a range of competing and complementary values and perspectives about what it means to be a child from media, peers, families and the many adults who work with children (Prout, 2005).

In western societies, the idea of a universal entity called a 'childhood' is less and less sustainable. Solberg (1997) suggested that it is within families that children determine what it means to be a child through a long series of negotiations between the adults who live with them, care for them and educate them. These negotiations take place on many different levels within families about specific practical matters (such as the division of household tasks). But, at another level, Solberg suggests that family members are simultaneously negotiating the meaning of individual childhoods:

> It is the organisation of daily life, the dividing up of tasks between family members, and the laying down of rules of conduct that implicitly determines what it means to be a child.
>
> (Solberg, 1997, p. 126)

In the third section of this chapter we will look at some of the ways children and adults negotiate what it means to be a child in relation to ideas of age, and other dimensions such as gender. But before that we need to consider a crucial dimension of children's lives: dependence.

Dependence is an important dimension of the social positioning of children, and childhood exists within a dynamic network of care relationships beyond that of parent and child. Children need care directly related to their age as their capacity for self-care, and their ability to care for others, develops.

Each individual child is likely to be both a recipient of care from adults and a provider of care as they grow older in a complex, negotiated, evolving dynamic. For Brannen and Moss (2003) children need greater recognition as a distinct social group with specific rights and a recognised position in their families and societies; a major contributor to this could be a re-analysis of care and dependency. Physical and emotional care and dependency are variable, fluctuating but fundamental to the child–adult relationship. All children are dependent at some time on adults. Dependency has been so closely linked with being part of the 'natural' state

Children also develop an ability to care for others

of children that it has become part of the way we define childhood, and children certainly require long-term, personalised and intimate care. Children's physical weaknesses, long period of growth and lack of skills and experience render them temporarily dependent on adults for their survival and wellbeing.

Ordinarily we look to families and to the education and care services to respond to a child's dependency in the most positive way and there remains a general sense of confidence in these to be dependable sources of socialisation, care and education. Children need to depend on close adults, primarily parents and carers, for care, consistency and stability, for emotional support and, in particular, for encouragement and praise. Primary carers can also act as interpreters, as listeners for children's concerns and feelings or as a 'container' for strange, or potentially overwhelming emotions. Children can learn a vocabulary for relationships that they take forward into adult life through these intimate, long-term relationships in early life. The great majority of families fulfil this crucial role: most parents feel a level of responsibility to provide the safe, rich environment a child needs to thrive and it is almost always parents who care most passionately for their children.

So care is what one generation provides for another and is seen as a prime function of the family. However, in the UK, the post-1997 Labour governments have given considerable prominence to childcare in public policy. This has strengthened the concept of care as a commodity, a series of discrete activities that can be defined and regulated, something to be bought and sold (Brannen and Moss, 2003). Indeed, the responsibility of providing safe care for children tends to dominate political attention and depletes adults' willingness to examine other, equally important, aspects of childhood. The concept of care, vital as it is to the lives of children, deserves more critical inspection. Brannen and Moss (2003) offer a more radical concept of care:

> Care as ethic moves us from care as a task performed by adults on children. Rather care is inscribed in all relationships – not only between adults and children (understood as an interactive and reciprocal relationship) but also between adults (parents, workers and others) and between children themselves. Adults *and* children care, and express this care in all relationships in the early childhood institution ... the same is often true of families, in which children are active carers, not dependent objects of care.
>
> (Brannen and Moss, 2003, p. 39)

This more interactive and reciprocal model of care has considerable potential for reconceptualising child–adult relations in the public and private sphere. Children and their parents, working with a small number of familiar adults, can create settings informed by subtly different understandings of children. The potential for a radically different perspective on care is already being realised by some.

The complex elements of adulthood and childhood are played out in institutions, social groupings and individual lives. The things that make children and adults different are real enough. There is, at the very least, a marked difference in levels of power over themselves and others. Most children lack an accumulation of knowledge and experience. But perhaps some divisions between children and adults are given too much emphasis; it might be more accurate to view children, young people and adults as on a continuum in relation to care, for example.

The concept of care is habitually discussed solely in terms of providers and receivers, obscuring the reciprocal nature of care relationships. Brannen et al. (2000) showed children acting on a sense of obligation to care for others. Their sensibility and their view of parental care showed children as actively involved in different levels of care. Children's ability to perceive and respond to emotions appeared to contradict adults' expectations, and children in this study said that respect from adults was sometimes absent, for example during important family discussions.

Of course, there are important differences between children, young people and adults. It is essential, for instance, that children are treated differently within the legal system. But dichotomous thinking could continue to slow down thinking about children and it may be more helpful to first see childhood and adulthood as situated on a continuum, across which the generations affect each other:

> the notion of a generational structure or order refers to a complex set of social processes through which people become (are constructed as) 'children' while other people become (are constructed as) 'adults' ... 'Construction' involves agency (of children and adults); it is best understood as a practical and even material process, and needs to be studied as a practice or a set of practices. It is through such practices that the two generational categories of children and adults are recurrently produced and therefore they stand in relations of connection and interaction, of interdependence: neither of them can exist without the other, what each of them is (a child, an adult) is dependent on its relation to the other, and change in one is tied to change in the other.
>
> (Alanen, 2001, pp. 20–21)

It is this construction of adulthood and childhood, involving agency, that we turn to next.

Key points

1 Children's services are developed according to perceptions of them as both 'human beings' and 'human becomings'.

2 The blurring of adult/child boundaries may be an uncomfortable and anxious part of life, but if it results in helping us to see adulthood and childhood as part of a continuum, this may be of benefit to children.

2 Adult–child relations: the influence of context

Recognising children's agency means recognising that children are not passive but act upon their familial and social worlds. From babyhood, children have a driving, biological and psychological motivation to be part of the social world; they want roles and tasks, to share interests, to have possessions, and to have recognised purpose and function alongside others. Children act out stories and tell jokes that reflect the world as they experience it. They strive to make new connections with people and to join in with older and younger children. Their experiences of guilt, triumph, conflict, cruelty or injustice are reflected through their art, play, literature and drama. They too consider universal human dilemmas, such as fairness and unfairness, fear and happiness, right and wrong, life and death.

There has been a growing recognition of the idea of children as social persons, 'social actors' and participants in a range of quite diverse settings (Hutchby and Moran Ellis, 1998; Prout, 2005). Work with children involves making a series of judgements that need to be focused on individual children, and groups of children, using skilled assessments of their experiences and their relationships within their own familial and social groupings (Mayall, 2002). Children are more widely recognised as engaging in the process of developing the tools and personal skills needed in life for the particular negotiation styles and rules that apply in their families, for example (Butler et al., 2005). This could, perhaps should, lead to some fundamental changes to children's services.

> Observing children's manipulation of the array of these resources allows us to see two things. First, that social competence is not a unitary phenomenon; nor is its 'possession' something that can be traced in a linear, developmental fashion. Rather, the possession, or display, of competence is something that is established in situ, for this particular here-and-now occasion ... The second thing we see is that social competence is therefore an intrinsically contextual matter. Competence cannot be separated from the structural contexts in which it is displayed or negotiated.
>
> (Hutchby and Moran Ellis, 1998, p. 16)

Further recognition that there is, qualitatively, no difference between the agency of adults and that of children, can come together with the challenge to the belief that competency comes only with age in a linear, developmental pattern.

Social spaces usually gradually increase through middle childhood. As children gain experience of organisations outside their homes, such as nurseries and schools, they begin to understand how places affect the people that come together in them. They may ask questions about the roles of people they meet and the function of the organisations they encounter. Recognising children's agency more fully and explicitly means acknowledging that children are experts in their own lives and participants in their own social and cultural world. Children try to make sense of their lives and of the world around them. Babies start to listen to, and learn about, people before they are even born; new-born babies give and receive cues based on the rhythms and intonations of speech, and even very young children can rapidly develop their inbuilt capacities for communication and participation in social settings.

Thinking point 4.6   In what ways could children's agency be further recognised in existing children's services – the care of babies for example? In what ways would mainstream practice be altered?

Skilled listening and observation should enable adults to find out about individual or groups of children: about their relationships and general wellbeing, whether they are happy, anxious or in some kind of distress. Working with groups of children provides opportunities to learn about how they approach and solve problems, how they learn from each other and how they enjoy themselves and have fun. A group of children playing, talking or learning together will contain a number of individuals acting in different, and often complementary, roles. One child may come up with the ideas or possibilities, another is technically inventive, another can put their finger on the weak spot of a plan, another will know where to find the people or things that are needed. These kinds of observations can be a useful thing to recognise, reflect upon, and, maybe, point out to the children themselves.

Relationships between adults and children are strongly influenced by the settings in which they take place. Everyone draws upon understandings of roles within specific contexts; children will search for clues as to what is possible, and what is expected of them, as an individual and as a child. They are likely to categorise adult status using the setting – parent, teacher, doctor, police officer, older person – and adapt what they say according to what they believe to be acceptable or safe. This means that adults need to interpret what children are saying in the light of the context in which they are speaking. Underpinning the social mores that children perceive is the strong inhibition arising from power relationships. Children understand power hierarchies and power imbalances. These children are talking about the police service:

> 'I don't think about the police much but they do their job right. I feel as safe around a police officer like I would around any other person. They are no different to anybody else. The police speak to me as a child because they don't act the same way they do

around adults. The police think that every teenager or young person is bad. I don't know my rights if I needed them in a police station. I do think that they help you sometimes.'

(Child quoted on Headliners, 2002, webpage)

'I think the police are canny good. They make me feel very safe. They never pick on me. It's the police that help you when you need them like if I got into a fight. I don't think there is anything bad about them although there doesn't seem to be many around. The police deal with serious issues. I think they should carry guns.'

(Child quoted on Headliners, 2002, webpage)

'I think the police are horrible and abuse their power. They think they can do anything, which they cannot and I don't feel very safe. If they were quicker getting to places where they were needed then that would help. They don't do enough for young people because they just don't care. They drive around thinking they are hard and stop you for no reason.'

(Child quoted on Headliners, 2002, webpage)

To get to grips with a particular issue or event, there is no substitute for talking to the people directly involved, be they children or adults or both. There is rarely a simple cause and effect relationship between particular events and certain behavioural or emotional reactions. Experiences are mediated through an individual's personality, family, community, and the wider context.

Teachers and children in schools, for example, could bring to light the effects on context by focusing on the patterns and rituals embedded in how they communicate with each other. Cullingford (1991) found that most children readily demonstrated that they wanted to speak and be listened to but, equally, they recognised the reality of the power hierarchy in schools. Schools are places with lots of rules and the children appeared to believe that external controls, plus explicit and implied rules and sanctions, are the way social behaviour is learnt. Children also approved of rules as an ethical tool that protects the weak from the strong (Cullingford, 1991).

In many settings talk is seriously underestimated as a thinking tool. Much of what children experience in education, for example, consists of posed questions but – as children are well aware – these are not always real questions which stimulate thought. They merely check on whether the transmission of information or knowledge has been successful. Children achieve much through talking but their talk can be dismissed by adults as 'just chatting'. It is often in prolonged conversation and discussion between children themselves that they work through ideas, yet talking is frequently undervalued as a means of thinking and learning (Cousins,

1999). Cousins (1999) found that children as young as five interrupted each other in the middle of discussions to remind each other to get back to work.

An assessment and developmental emphasis has perhaps led adults to focus too closely on the development of children's vocabulary, whereas conversational analysis leads researchers and observers to listen to children talking among themselves, engaged in their own learning and culture (Hutchby, 2005). Adults anxious to avoid what they see as distractions or irrelevancies, and to achieve particular end products, will feel impelled to interrupt their flow of thought and interaction. It will be difficult to change practice in this regard; perhaps much of what would be involved is beyond the control of practitioners themselves.

Giving children a voice enables them to understand and express their awareness; it is also vital for their growing understanding of their emotions and the emotions of others. For Sedgwick (1994) this is why the expressive arts are so crucial to children and young people; these children are using their writing to explore their feelings of anger:

> 'When I was angrey mummy woodet Let me play on my sega and I tride to get my own way. When it is bed time I say sory mummy then she ses tats arit my sasig [That's all right my sausage]'

> 'my bruf pols my her it fils lik I am getting a hed ak and I hit my bruf bak and when my mummy sey I cut't hava a pis of bred and in sid I fil pike [pink]'

> 'When I am angry my Bortha colls me a peg and I fill horde [horrible] and my face goes all red with agea and I poose him in the Buth and tone the tap on foll birst and I fill all red but then I sory and diy [dry] his coves [clothes].'

> (Six-year-old children quoted in Sedgwick, 1994, p. 95)

Connecting with children has the potential to deliver high returns, particularly for vulnerable groups of children, if practitioners use their skills to provide environments in which the children can think out loud. The implications of promoting children's wellbeing in this way require sustained commitment. Some individuals and agencies will be prepared to make radical changes in the way they work with children in the belief that supporting children's participation can address social divisions, particularly social exclusion. Some children continue to face high levels of disadvantage and discrimination. Children today live in a society which has become more diverse, and in some ways more tolerant, but is, perhaps, less cohesive and less respectful than in the past. They experience markedly differentiated childhoods in which differences of age, gender, disability, sexuality, ethnicity, ability, religion, class and culture, are associated with differences of power and quality of life. The intractable social divisions of the past have been joined by new divisions which will continue to determine many outcomes for children. Perhaps in view of this, using your own voice is something all children need to experience.

Key points

1 If children's agency was more fully and explicitly recognised it would recognise children as experts in their own lives and acknowledge them as participants in the social world.

2 Using your own voice is something all children need to experience.

3 Work with children should reflect their experience, maturity and evolving capacities.

3 Choices and choosing

Looking at how children are positioned as children gives a critical perspective with which to examine the social policies, practices and structures affecting them. This involves distinguishing between issues and processes that affect children as individuals and those that relate to them as a group. According to Dahlberg et al. (1999), we make choices about who we think children are. These choices are *productive*:

> Instead of waiting upon scientific knowledge to tell us who the child is, we have choices to make about who we think the child is, and these choices have enormous significance since our construction of the child and early childhood are *productive*, by which we mean that they determine the institutions we provide for children and the pedagogical work that adults and children undertake in these institutions.
>
> (Dahlberg et al., 1999, p. 43)

While it is important to gain a clearer understanding of the world of children, choosing to provide time and space to listen can result in more than just that. Inclusion means recognising children as people who know things too. In this way meaning is understood not as imparted but as co-constructed, and listening, as an active verb, is crucial to this process (Clark and Moss, 2001). In order to build a rapport with children, adults may need to reflect upon their own limited abilities to communicate and may have to recognise the many languages, codes and symbols that people, particularly children, use to express themselves (see Chapter 1, *Communicating with children*).

Christensen (2004) commented on children's use of language, their use of conceptual meanings and their actions. She describes how observation and engagement can enable adults to understand the connections that children make with people and learn how to behave and interact among children. Empathy or advocacy or mediation involving children who have had similar experiences can be especially valuable, as can other ways of child-to-child working. Sometimes, listening may involve taking a judicious step back and enabling another child to be your advocate.

Connecting with children, through language or another method, can be seen as part of a collective, social contribution to the emotional and mental welfare of children. The development of 'tuned-in' adults is important to children's emotional, social and mental health. Listening cannot wait until children grow up. It has to begin at birth and be adapted to their growing capacities for communication, conversation and participation. Connecting with children can be demanding. Adults need to be constantly reflecting, discussing, and considering their own understanding of children and, if appropriate, that of the institution and/or profession for which they work. These understandings may be hidden or fragmented or filtered.

Connecting with children requires a measure of awareness and the suspension of prejudices. For some adults, it may involve trying not to let memories of their own childhoods affect them. Others can be worried that they will be unable to meet a child's expectations, unable to change things for them. Adults' own anxieties, fears and frustrations may be reflected in the ways they respond to children, especially when dealing with traumatic experiences. And there may be times when children need to feel that the adult is more powerful and more able to cope with events and emotions than they are.

The children, young people and adults interviewed for research by Madge (2006) were asked whether their parents and carers listened to what they thought and took their views into account and whether adults and children listened to each other properly.

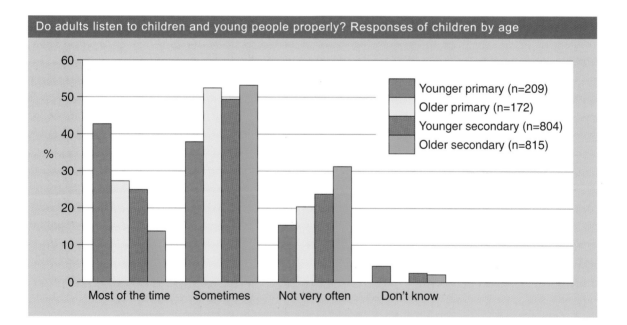

Do adults listen to children and young people properly? Responses of children by age

Younger primary (n=209)
Older primary (n=172)
Younger secondary (n=804)
Older secondary (n=815)

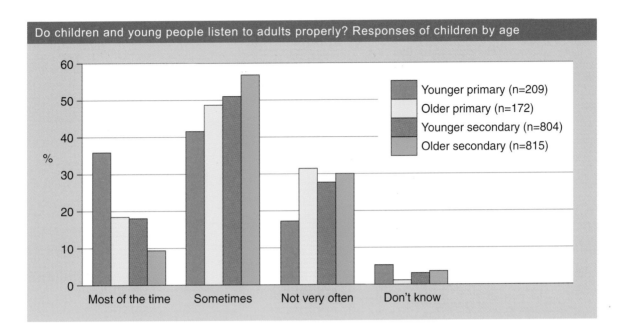

Do children and young people listen to adults properly? Responses of children by age

Legend:
- Younger primary (n=209)
- Older primary (n=172)
- Younger secondary (n=804)
- Older secondary (n=815)

Categories: Most of the time, Sometimes, Not very often, Don't know

Thinking point 4.7   What does this data show about listening across generations and how this changes as children grow older? What reasons may account for these changes?

The majority of primary school children answered 'most of the time' to the question about how often their views were taken into account but this percentage had reduced significantly among secondary children. The levels of listening between the generations generally seem not particularly good in the primary years and much worse in the secondary years. Most children feel that they should have a say in everyday matters. Consistent findings of studies of children in the middle years of childhood show that children want to have their voices heard and to be able to make choices about the things that affect them. These can include conditions in schools, how they spend their free time, public transport, health education, and, within the home, things such as looking after younger children, negotiations around doing chores and which secondary school to go to (Brannen et al., 2000; McNeish and Newman, 2002; Madge, 2006). If children have learnt how to weigh up choices and consider the implications of decisions in day-to-day matters, they are more likely to be ready, and perhaps more skilled, when bigger more complex decisions arise (see Chapter 5).

Butler et al. (2005) interviewed children aged between eight and eleven and concluded that they were involved in some subtle and complex processes through which families make decisions, both about day-to-day things, such as having a treat, and more major decisions such as moving house:

Int: Who chooses where you go?

Amy: We all decide together.

Int: What if all three children want something different?

Amy: We decide on one and on the next week we do the other and the week after that we'd do the other.

(Butler et al., 2005, p. 2)

Family decisions, including major ones, were negotiations in which children played a significant part:

Holly: All of us decided to move 'cos we didn't like where we were staying.

Int: Did you all go together and look at other houses?

Holly: Yeah. My mum said, 'If they choose this one and I choose that one, then I'll just go with their decision.'

Int: So the house you're moving to, did everyone like it?

Holly: Most of us.

Int: Who was less keen?

Holly: My mum.

(Butler et al., 2005, p. 2)

It is in these kinds of negotiations that age relations are played out. Changes in what is done can also be negotiated with reference to what others are doing at that age:

Int: Why do you think she's suddenly letting you go to town on your own?

Mandy: I think it's 'cos all my friends do and I keep saying it's not fair 'cos they're going, so she's starting letting me now 'cos I'm getting older.

Int: Why didn't you think it was fair?

Mandy: 'Cos all my friends were going and I wasn't. And I wanted to start buying my own stuff.

(Butler et al., 2005, p. 5)

One of the repeated subjects of child–adult negotiation is likely to be related to the negotiation of public space (Valentine, 2004). Valentine's study showed children 'performing' negotiation skills and what competence and tactics they had developed to outmanoeuvre restrictions placed on them. Children used different strategies to renegotiate adult restrictions. These might involve comparisons with peers, or siblings when they were of same age, or choosing to approach the parent who was considered more malleable. Sometimes children resorted to deception:

Girl: You say you're at my house, don't you, when you want to come in late. Like you'll phone home and say you're at my house ... yeah that's what I do when I want to come home late, I'll say 'Oh I'm phoning from Gemma's house and staying down there for a bit' and that's what gets me out of going home early ... If there's something you're definitely doing, they think you're doing, then they're not worried.

(Valentine, 2004, p. 63)

For children experiencing public care, whether it be residential care, foster care, family support or care in association with the youth justice system, it is just these levels of personal skills and knowledge of particular families' habits and rules that makes substitute family care so difficult (Butler et al., 2005).

Communication, voice and choice are as important in the lives of disabled children as in the lives of other children, although some practitioners still fail to address this issue and develop the skills they need. Disabled children get caught up in double constructions of dependency both as children and as people with disabilities. Cavet and Sloper (2004) found that good practice in involving disabled children in decision making was not widespread. They suggest that organisational systems, including the full and skilful use of advocacy, need to be addressed. Inclusive approaches to children generally need to be adopted, staff need training, and children and their families need more information. Involvement, particularly in the processes of assessment, having their wishes respected and being able to make choices, would be highly valued by disabled children (Beresford, 2002). Strategies employed to involve children in decision making may be ineffectual or unsuitable. However, some children, when not living with their families, may experience more involvement in decision making than they experienced in their own families.

Those children whose lives have acquired more usually adult problems, such as young carers, often find themselves living in painfully contradictory situations in which they have responsibility without control, support or acknowledgement. Refugee children can face particularly acute and severe problems.

Thinking point 4.8   Why should choice and choosing be a vital part of everyone's lives, including children's lives?

When we thought about and discussed this we came up with a few reasons:

- because it supports the development of the ability to think things through

- because it acknowledges that the interests of children and the interests of adults do not always coincide

- because it addresses the imbalance of power within groups of children and between children and adults
- because, with commitment, it is frequently possible to do and can make a real difference to children's lives
- because it contributes to an inclusive democratic process
- because if children learn how to make day-to-day choices in ordinary life, they might be better able to make choices and decisions in exceptional circumstances
- because making your own mistakes, contributing to your own successes and moving on from both is an important skill.

Adults need to be able to make decisions both for and with children, sometimes for, sometimes with. Sometimes adults will decide that the child (or children) can best make the decision themselves. Choice is strongly connected with power-sharing. People in a wide variety of roles need to make a contribution to children being seen as active, competent, strong and able to explore and find meaning – not as needy, fragile, incapable, hostile, out-of-control or ill-mannered.

Children already see their involvement as important; they consider it their right to be heard. There are now more adults listening, tuning in to children, even in the most difficult circumstances, in ways that are respectful, considered, moral and consistent. What children say may be different from what is expected or hoped for. But in their own terms, and about their own lives, children can be highly sensitive and aware, concerned about themselves and those around them, what happens around them and how they should make sense of it. However, children are also likely to be rightly sceptical about adults' commitment to listening and they may feel that even when they are listened to, their views have little effect.

Key points

1   Giving children a voice enables them to simultaneously form and express their views, and much of their understanding and awareness of their emotions will be generated through dialogue.

2   Connecting with children, through language or other methods, can be seen as part of a collective, social contribution to the emotional and mental welfare of children.

3   If children have learnt how to weigh up choices and consider the implications of decisions in day-to-day matters, they are more likely to be ready, and perhaps more skilled, when bigger, more complex, decisions arise.

4   Adults need to be able to make decisions for and with children, sometimes for, sometimes with. Sometimes adults will decide that the child (or children) can best make the decision themselves.

Conclusion

Being given choices and enabled to choose can, and should, add to a sense of wellbeing for children. With commitment and skill it is possible to involve children in just about every situation in which decisions are taken that affect them – but time is needed to build up trust and rapport between adults and children. Developing participation has to be a long-term commitment, not a one-off exercise but a permanent channel for communication.

The intimacy of children and the adults who care for them, made up of the biological, social and the psychological, makes relationships between adults and children particularly complex. Dependence and independence are features of everyone's lives, fluctuating throughout the life course. Dependency, so much a defining characteristic of childhood, tends to position children as those who are in receipt of actions and attention rather than people who are dependent on others but are capable of caring for others in their turn. Its variability from child to child, culture to culture, and life stage to life stage, makes the concepts of dependency and care shifting and ambiguous. It is, however, important that there is recognition of the real complexities of interdependence in relationships between children and adults over the course of their lives.

References

Aapola, S., Gonick, M. and Harris, A. (2005) *Young Femininity: Girlhood, Power and Social Change*, Basingstoke, Palgrave Macmillan.

Alanen, L. (2001) 'Explorations in generational analysis' in Alanen, L. and Mayall, B. (eds) *Conceptualizing Child-adult Relations*, London, Routledge Falmer.

Aldridge, J. and Becker, J. (2003) *Children Caring for Parents with Mental Illness*, Bristol, The Policy Press.

Armstrong, D. (1983) *The Political Anatomy of the Body*, Cambridge, Cambridge University Press.

Beresford, B. (2002) 'Preventing the social exclusion of disabled children' in McNeish, D., Newman, T. and Roberts, H., *What Works for Children? Effective Services for Children and Families*, Buckingham, Open University Press.

Brannen, J., Heptinstall, E. and Bhopal, K. (2000) *Connecting Children. Care and Family Life in Later Childhood*, London, Routledge Falmer.

Brannen, J. and Heptinstall, E. (2003) 'Concepts of care and children's contribution to family life' in Brannen, J. and Moss, P. (eds) *Rethinking Children's Care*, Buckingham, Open University Press.

Brannen, J. and Moss, P. (eds) (2003) *Rethinking Children's Care*, Buckingham, Open University Press.

Burman, E. (1994) *Deconstructing Developmental Psychology*, London, Routledge.

Butler, I., Robinson, M. and Scanlan, L. (2005) *Children and Decision Making*, London, National Children's Bureau.

Cavet, J. and Sloper, P. (2004) 'Participation of disabled children in individual decisions about their lives and in public decisions about service development', *Children & Society*, vol. 18, pp. 278–290.

Christensen, P. (2004) 'Children's participation in ethnographic research: issues of power and representation', *Children & Society*, vol. 18, pp. 165–176.

Clark, A. and Moss, P. (2001) *Listening to Young Children: The Mosaic Approach*, London, National Children's Bureau and Joseph Rowntree Foundation.

Cousins, J. (1999) *Listening to Four-year-olds: How They Can Help Us Plan Their Education and Care*, London, National Early Years Network.

Cullingford, C. (1991) *The Inner World of the School*, London, Cassell Educational Ltd.

Dahlberg, G., Moss, P. and Pence, A. (1999) *Beyond Quality in Early Childhood Education and Care: Postmodern Perspectives*, London, Falmer Press.

Donzelot, J. (1979) *The Policing of Families*, London, Hutchinson.

Ennew, J. (1994) 'Time for children or time for adults' in Qvortrup, J., Bardy, M., Sgritta, G. and Wintersberger, H. (eds) *Childhood Matters: Social Theory, Practice and Politics*, Aldershot, Avebury.

Foley, P. (2001) 'The development of child health and welfare services in England (1900–1948)' in Foley, P., Roche, J. and Tucker, S. (eds) *Children in Society: Contemporary Theory, Policy and Practice*, Basingstoke, Palgrave/Open University Press.

Gallagher, M. (2006) 'Spaces of participation and inclusion?' in Kay, E., Tisdall, M., Davis, J.M., Prout, A. and Hill, M., *Children, Young People and Social Inclusion. Participation for What?*, Bristol, The Policy Press.

Giddens, A. (1998) *The Third Way: The Renewal of Social Democracy*, Cambridge, Polity Press.

Goldson, B., Lavalette, M. and McKechnie, J. (eds) (2002) *Children, Welfare and the State*, London, Sage Publications.

Headliners (2001) *Junior Jury Children's rights*, available online at <http://www.headliners. org/storylibrary/stories/2001/juniorjurychildrensrights.htm>, accessed 1 June 2007.

Headliners (2002) *Junior Jury The police*, available online at <http://www.headliners.org/ storylibrary/stories/2002/juniorjurythepolice.htm>, accessed 1 June 2007.

Hendrick, H. (1997) *Children, Childhood and English Society 1880–1990*, Cambridge, Cambridge University Press.

Hutchby, I. (2005) 'Children's talk and social competence', *Children & Society*, vol. 19, pp. 66–73.

Hutchby, I. and Moran Ellis, J. (eds) (1998) *Children and Social Competence: Arenas of Action*, London, Falmer Press.

Hutchby, I. and Moran Ellis, J. (2001) 'Relating children, technology and culture' in Hutchby, I. and Moran Ellis, J., *Children, Technology and Culture. The Impacts of Technologies in Children's Everyday Lives*, London, Routledge Falmer.

James, A. and Prout, A. (eds) (1997) *Constructing and Reconstructing Childhood: Contemporary Issues in the Sociological Study of Childhood* (2nd edn), London, Falmer Press.

Leach, P. (1994) *Children First*, London, Michael Joseph.

Lee, N. (2001a) *Childhood and Society. Growing Up in an Age of Uncertainty*, Buckingham, Open University Press.

Lee, N. (2001b) 'The extensions of childhood. Technologies, children and independence' in Hutchby, I. and Moran Ellis, J., *Children, Technology and Culture. The Impacts of Technologies in Children's Everyday Lives*, London, Routledge Falmer.

Madge, N. (2006) *Children These Days*, Bristol, The Policy Press.

Mayall, B. (2002) *Towards a Sociology for Childhood: Thinking from Children's Lives*, Buckingham, Open University Press.

Mayall, B. (2006) 'Child-adult relations in social space' in Kay, E., Tisdall, M., Davis, J.M., Prout, A. and Hill, M. (eds) *Children, Young People and Social Inclusion. Participation for What?*, Bristol, The Policy Press.

McNeish, D. and Newman, T. (2002) 'Involving children and young people in decision making' in McNeish, D., Newman, T. and Roberts, H. (eds) *What Works for Children? Effective Services for Children and Families*, Buckingham, Open University Press.

Morrow, V. (2006) 'Understanding gender differences in context: implications for young children's everyday lives', *Children & Society*, vol. 20, pp. 92–104.

Mullender, A., Hague, G., Farvah Imam, U., Kelly, L., Malos, E. and Regan, L. (2003) '"Could have helped but they didn't": the formal and informal support systems experienced by children living with domestic violence' in Hallett, C. and Prout, A. (eds) *Hearing the Voices of Children. Social Policy for a New Century*, London, Routledge Falmer.

Office for National Statistics (ONS) (2006) *Social Trends 36*, Office for National Statistics, HMSO.

Osler, A. and Starkey, H. (2005) *Changing Citizenship: Democracy and Inclusion in Education*, Maidenhead, Open University Press/McGraw-Hill Education.

Parton, N. (2006) *Safeguarding Childhood: Early Intervention and Surveillance in a Late Modern Society*, Basingstoke, Palgrave Macmillan.

Prout, A. (2005) *The Future of Childhood. Towards the Interdisciplinary Study of Children*, London, Routledge Falmer.

Qvortrup, J. (1994) 'Childhood matters: an introduction' in Qvortrup, J., Bardy, M., Sgritta, G. and Wintersberger, H. (eds) *Childhood Matters: Social Theory, Practice and Politics*, Aldershot, Avebury.

Ridge, T. (2006) 'Childhood poverty: a barrier to social participation and inclusion' in Kay, E., Tisdall, M., Davis, J.M., Prout, A. and Hill, M., (eds) *Children, Young People and Social Inclusion. Participation for What?*, Bristol, The Policy Press.

Sedgwick, F. (1994) *Personal, Social and Moral Education*, London, David Fulton Publishing.

Solberg, A. (1997) 'Negotiating childhoods: changing constructions of age for Norwegian children' in James, A. and Prout, A. (eds) *Constructing and Reconstructing Childhood: contemporary issues in the sociological study of childhood* (2nd edn), London, Falmer Press.

United Nations (1989) *United Nations Convention on the Rights of the Child (UNCRC)*, available online at <http://www.unicef.org.uk/publications/pub_detail.asp?pub_id=133>, accessed 22 August 2007.

Valentine, G. (2004) *Public Space and the Culture of Childhood*, Aldershot, Ashgate Publishing.

Chapter 5

Children's participation

Stephen Leverett

Introduction

At a Children's Issues Conference in 1999 a group of children discussed the UN Convention on the Rights of the Child and collectively drew up the following statement concerning children's involvement and participation in decision making:

> * we can make responsible decisions if given a chance
> * it is okay for us to make the wrong decision sometimes, even if we know all the information
> * please listen to us instead of ignoring us, and take notice of what we have to say
> * expect an opinion from us, and ask for it
> * lastly, we need adults to guide us towards making good decisions, but we also need you to let us practise making the wrong decisions as well
>
> (Smith, 2000, quoted in Atwool, 2006, p. 264)

This statement reveals the extent to which children's collective voices can contribute to the development of positive adult–child relationships. These children clearly believe they have a right to be involved in decision making, but recognise that this involves both the support of adults and the creation of space in which to develop their capacities as decision makers. They are asking adults for guidance, patience and respect, as well as demanding that children's voices are heard.

McNeish and Newman (2002) identify different contexts of decision making:

* participation in individual decision making
* participation in service development and provision

- participation in research
- participation in communities
- participation in influencing policy or public awareness.

The first of these, a principle argued for by children and their advocates, is to be found in a range of policy and practice guidance (for example, the Children Act 1989, the Children (Scotland) Act 1995, the Special Educational Needs Code of Practice 2001, The Children and Family Court Advisory and Support Service (CAFCASS) 2006).

Children are also willing to participate in decision making that extends beyond their own immediate needs and individual interests, reflecting the other contexts in McNeish and Newman's list. It is these other contexts, reflecting children's involvement and participation in collective decision making, that will be examined in this chapter. The chapter will examine how participation has emerged, both politically and culturally, within practice across children's services. Case examples of projects, and a brief examination of selected methods, will be used to illustrate a range of potential benefits and challenges from participation. It is argued that effective participation requires specific skills and knowledge as well as critical reflection and evaluation of both processes and outcomes.

Core questions

- What are some of the different understandings of children's participation and involvement in collective decision making?
- In what ways is participation considered to be a good thing?
- How can we distinguish participation from non-participation?
- What has contributed to the original absence and eventual emergence of children's participation?
- What skills and processes contribute to effective participation in different contexts?

1 Participation and involvement

Participation and involvement in service development and practice, particularly with under-12s, is still evolving. The closer working ties within children's services create a context in which some organisations in the education and health sectors are finding opportunities to learn from sectors with longer histories of children's involvement, such as local authorities and voluntary organisations (Sloper and Lightfoot, 2003).

The existing body of knowledge confirms that, when done well, children's participation and involvement can:

- help children to develop a range of social and communication skills, including confidence-building and the capacity to participate in more sophisticated decision making (Taylor, 2003)

- help children become politically aware and active (Kellett et al., 2004)

- help parents, carers, policy makers and service providers improve their support for children (Department for Constitutional Affairs, 2004)

- provide children with a platform for learning about and demonstrating their capacities for good citizenship (Thomson and Holdsworth, 2003)

- provide children with space in which they can articulate their needs but also demonstrate their resources (Kay et al., 2006)

- help keep children safe – protection and participation are mutually reinforcing rights (Marchant and Kirby, 2004, in Kirby and Gibbs, 2006, p. 211)

- be important for children's self-reflective processes and identity constructions both at a personal and a collective level (Eide and Winger, 2005, p. 77)

- accord children the rights of respect and dignity as equal human beings (United Nations Convention on the Rights of the Child, 1989).

1.1 Defining participation

According to the international children's charity Save the Children (2007), participation is about having the opportunity to express a view, influence decision making and achieve change. Children's participation is an informed and willing involvement of all children, including the most marginalised and those of different ages and abilities, in any matter concerning them either directly or indirectly. Children's participation is a way of working and an essential principle that cuts across all programmes and takes place in all arenas – from homes to government, from local to international levels.

Kirby and Bryson (2002) suggest that the term participation can be used to describe a range of situations and processes. These include:

- one-off consultations in which children express their views and share experiences (for example, surveys, focus groups);
- regular or extended programmes of involvement at both the organisational (for example, school councils; students as researchers) and area-wide strategic levels (for example, council youth forums);
- integrated daily participatory approaches (for example, democratic schooling).

(Kirby and Bryson, 2002, p. 10)

Sinclair and Franklin (2000) suggest that participation can also include involvement in delivering services by acting as mentors, counsellors, volunteers or workers.

The evolution of participation and involvement has resulted in a range of innovative approaches and initiatives accompanied by an ongoing discussion and debate around what constitutes good and, in some cases, bad practice. The following reflects some of the issues raised in this debate.

Participation at different levels

Alderson (2000) describes how participation can operate at different levels. These levels include:

- individual settings, such as a school or nursery, when children are involved in making decisions about aspects of its day-to-day running, the wider environment or the curriculum

For example:

The Cardiff Sure Start centre involved parents, staff and children in designing a new sensory room. Part of the process involved children visiting other centres that had sensory rooms. The adults observed and recorded the children's reactions and interpreted photographs taken by the children of the things they enjoyed from their visit (Lancaster, 2006).

- individual service providers (such as social services, health authorities or schools) when deciding how to provide services

For example:

In England, the Children's Fund was set up to provide support to children aged five to thirteen who needed extra help. It was used for projects involving children's health, home life, education or leisure time. Children's organisations applied for money to implement project ideas. Children were involved in planning and monitoring the projects.

- government and governance bodies involved in the planning of services for children

For example:

Children and Young People: A Framework for Partnership is a strategy developed by the Welsh Assembly Government to organise and improve children's services. A central commitment is to listen to children and young people, resulting in participation at several different levels.

Nationally, the creation of the Funky Dragon website (http://www.funkydragon.org) by the Children and Young People's Assembly of Wales has enabled children and young people from across Wales to share their concerns with government ministers. Locally, every local authority is encouraged to set up a children and young person's forum for children aged eleven and over.

In Welsh schools, there is a requirement that the governing bodies of all junior and secondary maintained schools establish school councils.

- national government departments and parliaments responsible for introducing new legislation that may impact upon the lives of children

> For example:
>
> In England, government departments were issued with guidance on how to encourage children's participation. Responses from national consultations were used by the Government to develop the 2003 Green Paper *Every Child Matters*.
>
> • international bodies such as the United Nations (UN) and non-governmental organisations
>
> For example:
>
> International organisations were set up by and for street children campaigning for better conditions.
>
> (Connolly and Ennew, 1996, quoted in Alderson, 2000).

Thinking point 5.1   Can you identify similar examples of participation initiatives at a range of different levels?

Participation as a process

The tendency to reduce participation to one-off consultations or events, which remain detached from wider decision making processes, has been widely criticised (Shephard and Treseder, 2002, p. 6).

Alternatively it is suggested that participation should be a planned process allowing the expression and recording of children's views (Crowley, 2004), followed by action, including feedback on the potential impact of the children's ideas on policy and practice (Aspinwall and Larkins, 2002).

Participation as process has been promoted within the *Hear By Right* standards produced in conjunction with children and young people by the National Youth Agency (Badham and Wade, 2005). These include the following values which illustrate very clearly both the process and level of commitment required for participation:

- Children and young people's involvement is a visible commitment that is properly resourced
- Children and young people's involvement is valued
- Children and young people have equal opportunity to get involved
- Policies and standards for the participation of children and young people are in place, evaluated and improved

(Badham and Wade, 2005, p. 8)

1.2 Participation and non-participation

[Those consulting] want to be seen to be doing something. I know from experience it is/You see in the newspapers they've consulted a certain number of young people—but then where does the report go? And then nothing is done about it/It's just campaigning for the Government to make it seem they're doing something worthwhile.

(Young person quoted in Stafford et al., 2003, p. 365)

It is acknowledged that many children have had bad experiences of being 'consulted' (Peter Clarke, the Children's Commissioner for Wales, in Aspinwall and Larkins, 2002). Hart (1992) developed a highly influential model of participation. It expresses the interrelationship between adults and

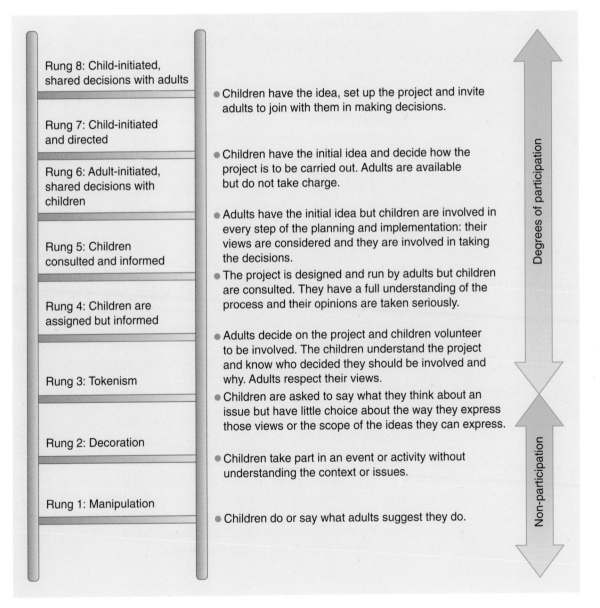

Rung 8: Child-initiated, shared decisions with adults
● Children have the idea, set up the project and invite adults to join with them in making decisions.

Rung 7: Child-initiated and directed
● Children have the initial idea and decide how the project is to be carried out. Adults are available but do not take charge.

Rung 6: Adult-initiated, shared decisions with children
● Adults have the initial idea but children are involved in every step of the planning and implementation: their views are considered and they are involved in taking the decisions.

Rung 5: Children consulted and informed
● The project is designed and run by adults but children are consulted. They have a full understanding of the process and their opinions are taken seriously.

Rung 4: Children are assigned but informed
● Adults decide on the project and children volunteer to be involved. The children understand the project and know who decided they should be involved and why. Adults respect their views.

Rung 3: Tokenism
● Children are asked to say what they think about an issue but have little choice about the way they express those views or the scope of the ideas they can express.

Rung 2: Decoration
● Children take part in an event or activity without understanding the context or issues.

Rung 1: Manipulation
● Children do or say what adults suggest they do.

Degrees of participation

Non-participation

Hart's Ladder of Participation (1992)

children at different levels (or rungs of a ladder) along a continuum that starts with manipulation and ends with child-initiated decision making with adults.

Thinking point 5.2   Identify some examples of participation from your own experience and consider where on the ladder model they might be placed.

The ladder model is particularly useful at measuring the extent to which children are participating within particular contexts. According to Shier (2001), one of the most useful contributions that Hart's model makes is to help to identify non-participation. The three lowest rungs on the ladder (Manipulation, Decoration and Tokenism) represent this and can be a reminder for adults intending to carry out participation work with children that it is easy to get it wrong:

Manipulation

> One young woman who had been in care told us about her experience of being interviewed by a newspaper about the newsletter they were producing. She felt that all of her quotes had been taken out of context. She was very unhappy about the result as the journalist had made the article just about her own life. This could be seen as manipulation as she gave her opinion but had it taken out of context.
>
> (McNeish et al., 2000, p. 61)

This extract, taken from a focus group discussing participation, demonstrates how, rather than reporting the young person's account of her experience as an active participant within a productive young persons group, the media manipulated her account into their own predetermined stereotype. It is frequent for the media to portray children in care, disabled children and others, as exceptional or brave children (Headliners, 1998).

Decoration

In May 1990, at the height of public anxiety about Mad Cow Disease, the Conservative Minister for Agriculture, John Gummer, was photographed eating beefburgers at a boat show with his four-year-old daughter Cordelia.

His actions appeared to be an attempt to reassure the public that eating beef, and feeding beef to their children, was totally safe. His daughter's views on eating beef and her involvement in the publicity stunt were not reported at the time. Sinead Kirwan from Headliners identifies other examples in the media of children being used to decorate adults.

Using children as decoration: John Gummer, then agriculture minister, with his daughter

She says:

> kids are like a hat you bring out on special occasions and put back in the closet when you've finished showing it off.
>
> (Headliners, 1998, webpage)

Tokenism

> When you go into a room ... and sat round in a board meeting ... and put my points across and the director hasn't taken them or just brushed them aside because he's got other issues that are more important to him ... that sort of situation makes me angry.
>
> (Young person quoted in McNeish et al., 2000, p. 61)

This quote highlights a common experience for some children who are expected to express their views in an unwelcoming and unfamiliar adult-orientated environment (in this case a formal board meeting). Alderson (2000, p. 93) says children are very 'aware of tokenism'. They know they are carrying out a 'symbolic function' (Hart, 1997, p. 42) in that the adults want to be seen to be involving children.

Participation within context

Although Hart's model is useful in identifying examples of non-participation, its tendency to categorise participation hierarchically has been questioned. Comeau (2005), for example, is concerned that it could promote the view that participation at the level of the top rungs is dependent upon satisfactory completion of the interactions described in the lower rungs. In other words, participation projects could work their way up the ladder one rung at a time rather than choose an approach that suits the context in which they are working.

In response to this perceived weakness, Treseder (1997) developed a non-hierarchical and context-specific model reflecting that, within certain contexts (for example, in schools), children may not have control and therefore never reach the top rung of Hart's model. Treseder's model also acknowledges that although some children may wish to participate, they may choose to do so at a level that best reflects their abilities, resources and ambitions. Just as levels of participation may depend on individual contexts, children are not a homogenous group (Lansdown, 2001, p. 14).

Consulted and informed
The project is designed and run by adults but children are consulted. They have a full understanding of the process and their views are taken seriously.

Child-initiated, shared decisions with adults
Children have the ideas, set up projects and come to adults for advice, discussion and support. The adults do not direct but offer their expertise for children to consider.

Degrees of involvement

Assigned but informed
Adults decide on the project and children volunteer for it. They know who decided to involve them and why. Adults respect children's views.

Child-initiated and directed
Children have the initial idea and decide how the project is going to be carried out. Adults are available but do not take charge.

Adult-initiated, shared decisions with children
Adults have the initial idea but children are involved in every step of the planning and implementation. Not only are their views considered but children are also involved in taking the decisions.

Treseder's Degrees of Involvement Model (1997)

For some children and young people, being involved in a group with others who have shared similar experiences is important.

> Peer support encourages children and young people to take responsibility for each other and to actively participate in developing positive relationships and community well-being.
>
> (Kirby et al., 2003, p. 97)

This is particularly relevant to Black, disabled and refugee children who are also in the Looked After care system (Voice for the Child in Care, 2004). Some experiences, such as poverty and disability (as we show in Chapter 7), affect both children and adults and may require support and decision making involving whole families or communities. On the other hand, some children do not feel comfortable working in groups with peers or adults. Despite some perceived benefits in splitting children into sub-groups based on interest or experience, Lansdown suggests that:

> it is also important to recognise that many issues affecting children are common to them all and that it is not always appropriate to focus on children in terms of 'problems'.
>
> (Lansdown, 2001, p. 14)

Adults need to enter into dialogue with children to ascertain if and how, and with what kind of support, they would like to become involved.

> This may shift from moment to moment, and from child to child, as well as between tasks and projects.
>
> (Kirby and Gibbs, 2006, p. 212)

Effective participation projects work with the different strengths and experiences that children bring and provide:

> a number of different roles that children can fulfil according to their aptitudes, interests and abilities, each of which should be promoted and valued equally.
>
> (Lansdown, 2001, p. 14)

Empowering children

It is evident from children's accounts that they are acutely aware of power, and the hierarchy of power in which adults place themselves firmly above children:

> 'Adults make the decisions of children and children make the decisions of babies. And then babies make the decisions of a mouse, and then a mouse makes it for ants, and then ants make it for a small crumb.'
>
> (Child quoted in Kirby and Gibbs, 2006, p. 212)

Real participation will shift that balance of power: 'The outcome of any successful participation process will be empowered children' (Shephard and Treseder, 2002, p. 4).

Empowerment generally refers to the process by which power is developed and gained by people who lack it (Braye and Preston Shoot, 1995, quoted in Ward, 2000). At its simplest level 'it refers to gaining greater control over one's life and circumstances' at the psychological, political and social level (Thompson, 2000, p. 120). For some people working with children (for example, social workers) the term 'empowerment' is a familiar challenge embedded into the professional value base. For others, empowerment is perhaps a less obvious part of the role they play in children's lives: 'it's giving up control, a certain amount of control, which is not necessarily very easy for a teacher' (educational professional quoted in Kirby and Gibbs, 2006, p. 214). It is a 'challenge' to 'really hold back and let the children come out with what they want' (parent volunteer quoted in Kirby and Gibbs, 2006, p. 214).

Empowerment challenges the view that children are totally dependent upon adults to support them. A more positive interpretation, that acknowledges children's agency, is to construct the child–adult relationship as interdependent, see Chapter 4.

Interdependence is evident even in relationships between adults and small children (Alderson, 2000). Babies and toddlers are able to communicate when they need support and provide opinions on the support that they are given. By responding sensitively and appropriately, adults, perhaps without realising it, are involving and empowering very young children.

Participation is, similarly, an interdependent relationship requiring work with, rather than for, children. Adults play a crucial part in these empowering relationships by 'accepting responsibility' for children without 'taking responsibility away from them' (Kirby et al., 2003, p. 20). The following example illustrates interdependence and empowerment in operation:

The Children's House Nursery, in north east Lincolnshire, actively enabled children's participation in collective decision making. In particular, children were involved in issues involving food and eating. The adult workers promoted discussion with children about healthy eating and involved children in tasting sessions. The children themselves went to the supermarket and helped choose the food for the tasting. Children were also encouraged to discuss what, with whom and how they eat at home. The staff noted how children involved food in role plays, making meals from photographs cut out of food magazines, and from dough which they then served to each other. This role play was observed and videoed and notes kept on the kinds of food children preferred or disliked. This information was used to plan menus with the nursery cook.

(Case study by McAuliffe and Lane, 2005)

Thinking point 5.3   To what extent can all the relationships that you form with children be described as interdependent?

Involving everyone

Criticism has been levelled at participation initiatives that appear to only involve certain children whilst excluding others. 'It's always the same people that get picked for everything' (young person quoted in Hill, 2006, p. 77).

Hill (2006) found that many children were driven by a sense of fairness and would question why, in certain contexts, only more confident or older children were given opportunities to participate. Other factors associated with children's gender, ethnicity, social class or disability can also impact on their invisibility in participation work.

In one study of school consultations, children presented their own ideas about how inclusive participation could be achieved:

- picking young people for consultation on a random basis rather than at the discretion of adults;
- involving whole schools in consultation;
- rotating consultation round different schools and areas of Scotland so that each gets a turn;
- encouraging young people to take part, using publicity, for example TV adverts.

(Stafford et al., 2003, p. 364)

Key points

1   Participation is a process that can operate at different levels with many positive benefits for children.

2   Models of participation are useful for highlighting different ways of working with children and exposing bad practice.

3   Participation benefits from inclusive, empowering and interdependent adult–child relationships.

2   The philosophical basis of participation

The pace of change in accepting children's participation in practice has been slow – and in some cases non-existent. To understand why, it is necessary to examine, first, how and why children have been denied a voice and, secondly, the various discourses from which the idea of children's participation has emerged.

By the early twenty-first century the rhetoric of participation in public decision making had achieved a 'high profile, with a growing body of literature' (Shier, 2001, p. 107) and 'a sustained commitment in government policy' (Cavet and Sloper, 2004, p. 614). Turning this into a reality remains a challenge for the children's workforce. Prior to this it was possible to describe children as having 'muted voices' (Ennew, 1994, p. 125). This section will explore ways in which adults have contributed to this situation.

Actively muting children's voices

> Infected by the strike contagion at present passing over Scotland many of the boys at Rattray School refused to resume lessons on Tuesday forenoon and proceeded to Craigmill and subsequently to Blairgowrie but failed to induce the scholars at these places to join their ranks. The strikers caused considerable disturbance but the movement was short lived most of them returning to school the same day, where they were duly rewarded for their pains.
>
> (*Blairgowrie Advertiser*, 11 October 1889, quoted on Perthshire Diary, 2007, webpage)

Although it is fair to say that children's voices have been muted, it is not the case that they have been silent. History is full of examples of children who have protested, commented, argued and offered constructive criticism on the services provided for them and the wider world in which they live. The article in the *Blairgowrie Advertiser* was written when a school strike movement spread throughout Britain with children demanding: 'free education, less rote learning and the abolition of corporal punishment' (Cunningham and Lavalette, 2002, p. 172).

Subsequently the children were portrayed unfavourably in the media and the police were posted at school entrances. Some of the strikers were taken to court, fined and 'bound over' with threats of imprisonment or flogging should they repeat their actions (Cunningham and Lavalette, 2002).

A further series of national strikes occurred in 1911, initially as a response to a school strike at Bigyn School in Llanelli which was sparked off by a teacher beating a student for passing paper around the class (Bigyn School, 2006). A school in Liverpool went out on strike in sympathy, adding their own demands including abolition of the cane, abolition of home lessons and an extra half day's holiday (Cunningham and Lavalette, 2002, p. 176). A further sixty schools across the country also joined the strike.

Newspaper cartoons belittling children's protests: *Sunday Express*, 14 May 1972 (left) and *The Times*, 20 March 2003 (right)

Thinking point 5.4   In what ways are these two cartoons, published thirty years apart, conveying a similar message about children's participation?

The reaction to these children's protests demonstrates the different ways in which children's collective voices have been silenced. Both the 1889 and 1911 strikes resulted in children being physically punished. Later protests, including further anti-corporal-punishment strikes in 1972 and the Gulf war protests by schoolchildren in 2003, were belittled in the press with a suggestion that children were, in some way, mimicking adults or using the protests as an opportunity to miss school lessons.

Learning and valuing the languages of childhood

I've got a load to give you

But I don't know how

I've got load to say to you

But I don't know how.

Well, you wouldn't understand

(Child's poem in Foster Care Associates, 2000, p. 52)

Text messaging: one of the creative ways in which children communicate with each other

Children find creative ways of expressing their feelings and ideas that both include, and move beyond, verbal and written communication. Their views 'can be expressed in many ways, for example, through emotions, drawing, painting singing, drama'

(Lansdown, 2005, p. 4)

Drawing, particularly, has been referred to as the universal language of childhood (Rubin, 1984, quoted in Rollins, 2005) and is particularly useful for younger children 'who may not have the cognitive ability to express themselves in words' (Malchiodi, 1999, quoted in Rollins, 2005). As we saw in Chapter 1, adults can connect with children through a broad range of communication methods. This is sometimes described within the Reggio Emilia approach as the 'hundred languages of childhood'. Arguably it has been the refusal of adults to learn and value the languages of childhood that has historically contributed to the muting of children's voices.

With this in mind it becomes possible to reappraise the national protests and strikes by children. Much has been made of the fact that these exceptional instances of children achieving a national voice appeared to coincide with major political unrest by trades unions or other protesters. The implication is that children were either being misled by adults or were participating in some kind of copycat activity. The appropriation of the adult methods of striking and marching to make a political point is, itself, an example of creative expression. Mimicking in this sense is a positive attribute, a familiar part of the process of learning and developing communication. Adults have a responsibility to model behaviour to children and should expect such observed behaviour (whether judged good or bad) to be appropriated. This strengthens the case for adults to model effective democratic processes and to provide opportunities for children to do likewise.

Adults replacing children's voices with their own

Beresford (1997) describes the difficulties of hearing the views of disabled children. In many cases adult carers present what she refers to as the proxy views of these children, denying them a true voice. Political and media-led debates about the treatment of disabled children increasingly provide parents and carers with a platform to air their views, yet rarely include the views of disabled children.

Carter (2002) undertook research around medical encounters (that is, consultations and meetings with medical professionals) where children were suffering from chronic pain. The children in her study (aged seven to thirteen) were able to be both articulate and animated. However, despite the fact that the children felt they had a lot to offer in the medical encounter they reported being marginalised or overwhelmed by the professionals.

> Communication between doctors and children was mostly restricted to children answering specific, medical-diagnostic questions. Frequently, the parents were used as the conduit for the children's experiences, a form of adult–child ventriloquism, even though the children would have welcomed more direct and appropriate involvement.
>
> (Carter, 2002, p. 35)

Significantly, the children's experiences in these accounts replicate those of some adults who also have chronic pain. It suggests that these children are doubly disadvantaged and discriminated against.

> '[Doctors should] talk to me more, not just my mum.'
>
> (Child, interviewed by Carter, 2002, p. 35)

> 'Listen!!!!! [...] Listen to what the people [with chronic pain] have to say and take notice of it. Treat them as people no matter how young they are [...] [Doctors] get really patronising [...] I just get really fed up with it.'
>
> (Child interviewed by Carter, 2002, p. 35)

At the collective level the same process is evident when professionals express a view that is supposed to be representative of all children in their setting, or where large organisations supposedly speak on behalf of children.

Because adults hold a more powerful position in society, they can be useful advocates for children's voices. A good example of this is the Children are Unbeatable Alliance which consists of over 400 mainly adult-led organisations campaigning against smacking. The important distinction here is that the issues are led by the views and wishes of children.

Key points

1   Historically, children's voices have been suppressed.

2   Adults wanting to encourage children's involvement need to understand and work with the many different languages of childhood.

3   Adults must learn not to replace children's voices with their own.

4   Some children are silenced as a result of double or multiple forms of discrimination.

3   The emergence of children's participation

In this section we will consider a number of interrelated processes, themes and discourses that have contributed to the present day emphasis on children's participation.

3.1 New ways of understanding children's evolving capacity

The political changes promoting participation are the product of new ways of understanding children and childhood. The ideas behind participation can be received as a challenge to deeply held cultural attitudes and practices.

> Even adults who are utterly sympathetic to the principle of enabling children to express their views may often feel uncomfortable with the ways, means and implications of putting this into practice. Indeed, children themselves frequently experience similar feelings of unease.
>
> (Lansdown, 2001, p. v)

These feelings are not surprising because they run counter to the dominant framework that constructs how we understand childhood.

In the introduction to this book we outlined the emergence of a new sociology of childhood providing a theoretical challenge to the dominant framework. In order to push forward policies that promote children's participation and involvement, some advocates have found it useful to place their projects within this alternative theoretical framework, as this extract from publicity material for the Norfolk Children's Fund demonstrates:

> This approach draws on new models of children as 'social actors'; as innovative and creative users of the world around them and as having social rights conferred upon them through the UN Convention on the Rights of the Child ... It is believed that sensitivity to the 'child's view' will add value to the design and delivery of services and increase sustainability.
>
> (Norfolk Children's Fund, 2003, webpage)

Despite some evidence of changes in attitude towards children there is still some uncertainty about the relevance of participation to younger or disabled children. It is 'widely accepted that some significant changes in physical strength, agility, and cognitive and social competencies take place during a child's second year, at around 6–7 and again at puberty' (Lansdown, 2004, p. 4). Most societies have some kind of age-based transition in their expectations of children between the ages of seven and twelve (Thomas, 2002). Unsurprisingly, most participation work is undertaken with teenagers.

Lansdown (2005) suggests that the concept of *evolving capacity* could be used as an alternative to age-based ideas about competency. This concept is drawn directly from Article 5 of the UNCRC and extends the consensus, found in all theories of childhood, which recognises change and evolution in children's capacities.

> Children's physical immaturity, relative inexperience and lack of knowledge do render them vulnerable and necessitate specific protections.
>
> (Lansdown, 2005, p. 31)

Yet they can still be introduced to experiences of participation within a safe context with 'appropriate direction and guidance' (United Nations, 1989).

Once again, this promotes the potential for interdependent adult–child relationships. As Vygotsky (1978) identified, even very young children can learn and develop new capacities through collaboration and interaction with adults. Marchant et al. (1999) used innovative communication methods enabling young learning disabled people to collectively express views about respite care. It appears that the *capacity to participate* can be learnt through being provided with *opportunities to participate* (Lansdown, 2005). Miller (2003) describes a very good example of this in practice:

Practice box 5.2

At Wood End Family Project in Coventry, crèche staff set up a drinks and fruit bar, available at all times, so that children could decide for themselves when to have a drink and something to eat. There were 20 children in the group, aged 0–4 years.

At first the children kept asking if they could have fruit and water rather than helping themselves, but they soon realised that it was there for them to have when they wanted it. Initially the children kept spilling water, but as they got used to pouring they became proficient and less was spilt. The children helped staff to wipe up spillages where they occurred. The children told the staff that they really enjoyed eating the fruit.

Staff comment that the activity went very well and feel that in time the children will get used to this as a regular part of the session.

(Miller, 2003, p. 38)

Participation as a universal children's right

The UNCRC has been one of the most significant influences on children's rights, in particular the development of children's participation. It was adopted by the UN in November 1989 and ratified by the UK government in December 1991.

The UNCRC's status in law is often overstated and, whilst it can be used to prompt member countries into improving their rights record, the UK continues to fall short in several areas – such as the reasonable chastisement laws and treatment of young refugees. The UN has also been accused of promoting a globalised standard childhood at the expense of the multitude of diverse childhoods that exist (Woodhead, 1999). Ironically, although it has promoted a wide range of participation initiatives, the Convention itself was drawn up without children's involvement (Freeman, 2000).

The UNCRC is made up of fifty-four separate articles, each conveying a particular area of rights. These articles can be categorised into three general areas:

- Provision
- Protection
- Participation

Franklin (2002, p. 21) makes a helpful distinction between welfare rights and liberty rights. Welfare rights tend to prioritise the *provision* for, what are seen at particular times and places, children's welfare needs (education, healthcare and housing) and their *protection* (health and safety, child protection). Franklin notes that in some cases this involves restricting children's choices and behaviour and for this reason can be described as paternalistic. For example, a child's 'right' to education provision involves being compelled to follow a specific curriculum or to attend school between specified hours. Similarly, a child's right to protection from harm involves being denied the opportunity to watch certain television programmes after the 9 p.m. watershed.

Liberty rights, on the other hand, focus on children's rights to self-determination which could include, for example, the right to *participate* in decision making. This more radical idea might involve children in determining a curriculum, negotiating the school day or helping the government decide if and when a television watershed should be created. By introducing participation, alongside protection and provision, the UNCRC challenged adults to build interdependent and empowering relationships with children.

Franklin (2002) concludes that children's claims to protection and provision rights 'are rarely contested' whilst 'their claims for liberty rights invariably are'. Lee (2005) suggests that this results from a tendency to view participation as creating complete separation between adults and children and therefore undermining adults' possession of children. Protection and provision both conjure up images of adults surrounding and possessing children who are unable to act for themselves. The wording of Article 12, Lee claims, is designed both to protect children from 'exploitative forms of possession' (that is, adults who do not act to ensure the child's best interests are met) and to promote 'good forms of adults' possessive concern' (that is, adults who find a balance between children's rights to participation and protection) (Lee, 2005, p. 18). He suggests that separation could be replaced by the more flexible concept of *separability* which represents both the connectedness that exists between children and adults and also the space for children to be valued in their own right with their own voices.

The following is an extract forming part of the conclusions from some direct research with children about their experiences of childcare provision. It provides an insight into how children's views can provide a basis for improving standards and, therefore, how participation can potentially overlap with provision:

> Younger children (under 5) were more likely to complain about not having enough toys or having to sit on the carpet too long (a particular feature of pre-school centre-based settings where children sit on carpet squares or a rug for story or circle time) and not being able to go outside. Older children (8+) were more likely to complain of being bored due to insufficient choice of activities, no one of their age to play with, or activities that were not age appropriate. There is a feeling that they do not have enough to do because the club is structured for younger children (5–7). Some considered they were not given sufficient freedom and responsibility for their age.

> (Mooney and Blackburn, 2003, pp. 20–21)

Thinking point 5.5   What practical changes could be made to service provision based upon these children's views?

Alderson (2000) argues that protection, provision and participation rights overlap. Rather than viewing participation as radical and different she argues that it is an integral part of good-quality provision and protection. Article 3.3 of the UNCRC focuses on the need to have standards against which services involved in provision and protection can be measured. These standards can include and be informed, she argues, by regular consultation with parents and children who use the services.

3.2 Service user involvement

Nothing about us, without us

(Popular slogan of the disability rights movement)

The development of children's participation has also been influenced by the ongoing interest and activity associated with service user involvement.

Service user involvement has developed in part through the historic grass roots activism of pressure groups, including physically disabled people, older people, people with learning difficulties, and people who use mental health services. A desire to see improvements to welfare services has become the focus of campaigning activity by many of these groups.

Children who come into contact with welfare services have likewise developed their own grass roots organisations. This has been evident in the campaigning carried out by local or regional Young Carers projects. Children from the Looked After care system have also been actively involved historically through the National Association of Young People in Care (NAYPIC) and more recently by A National Voice (ANV). These organisations also focus on promoting awareness and campaigning on specific issues, such as the use of restraint by social care workers.

Thinking point 5.6   In what ways might organisations run by and for young people differ from traditional children's rights organisations like the National Society for the Prevention of Cruelty to Children (NSPCC) or Save the Children?

More recently, service user involvement has been stimulated by a top-down approach inspired by government social policy requiring welfare organisations to improve the quality of their provision by actively seeking the views of service users. Initiatives such as Patient and Public Involvement (PPI) in the National Health Service (NHS) have resulted in large-scale organisational infrastructures and government funds designed to create a listening culture within health service design and delivery. The attempt by governments to promote the perception that welfare service users can choose between services has also reinforced the construction of service users as empowered consumers or customers.

This vision of involvement is difficult to sustain, particularly as some service users (Looked After children or people sectioned under the Mental Health Act 1983) are not necessarily choosing to 'use' services. Furthermore, many other people lack the confidence, ability or resources to express a view or make choices between services. There is a suspicion in some quarters that these initiatives are little more than:

mechanisms by which state agencies give their decision-making processes legitimacy, in the process failing to address inherently problematic structural issues and excluding voices that are not deemed acceptable.

(Hodge, 2005, p. 164)

Involvement and participation in children's services has also been stimulated by government policy. However, this was pre-dated by a longer tradition of participatory and empowering activity particularly in the voluntary sector and amongst youth and community workers. This bank of good practice and knowledge has the potential to be shared across different areas of the children's workforce. Such innovation and diffusion of ideas is evident in the wide range of projects emerging from the locally based Children's Fund initiative. The following two examples illustrate this:

Project	Details of activity	More information
South Gloucestershire Council Participation Project	A Children's Fund project using a project worker to support children's involvement in design delivery and evaluation of preventative services.	South Gloucestershire Council (2007)
St Helens 'Kidz Time'	Children in a refuge for homeless families are supported to have their say on what they would like to happen to themselves and their families. Supported by the St Helens Involvement & Participation Team (SHIP) and the Children's Fund.	Mittler and May-Chahal (2004)

Unsurprisingly, service user involvement with children can be challenging to both children and adults. Many well-meaning policy makers and service providers fail in their attempts to seek children's views through lack of resources or by adopting inappropriate approaches and working methods. Sometimes, where successful user groups of children have been established, they may become overburdened with requests for consultation. Such groups can often be dismissed as unrepresentative. The views of certain groups of children (such as residents of children's homes) are easier to access than others (such as foster children who are dispersed in individual households across a wide geographical region). Furthermore children themselves often lack the communication skills suited to participation activities, and their voices can be viewed by some adults as confrontational, challenging and even rude.

Democratic schools and active citizenship

> I think that a lot of schools would benefit from listening to pupil voice. That way pupils feel better by knowing that teachers will listen to them. I know that almost everybody in our school does. (Oliver, Year 6 student, Wheatcroft School)
>
> I think it is important that the children and teachers have a good relationship – it makes working much easier. (Nicola, Year 6 student, Wheatcroft School)
>
> (Peacock and Wheatcroft School, 2001, pp. 51–52)

Concern has been expressed at the reluctance of young people to understand, see the importance of, or get involved in the democratic political process. This is evidenced by the decline of under-25s as voters in general elections and as members of political parties (Hannam, 2001, p. 5). One response following the Crick Report (Qualifications and Curriculum Authority, 1998) was to introduce citizenship into the school curriculum in the hope that children would learn to understand and value democratic processes. This was felt to be particularly important after a government survey revealed that students possessed a 'limited' understanding of 'fundamental democratic values and institutions' (Kerr et al., 2003, p. iv).

The government's concerns about the future of democracy have resulted in a further process influencing the development of participation. Evidence that 'successful education for democracy needs to be at least in part experiential' (Hannam, 2001, p. 5) has led to the view that children should be encouraged to participate in decision making bodies within schools. For some this is less about preparing children for the future than an opportunity to make schools more democratic.

In the main, most developments have occurred in secondary level education, including the introduction of citizenship education and guidance for school governing bodies and local education authorities (LEAs) on involving children in decision making (Department for Education and Skills, 2004, p. ii). In Wales, all schools beyond infant level are expected to have a school council. However, English primary schools also have to show how they are preparing children for citizenship. Despite being a lesser priority for social policy, a number of infant and primary schools have developed participatory activities:

Project	Details of activity	More information
Peer Support at Stubbings Infant School	Year 2 children are trained to support other children who are lonely or in need of help. One of several strategies to prevent bullying.	Save the Children (2006c)
Children as Governors at Isambard Brunel Junior School	One pupil from years 4, 5 and 6 is recruited to attend Governors' Curriculum Committee meetings. These meetings are adapted to ensure children can participate in curriculum and budget decision making.	Save the Children (2006a)
Children as Inspectors at Cannon Lane First School	Selected children write reports based upon their observations of lessons and surveys of other pupils and parents. These are shared with governors, staff and other pupils and parents and are used for setting targets.	Save the Children (2006b)
School Court at Isambard Brunel Junior School	Local community police officers train selected pupils with mentorship skills, enabling them to support other children referred by teachers for being disruptive in class.	Save the Children (2006a)

Children report great satisfaction and personal gains from participation in schools:

> 'I never used to like school, but now because I've got this important job I'm starting to mix in quite a bit now.'
>
> (Peer mediator quoted in Save the Children, 2006a)

> 'I am a pupil at Wheatcroft Primary and I am chairman of our School Council. I think that being chairman gives me a responsibility and it makes me feel important and having that feeling makes me want to do better at things so I don't let myself down.'
>
> (Year 6 child quoted in Peacock and Wheatcroft School, 2001, pp. 51–52)

According to some headteachers participation also:

> impacts beneficially on self-esteem, motivation, sense of ownership and empowerment, and ... this in turn enhances attainment.
>
> (Hannam, 2001, p. 7)

Studies have shown that despite the misconception that participation leads to an undermining of teachers' authority, it can in fact enhance discipline (Taylor and Johnson, 2002; Ekholm, 2004, in Osler and Starkey, 2005,

p. 142) by creating a situation in which teachers have to provide justification for their rules and actions. Hannam (2001) found that although participatory activities increased teachers' workload, this was outweighed by the great benefits produced for students. Evidence from Baginsky and Hannam's (1999) research for the NSPCC argued that the development of democratic structures in schools is one way of making schools safer places for children.

Despite the perceived benefits, concerns have been expressed that citizenship in schools is no more than a 'mantra being repeated' (Leighton, 2004, p. 179). A discrepancy has been noted between what children learn in citizenship classes and the undemocratic experience of school itself (Osler and Starkey, 2005) with students indicating that they can easily see through tokenism or manipulation:

> 'There is a pupil council but the headteacher comes to the meetings so you really can't say what you think, well you can, but he always says you're wrong.
>
> We do get a say and they do listen, but not necessarily anything is done about it. It's as if they're trying to prove they're listening but they don't pay attention to what we think'
>
> (Student quoted in MacBeath and Mortimore, 2001, p. 78)

If, as Willow and Neale (2004, p. 8) suggest, citizenship involves 'recognition, respect and participation', the fostering of respectful interdependent relationships between children and their teachers is a necessary precondition. This is particularly challenging because schools 'remain essentially authoritarian in their structures and organisation' (Osler and Starkey, 2005, p. 137).

> It is not simply that schools do not practice the human rights and democratic values they preach. It is that many schools consistently contravene them.
>
> (Alderson, 1999, p. 194)

Key points

1 The dominant theoretical framework has been challenged by new ways of understanding childhood which, in turn, have helped the development of participation.

2 Children's participation has been influenced by policies promoting service user involvement and citizenship.

3 Models of participatory activities from practice indicate potential gains for both adults and children.

4 Putting participation into practice

For anybody intending to undertake participatory activities with children, a large body of material has been generated offering advice on methods, techniques and approaches. This section considers the importance of relating techniques to contexts and provides an example of one widely used approach, referred to as circle time. It also highlights the importance of understanding participation as a total process requiring planning, reflection and evaluation.

Suitability for purpose

One study into quality within early childhood services (Mahony and Hayes, 2006) attempted to utilise 'multiple perspectives' which included children's views alongside those of parents and professionals. In order to access a wide range of children, the project team used a range of techniques including:

- structured conversation
- supported conversations
- the use of line drawings depicting facial expressions (happy, sad, sleepy and cross/angry)
- puppetry
- cameras
- arts and crafts.

These approaches were well-suited for children aged three to six but were not considered suitable for:

> a number of children who were too young, developmentally immature or lacked understanding/comprehension of the use of the method.
>
> (Mahony and Hayes, 2006, p. 12)

An alternative approach was therefore adopted for these children, involving observation of their language and behaviour.

This highlights the importance of having available approaches that are specifically suited to both task and children. Having a range of possible approaches also enables children themselves to have options in terms of which approach they would like to participate in.

Thinking point 5.7   How would you go about ensuring that a particular participation technique was suited to individuals within a group of children?

4.1 Practice example: circle time

Circle time is only one of many approaches to enable children's participation. However, within the context of this chapter, it is useful as an example to raise some of the practical issues that need to be considered when undertaking participatory work with groups of children. Circle time is used in early years settings and schools for helping children develop communication and self-confidence within groups. Variations of circle time are also applicable to a range of participatory contexts, including young carers groups and resident groups in children's homes.

> 'If there's a problem between friendship ... because our friend Sam ... we once had an argument, we called each other names, but we made up in Circle Time, sorted out our problems ... We shook hands in the middle of the circle ... it made me feel better about myself, it got, like, a lot off my shoulders.'
>
> (Child quoted in Taylor, 2003, p. 3)

It is particularly valuable in helping younger children develop social awareness, which is a prerequisite for any kind of social participation or involvement. According to Tait:

> social awareness comes about gradually through experiences of meeting and interacting with others, influencing one's ability to 'decentre'
>
> (Tait, 2005, p. 24)

The ability to decentre means being able to take on board alternative viewpoints.

One study identified several ways for dealing with emotions and using games, including structured, activity-based, spontaneous and problem-centred models (Taylor, 2003). The circle format is a symbol of unity. 'It enables everyone in the group to have a clear physical view of everyone else and hopefully, in time, this will also become a clear psychological view' (Tait, 2005, p. 24). For some children, circle time is valued ahead of other forms of collective participation because it enables everyone to have a say:

> Child: Before the school council voted for children in class – to be governors – people tell them what they wanted. It was always the same people, it wasn't all of us, just two people from each class,

sitting around the table talking 'blah blah blah'. Child: We decided we didn't like it. In circle time we all have a go, go around the circle.

(Kirby et al., 2003, p. 65)

Participation in circle time varies according to group size and children's existing relationships with their peers (Taylor, 2003). Mosley (in Tait, 2005, p. 25) suggests an optimum group size of six to eight children for three- to four-year-olds and twelve to fourteen children for five- to six-year-olds. Some children find it more difficult to participate than others.

> We can suggest that children raise a hand to signal their wish to speak but need to make sure we don't always pick the same people. We can encourage the less confident children to join in by occasionally addressing questions directly to them, though we should never place them under any pressure to talk

(Tait, 2005, p. 25)

Circle time encourages adults to listen to and empathise with children's views. Children themselves value the opportunity to talk, learn about other people and have fun. They do, however, express concern that some children can undermine circle time by being disruptive, which highlights the need for ground rules and good facilitation skills (Taylor, 2003). Mosley (in Tait, 2005) highlights the dangers of constantly reprimanding children during circle time and promotes a more indirect and sensitive approach to dealing with disruptive behaviour. For example:

Circle time: an opportunity to encourage children's participation

> Remember, talking stops us from hearing what others are saying is better than: Damien, it's very rude to talk when someone else is speaking!

(Mosley, in Tait, 2005, p. 25)

Taylor's (2003) study highlighted a lack of formal training amongst teachers in how to facilitate circle time. The adult leading the circle time is a crucial role model for the children (Tait, 2005, p. 24) and requires appropriate facilitation skills in order to attend to issues of confidentiality and disclosure. The type of support most wanted was when adults 'let you do what you want and only helped you in the things you want to be helped in' (one child's view of adult facilitation, in Kirby and Gibbs, 2006, p. 215).

Kirby and Gibbs (2006, p. 215) suggest that facilitation of participatory activities (including circle time) needs to be adapted to the particular context. A skilled participatory facilitator is able to give the children 'maximum control' while maintaining 'sufficient adult input'. In some cases it involves stepping in to ensure effective group functioning and equal opportunities to participate:

Child: I'm presenting

Professional: No, you did it last week.

Child: I'm the best at presenting, I've got a loud voice.

Professional: You did very well last week, but how about giving others a chance to develop the skills as well?

(Kirby and Gibbs, 2006, p. 218)

To illustrate the range of facilitator roles in participation work, Kirby and Gibbs (2006) developed the model opposite. It identifies eight possible roles that adults could move between, depending on the specific context.

Thinking point 5.8   In what ways does this model relate to Hart's Ladder of Participation or Treseder's Degrees of Involvement?

Most participatory facilitators, including those leading circle time, consider it important to set ground rules that promote positive communication. These can include:

> Listen when someone else is speaking in the group.
>
> Wait one's turn to speak or act (not when others are speaking or doing things).
>
> Look at what is going on.

(Tait, 2005, p. 24)

Non-directive	Abstainer	Leave children alone to do activities, discuss and develop ideas and materials without adult intervention.
	Observer	Reflect and feed back on what is happening in the group.
	Enabler	Ask questions to find out what children want to do. Encourage inclusion. Provide resources to take action.
	Activator	Challenge ideas and encourage children to develop their ideas further. For example, may play devil's advocate.
	Adviser	Suggest ways in which events can move forward.
	Informer	Tell children what is happening. Provide further information. May include adults' own views.
	Instructor	Tell children what to do and how to do it. For example, ensure structure, discipline and safety.
Directive	Doer	Take action on behalf of children.

Facilitation roles within participatory projects, adapted from Klein (2001) by Kirby and Gibbs (2006)

Miller (2003) suggests two further rules:

- No one will be ridiculed or put down.

- Everyone has a right to 'pass'.

Tait (2005, p. 24) suggests that these can be presented and reinforced through the use of activities such 'Follow Me':

Practice box 5.3

Follow Me: A 'looking and turntaking' game

The adult holds a 'wand' and raises and lowers it at varying speeds. The children must watch closely and follow the movements of the wand, responding with high and low movements. Children can also take turns controlling the wand.

Once ground rules have been established and children have developed more confidence, Tait suggests that new themes can be introduced into circle time:

Practice box 5.4

The Special Person Box is designed to build self-esteem. Use a small, attractive box with a mirror fitted into its base. Keep the lid closed as you introduce the box to the children, explaining that you are going to pass it around the circle and that each child in turn is to look inside where they will see someone who is very special. No-one is to speak as the box is passed around!

Show Me How You Feel is an activity in which children choose badges depicting a facial expression representing the way they are feeling. It helps children to identify and reflect upon different emotions – their own and others – by focussing on body language. We can begin by asking the children to make a happy face, sad face, angry face. (Don't explore too many feelings at once!) We can ask them to say what might make them feel happy, sad and so on. It is important that the adult accepts what each child says in a non-judgemental and calm way. We can then introduce badges depicting certain expressions and ask the children to identify the emotion represented on each badge. Explain that you will leave the badges in a certain place in the classroom and that any child may choose a badge to wear, to let others know how s/he is feeling. Eventually the use of pictures will become redundant as children become more able to recognise and verbalise their feelings. The adult can create opportunities for discussion at circle time by saying 'Would anyone like to talk about how they feel today?'

(Tait, 2005, p. 26)

Thinking point 5.9   How might you feel as an adult being asked to take part in a 'show me how you feel' activity? Do you think that children might have similar feelings?

4.2 Evaluating participation

At the start of the chapter we listed a number of reasons why participation is considered a good idea. It is evident that policy makers and practitioners are convinced by many of these arguments. More opportunities appear to be open for children's participation and involvement in public decision making. There is also an evolving body of good practice literature and guidance for people working with children.

In order to develop these opportunities further, and expand the practice literature, it is necessary to evaluate the scope, quality and impact of participation (Lansdown, 2004). Hart's model of participation can be a useful measure of scope, while quality can be measured with reference to standards such as *Hear by Right* (Badham and Wade, 2005).

Evidence can be easily found demonstrating the beneficial impact of participatory work on children's personal and social development including 'confidence, self-belief, knowledge, understanding and changed attitudes, skills and education attainment' (Kirby and Bryson, 2002, p. 6). Participation and involvement can also be fun for children and an opportunity to make new friends.

Children's active involvement has impacted on the growth in service-user-led training for professionals (Children's Rights Officers and Advocates, 2000) and the mainstreaming of service user involvement, particularly in social care (*Hear By Right*, Badham and Wade, 2005). Children's collective voices conveyed through research (for example, the Children's Research Centre) and media (for example, Headliners) have helped challenge traditional views of childhood and promoted children instead as competent social agents.

Despite these positive results, Wyness (2006) alerts us to the danger of 'sentimentalising' children's voices as an end in itself rather than as a means to change policy. Of particular concern is the scarcity of evidence about the impact of children's involvement on service development (Cavet and Sloper, 2004). The continued involvement of children can only be achieved, and sceptics (both children and adults) won over, if participation is shown to result in improvements to children's quality of life.

If participation becomes an end in itself, there is an inherent danger that people will not be open and honest about what does and does not work. Ackermann et al. (2003) identify that some organisations are under pressure from funding bodies and policy makers to demonstrate successful participation.

> Therefore, many of the most valuable learning experiences, which came out of apparent 'failure' may not be shared openly for the benefit of all
>
> (Ackermann et al., 2003, p. 17)

Effective participatory practice will only be developed through honest and open evaluation linked to critical reflection and review. Also, because participation is a process rather than a one-off event (Crowley, 2004) it is important that these evaluations look at changes over time (Ackermann et al., 2003).

More research is needed to understand why some children participate more than others. This may be because some children have no interest in becoming involved, or because traditional participation approaches do not reach some children. It is noticeable that very few studies have sought the views of children who do not participate (Kirby and Bryson, 2002).

Adults working with children may need help in recognising that participation is not an off-the-shelf technical approach. Neither is it built upon a universal fully-formed area of practice knowledge. Even experienced participatory workers learn a great deal through evaluating their methods and being willing to share their experiences with others. Ackermann et al. (2003) suggest that because the aims of participatory projects are often context-specific, 'extreme caution should be exercised in the promotion of universal indicators for the impact of participatory projects' (Ackermann et al., 2003, p. 11).

One way around this is to build evaluation into participatory projects from the start and involve children themselves in the evaluation process. A number of ethical principles can guide evaluation of participation with children:

- *participant centred*: based on children's own meanings and understandings

- *informed consent*: children should be fully aware of the purpose and process of evaluation

- *confidentiality*: children should know and understand the boundaries of confidentiality

- *risks* to children by being involved should be anticipated and averted

- *appropriate organisation and working space*: to ensure an environment in which children feel comfortable and safe enough to be creative and honest

- *transparency*: staff should be open and honest about the evaluation purpose process and with whom information will be shared

- *feedback*: children are entitled to have the findings fed back to them in an appropriate format and be informed about any outcomes resulting from their involvement.

The following example is adapted from Shephard and Treseder, who provide a number of evaluative activities that can involve children.

Practice box 5.5

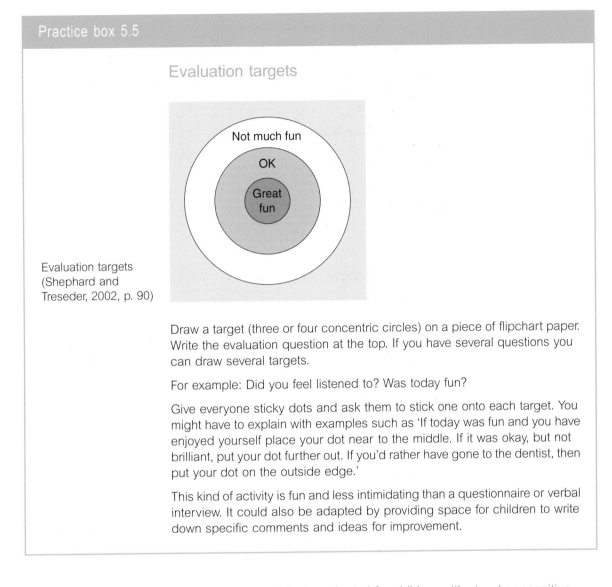

Evaluation targets
(Shephard and
Treseder, 2002, p. 90)

Draw a target (three or four concentric circles) on a piece of flipchart paper. Write the evaluation question at the top. If you have several questions you can draw several targets.

For example: Did you feel listened to? Was today fun?

Give everyone sticky dots and ask them to stick one onto each target. You might have to explain with examples such as 'If today was fun and you have enjoyed yourself place your dot near to the middle. If it was okay, but not brilliant, put your dot further out. If you'd rather have gone to the dentist, then put your dot on the outside edge.'

This kind of activity is fun and less intimidating than a questionnaire or verbal interview. It could also be adapted by providing space for children to write down specific comments and ideas for improvement.

Thinking point 5.10   How might this activity be adapted for children with visual or cognitive impairments?

Key points

1   Participation methods should be carefully chosen to reflect both context and purpose and not be forced upon unwilling participants.

2   Different participatory methods require adults with appropriate facilitation skills.

3   Both the processes and outcomes of participation require evaluation.

Conclusion

In this chapter we have examined the potential for children's participation in collective decision making. It is evident that adult–child relations, particularly within the provision of services, can be enhanced when children are valued and involved. Services themselves are more likely to meet the needs of children if they are designed with their views in mind. Although the historic attitudes about children and childhood still linger, it is possible to find examples of spaces where children are provided with opportunities to show their true capacity and competence. It is important that these are evaluated and the findings shared so that others can build effective participatory relationships.

References

Ackermann, L., Feeny, T., Hart, J. and Newman, J. (2003) *Understanding and Evaluating Children's Participation: A Review of Contemporary Literature. Children in Development*, Plan UK, Plan International.

Alderson, P. (1999) 'Human rights and democracy in schools; do they mean more than "picking up litter and not killing whales"?', *International Journal of Children's Rights*, vol. 7, no. 2, pp. 185–205.

Alderson, P. (2000) *Young Children's Rights: Exploring Beliefs, Principles and Practice*, London, Jessica Kingsley.

Aspinwall, T. and Larkins, C. (2002) *Breathing Fire Into Participation, The Funky Dragon Guide Good Practice Guidelines on Supporting Groups of Children and Young People to Participate*, Cardiff, Funky Dragon/Children and Young People's Assembly For Wales.

Atwool, N. (2006) 'Participation in decision-making: the experience of New Zealand children in care', *Child Care in Practice*, vol. 12, no. 3, pp. 259–267.

Badham, B. and Wade, H. (2005) *Hear By Right: Standards for the Active Involvement of Children and Young People* (revised edn), Leicester, National Youth Agency and Local Government Association.

Baginsky, M. and Hannam, D. (1999) *School Councils: The Views of Students and Teachers*, London, NSPCC.

Beresford, B. (1997) *Personal Accounts Involving Disabled Children in Research*, London, Social Policy Research Unit.

Bigyn School (2006) *School History 1898–1920*, available online at <http://www.ysgolccc.org.uk/bigyn/ourschool/history7.html>, accessed 6 June 2007.

Braye, S. and Preston Shoot, M. (1995) *Empowering Practice in Social Care*, Buckingham, Open University Press.

Carter, B. (2002) 'Chronic pain in childhood and the medical encounter: professional ventriloquism and hidden voices', *Qualitative Health Research*, vol. 12, no. 1, pp. 28–41.

Cavet, J. and Sloper, P. (2004) 'The participation of children and young people in decisions about UK service development', *Child: Care, Health and Development*, vol. 30, no. 6, pp. 613–621.

Children Act 1989, Crown copyright, HMSO.

Children and Family Court Advisory Support Service (CAFCASS) (2006) *Putting Children and Young People First: Children's Rights Policy*, London, CAFCASS.

Children's Rights Officers and Advocates (CROA) and Department of Health (DH) (2000) *Total Respect Training Manual: Ensuring Children's Rights and Participation in Care*, London, CROA and DH.

Comeau, K. (2005) *Involving Children in Decision Making. A Model for Developing Children's Participation*, Surrey, Children's Fund.

Connolly, M. and Ennew J. (1996) 'Introduction: children out of place', *Childhood*, vol. 3, no. 2, pp. 131–146.

Crowley, A. (2004) *Children and Young People's Participation: Working Towards a Definition. A Discussion Paper*, Save The Children and Participation Consortium (Wales), available online at <http://www.savethechildren.org.uk/scuk_cache/scuk/cache/cmsattach/2003_Part_Discussion_Paper.Eng.FINAL.Oct.04.pdf >, accessed 6 June 2007.

Cunningham, S. and Lavalette, M. (2002) 'Children, politics and collective action: school strikes in Britain' in Goldson, B., Lavalette, M. and McKechnie, J. (eds) *Children, Welfare and the State*, London, Sage.

Department for Constitutional Affairs (DCA) (2004) *Involving Children and Young People: Action Plan 2004–05*, London, Youth Parliament and National Children's Bureau.

Department for Education and Skills (DfES) (2004) *Working Together: Giving Children and Young People a Say*, London, DfES.

Eide, B.J. and Winger, N. (2005) 'From the children's point of view: methodological and ethical challenges' in Clark, A., Kjorholt, A.T. and Moss, P., *Beyond Listening: Children's Perspectives on Early Childhood Services*, Bristol, The Policy Press.

Ekholm, M. (2004) 'Learning democracy by sharing power' in MacBeath, J. and Moos, L. (eds) *Democratic Learning: The Challenge to School Effectiveness*, London, Routledge Falmer.

Ennew, J. (1994) 'Time for children or time for adults' in Qvortrup, J., Bardy, M., Sgritta, G. and Wintersberger, H. (eds) *Childhood Matters: Social Theory, Practice and Politics*, Aldershot, Avebury.

Foster Care Associates (FCA) (2000) *It's Mad That's All. A Collection of Poems about Being Looked After*, Bromsgrove, Foster Care Associates.

Franklin, B. (ed.) (2002) *The New Handbook of Children's Rights: Comparative Policy and Practice*, London, Routledge.

Freeman, M. (2000) 'The future of children's rights', *Children & Society*, vol. 14, pp. 277–293.

Hannam, D. (2001) *A pilot study to evaluate the impact of the student participation aspects of the citizenship order on standards of education in secondary schools. Report to the DfEE*, available online at <http://www.csv.org.uk/csv/hannamreport.pdf>, accessed 23 August 2007.

Hart, R. (1992) 'Participation from tokenism to citizenship', *Innocenti Essays*, no. 4, Florence, UNICEF.

Hart, R. (1997) *Children's Participation: The Theory and Practice of Involving Young Citizens in Community Development and Environmental Care*, London, Earthscan.

Headliners (1998) *Kids: what the papers say*, available online at <http://www.headliners.org/storylibrary/stories/1998/kidswhatthepaperssay.htm>, accessed 6 June 2007.

Hill, M. (2006) 'Children's voices on ways of having a voice: children's and young people's perspectives on methods used in research and consultation', *Childhood*, vol. 13, no. 1, pp. 69–89.

Hodge, S. (2005) 'Participation, discourse and power: a case study in service user involvement', *Critical Social Policy*, vol. 25, pp. 164–179.

Kay, E., Tisdall, M., Davis, J.M., Prout, A. and Hill, M. (eds) (2006) *Children, Young People and Social Inclusion. Participation for What?*, Bristol, The Policy Press.

Kellett, M., Forrest, R., Dent, N. and Ward, S. (2004) '"Just teach us the skills please, we'll do the rest": empowering ten-year-olds as active researchers', *Children & Society*, vol. 18, no. 1, pp. 329–343.

Kerr, D., Cleaver, E., Ireland, E. and Blenkinsop, S. (2003) *Citizenship Education Longitudinal Study: First Cross-sectional Survey 2001–2002*, Research report RR416, London, DfES.

Kirby, P. and Bryson, S. (2002) *Measuring the Magic? Evaluating and Researching Young People's Participation in Public Decision-making*, London, Carnegie Young People Initiative.

Kirby, P. and Gibbs, S. (2006) 'Facilitating participation: adults' caring support roles within child-to-child projects in schools and after-school settings', *Children & Society*, vol. 20, no. 3, pp. 209–222.

Kirby, P., Lanyon, C., Cronin, K. and Sinclair, S. (2003) *Building a Culture Of Participation. Involving Children and Young People in Policy, Service Planning, Delivery and Evaluation*, London, DfES.

Lancaster, Y.P. (2006) *RAMPS: A Framework for Listening to Children*, London, Daycare Trust.

Lansdown, G. (2001) *Promoting Children's Participation in Democratic Decision Making*, Florence, UNICEF Innocenti Research Centre.

Lansdown, G. (2004) *Evolving Capacities and Participation*, prepared for the Canadian International Development Agency, Victoria, Canada, International Institute for Child Rights and Development.

Lansdown, G. (2005) *The Evolving Capacities of Children*, Florence, UNICEF Innocenti Research Centre.

Lee, N. (2005) *Childhood and Human Value Development. Separation and Separability*, Maidenhead, Open University Press.

Leighton, R. (2004) 'The nature of citizenship education provision: an initial study', *Curriculum Journal*, vol. 15, no. 2, pp. 167–181.

MacBeath, J. and Mortimore, P. (eds) (2001) *Improving School Effectiveness*, Buckingham, Open University Press.

Mahony, K. and Hayes, N. (2006) *In Search of Quality: Multiple Perspectives, Executive Summary*, Dublin, Centre for Early Childhood Development and Education.

Malchiodi, C. (1999) 'Understanding somatic and spiritual aspects of children's art expressions' in Malchiodi, C. (ed.) *Medical Art Therapy with Children*, London, Jessica Kingsley, pp. 173–196.

Marchant, R., Jones, M. and Martyn, M. (1999) *Tomorrow I Go: What You Told Us about Dorset Road. Young People's Views about a Residential Respite Care Service*, Brighton, Triangle and East Sussex County Council.

Marchant R. and Kirby P. (2004) 'The participation of young children: communication, consultation and involvement' in Neale, B. (ed.) *Young Children's Citizenship: Ideas into Practice*, York, Joseph Rowntree Foundation.

McAuliffe, A-M. and Lane, J. (2005) *Listening and Responding to Young Children's Views on Food. Listening as a Way Of Life*, London, NCB and Sure Start.

McNeish, D., Downie, A., Newman, T., Webster, A. and Brading, J. (2000) *The Participation of Children and Young People: Report for Lambeth, Southwark and Lewisham Health Action Zone*, Ilford, Barnardo's.

McNeish, D. and Newman, T. (2002) 'Involving children and young people in decision making' in McNeish, D., Newman, T. and Roberts, H. (eds) *What Works for Children? Effective Services for Children and Families*, Buckingham, Open University Press.

Miller, J. (2003) *Never Too Young. How Young Children Can Take Responsibility and Make Decisions*, London, Save the Children.

Mittler, H. and May-Chahal, C. (2004) *Evaluation of St Helen's Children's Fund: Final Report 2002–04*, University of Central Lancashire, available online at <http://www.lancs.ac.uk/fss/apsocsci/research/documents/shcffinalreport2002-04.doc>, accessed 6 June 2007.

Mooney, A. and Blackburn, T. (2003) *Children's Views on Childcare Quality*, Research report RR482, Norwich, DfES.

Neustatter A. (1998) *Kids: what the papers say*, Headliners Story Library, available online at <http://www.headliners.org/storylibrary/stories/1998/kidswhatthepaperssay.htm>, accessed 6 June 2007.

Norfolk Children's Fund (2003), *The Children's Fund*, available online at <http://www. norfolkchildrensfund.co.uk/aboutus/index.jsp>, accessed 6 June 2007.

Osler, A. and Starkey, H. (2005) *Changing Citizenship: Democracy and Inclusion in Education,* Maidenhead, Open University Press/McGraw-Hill Education.

Peacock, A. and Wheatcroft School (2001) 'Working as a team: children and teachers learning from each other', *FORUM*, vol. 43, no. 2, pp. 51–53.

Perthshire Diary (2007) *Striking schoolchildren*, available online at <http://www. perthshirediary.com/html/day1011.html>, accessed 2 August 2007.

Qualifications and Curriculum Authority (QCA) (1998) *Education for Citizenship and the Teaching of Democracy in Schools: Final Report of the Advisory Group on Citizenship (The Crick Report)*, London, QCA.

Rollins, J.A. (2005) 'Tell me about it: drawing as a communication', *Journal of Pediatric Oncology Nursing*, vol. 22, no. 4, pp. 203–221.

Rubin, J. (1984) *Child Art Therapy: Understanding and Helping Children Grow Through Art* (2nd edn), New York, Van Nostrand Reinhold.

Save the Children (2007) *Child Participation*, Save the Children Canada, available online at <http://www.savethechildren.ca/whatwedo/rights/participate.html>, accessed 2 August 2007.

Save the Children (2006a) *Participation for schools: Isambard Brunel School*, available online at <http://www.participationforschools.org.uk/case-isambard.html>, accessed 2 August 2007.

Save the Children (2006b) *Participation for schools: Cannon Lane First School*, available online at <http://www.participationforschools.org.uk/case-cannon.html>, accessed 2 August 2007.

Save the Children (2006c) *Participation for schools: Stubbings Infant School*, available online at <http://www.participationforschools.org.uk/case-stubbings.html>, accessed 2 August 2007.

Shephard, C. and Treseder, P. (2002) *Participation: Spice it Up! Practical Tools for Engaging Children and Young People in Planning and Consultation*, Cardiff, Achub y Plant/Save the Children.

Shier, H. (2001) 'Pathways to participation: openings, opportunities and obligations: a new model for enhancing children's participation in decision making in line with Article 12.1 of the United Nations Convention on the Rights of the Child', *Children & Society*, vol. 15, pp. 107–117.

Sinclair, R. and Franklin, A. (2000) *Young People's Participation, Quality Protects*, Research Briefing, London, IPPR.

Sloper, P. and Lightfoot, J. (2003) 'Involving disabled and chronically ill children and young people in health service development', *Child: Care, Health and Development*, vol. 29, no. 1, pp. 15–20.

Smith, A.B. (2000) 'Children's rights: an overview' in Smith A.B., Gollop, M., Marshall, K. and Nairn, K. (eds) *Advocating for Children*, Dunedin, University of Otago Press, pp. 13–18.

South Gloucestershire Council (2007) *Participation of children and young people*, available online at <http://www.southglos.gov.uk/NR/exeres/11861b6b-3176-45de-9d0f-d65c0a62cb16>, accessed 24 August 2007.

Stafford, A., Laybourn, A., Hill, M. and Walker, M. (2003) '"Having a say": children and young people talk about consultation', *Children & Society*, vol. 17, no. 5, pp. 361–373.

Tait, M. (2005) 'Circle time', *Montessori International*, July–September, pp. 24–26.

Taylor, M.J. (2003) Going Round in Circles: Implementing and Learning from Circle Time, Slough, National Foundation for Educational Research.

Taylor, M.J. and Johnson, R. (2002) *School Councils: Their Role in Citizenship and Personal and Social Education*, Slough, National Foundation for Educational Research.

Thomas, N. (2002) *Children, Family and the State: Decision-making and Child Participation*, Bristol, The Policy Press.

Thompson, N. (2000) *Understanding Social Work: Preparing for Practice*, Basingstoke, Palgrave.

Thomson, P. and Holdsworth, R. (2003) 'Theorising change in the educational "field": rereadings of "pupil participation" projects', *International Journal of Leadership in Education*, vol. 6, no. 4, pp. 371–391.

Treseder, P. (1997) *Empowering Children and Young People Training Manual: Promoting Involvement in Decision-making*, London, Save the Children.

United Nations (1989) *United Nations Convention on the Rights of the Child (UNCRC)*, available online at <http://www.unicef.org.uk/publications/pub_detail.asp?pub_id=133>, accessed 22 August 2007.

Voice for the Child In Care (VCC) (subsequently renamed Voice) (2004) *Time 4 Change – Young People as Partners in the Blueprint Project – What Young People Had To Say*, London, National Children's Bureau/VCC.

Vygotsky, L.S. (1978) *Mind in Society: The Development of Higher Mental Processes*, Cambridge, MA, Harvard University Press.

Ward, D. (2000) 'Totem not token: groupwork as a vehicle for user participation' in Kemshall, H. and Littlechild, R. (eds) *User Involvement and Participation in Social Care*, London, Jessica Kingsley.

Willow, C. and Neale, B. (2004) *Young Children's Citizenship: Ideas into Practice*, York, Joseph Rowntree Foundation.

Woodhead, M. (1999) 'Reconstructing developmental psychology: some first steps', *Children & Society*, vol. 3, pp. 3–19.

Wyness, M. (2006) *Childhood and Society*, London, Palgrave.

Chapter 6

Understanding transitions

Stephen Leverett

Introduction

> He pushed his trolley round and stared at the barrier. It looked very solid. He started to walk towards it. People jostled him on their way to platforms nine and ten. Harry walked more quickly. He was going to smash right into the ticket box and then he'd be in trouble – leaning forward on his trolley he broke into a heavy run – the barrier was coming nearer and nearer – he wouldn't be able to stop – the trolley was out of control – he was a foot away – he closed his eyes ready for the crash –
>
> It didn't come ... he kept on running ... He opened his eyes.
>
> A scarlet steam engine was waiting next to a platform packed with people. A sign overhead said Hogwarts Express, 11 o'clock. Harry looked behind him and saw a wrought-iron archway where the ticket box had been, with the words Platform Nine and Three Quarters on it. He had done it.
>
> (Rowling, 1997, pp. 70–71)

For anybody reading (or watching) one of the Harry Potter series of books or films, a most memorable sequence is the transition through platform Nine and Three Quarters. It is here that Harry Potter departs for 'Hogwarts', his boarding school for witches and wizards. The move from home to school is a transition familiar to many children. The significance of the first day at school is borne out by the fact that many of us much later in life still retain vivid memories (both good and bad) of the sights, sounds and smells that confronted us in the strange new world of formal education.

For Harry Potter, school is more than a place to learn, it is also the place where he will be temporarily living and a refuge from his life in Privet Drive with his cruel uncle, aunt and cousin. Harry also undertakes a transition between a world inhabited by non-magic 'muggles' to one where witches and wizards live. Harry not only moves back and forth but has to deal with situations where the two worlds, with their different value systems, collide. Being caught 'in the middle' leaves Harry vulnerable to prejudice and misunderstanding and, at times, his own identity is in doubt. Harry's experience echoes something of the lives of real children who perhaps move to foster families or, in the case of refugees and migrants, to new countries, in order to find safety or better opportunities. They too are confronted with powerful feelings of loss, change and uncertainty.

The character of Harry Potter is presented to us as a resilient, socially active child with great inner strength and adaptability. These qualities, combined with a network of caring adults and loyal friends, enable Harry to overcome great adversities including the death of his parents and life as an orphan. Harry, of course, is a fictional character, the product of author J.K. Rowling's imagination, yet he also reflects the lives of many real children who experience similar challenges and transitions and exhibit their own qualities of resilience and social agency. This chapter will introduce you to some of their stories.

In order to support children it is important that adults listen to and respond to their feelings and concerns. Children are social beings and much of what they experience, and have feelings about, occurs within and across different contexts. As with Harry Potter, children move between different 'worlds'. Each 'world' or cultural context is likely to possess a different 'cultural model' (Lam and Pollard, 2006, p. 124), made up of different expectations, values and ways of being. It is therefore unsurprising to find that transitions into new environments or contexts provoke powerful feelings associated with change.

Children may experience, yet have difficulty naming, a range of feelings including bewilderment, curiosity, excitement, fear, grief and anger. Adult empathy and support (as we show in Chapter 7) can help children identify and clarify their feelings.

Thinking point 6.1   What is your earliest memory of a transition (for example, your first day at nursery or at school)? What significant feelings do you remember?

Moss and Petrie (2002) suggest that adults who are reflective practitioners, researchers and thinkers are well-placed to support children. They propose a model of adult–child relations in which the child is valued equally as a source of knowledge, alongside the adult's own experiences and learning.

Reflection involves contemplating and reviewing an experience and analysing how it makes both the individual and others feel. In some cases it is possible to relate this process to academic theories and existing practice knowledge. Reflection can confirm or transform our understanding of a situation or phenomena and is, therefore, the basis of further learning and action. It also enables us to gain a deeper understanding of what transitions mean to children.

As we saw in previous chapters, reflection on how we connect and interrelate with children can bring us closer to their worlds and create a platform for providing appropriate and sensitive support with transitions. The following two accounts demonstrate the potential of also reflecting on our own experiences from the past:

> I can remember very clearly my first day at middle school; I was eight years old. I had been really excited in the days leading up to school opening and had spent time choosing a bag and buying stationery and I loved my new school clothes. By the night before I started to worry, because I wasn't sure if you were allowed to go to the toilet during lessons, like we could at first school. By the time I reached the school gate I was really worried and was shaking. My best friend asked me what was wrong and was really sweet when I explained. She said that she would ask the teacher for me. I instantly felt better as we walked into school hand-in-hand.
>
> (Nicole, stay-at-home mum, informal interview 2007)

> I remember playing at a stand-up sand-pit and another boy, whose name I still remember, pushing me so that I banged my nose and it started to bleed. I had two older sisters and I am told I couldn't wait to start school like them but I feel that my memory is a negative one. The sand-pit is maybe vivid because it was a new experience for me and the fact that I still remember the boy's name maybe stems from being brought up in an all-girl environment until then so I wasn't prepared for rough-and-tumble kind of play or keeping myself safe to avoid conflict.
>
> (Brenda, playleader, informal interview 2007)

These accounts give us insight into important details about children's transitions. Nicole reveals how an impending transition can be both a time for pleasure and ritual (buying new clothes) and also a time of anxiety and uncertainty. Brenda describes the disappointment of a negative experience that dampened her expectations of what school was supposed to be like. Her reflection on this experience leads her to consider the impact of wider family and gender issues on her transition. In both accounts we can recognise the challenge children face as they move into new worlds and try their best to learn and adapt to change.

By reflecting on their own experiences, Brenda and Nicole make connections with what it was like to be a child, in particular before, during and after important transitions. This potentially gives them an additional resource with which to empathise and provide appropriate support to children for whom they have responsibility.

Core questions

- What are some of the different meanings, definitions and consequences of transitions in the lives of children and their families?

- What can be learned about the experience of transition from children, their families and professional accounts?

- How can both personal reflection and theoretical ideas and models assist in critically analysing the process and experience of transition?

1 Definitions and meanings of transition

The concept of transition has many meanings and applications when applied to children's lives. Newman and Blackburn (2002, p. 1) define transition as: 'any episode where children are having to cope with potentially challenging episodes of change, including progressing from one developmental stage to another, changing schools, entering or leaving the care system, loss, bereavement, parental incapacity or entry to adulthood'.

Niesel and Griebel (2005) argue that, compared to previous generations, children and their families in the twenty-first century are 'confronted with more and different disruptions to their biographies'. A range of issues, such as parental separation, divorce, remarriage, moving house, migration, the increased number of mothers who work and phases of unemployment and poverty, mean that children today 'have a higher probability of being confronted with increasing personal demands resulting from transitions in their own, and in their family's, development' (Niesel and Griebel, 2005, p. 4).

1.1 Transitions within an ecological context

Children's transitions can be complex and diverse and derive from multifarious influences and causes. This is because children live interdependent and interconnected lives within a series of environmental systems that include people, places, culture, ideas, beliefs, and other social and economic factors (Bronfenbrenner, 1979). Transitions occur as children move between, and adapt to, different environmental systems (Colton et al., 2001), through both space and time. This context, or environment, is both dynamic (changing) and specific to each child.

Ecology describes the relationship between individuals and their environments. Bronfenbrenner's ecological model (overleaf) represents the environment as a series of systems that interact with each other, and the child. The 'nested arrangement of concentric structures' (Bronfenbrenner, 1979, p. 22) is often portrayed as a bull's-eye or Russian doll model. Each circle or ring represents a different environmental system, and interaction occurs both within each system and between each system.

Bronfenbrenner's ecological model is often portrayed as a series of nested Russian dolls

Thinking point 6.2   Can you relate this model to a child you know?

According to Bronfenbrenner, the immediate environment (or microsystem) for very young children usually consists of primary carers and close family within the home setting. As children become older this expands to include, for example, other family members, friends, peers, early years

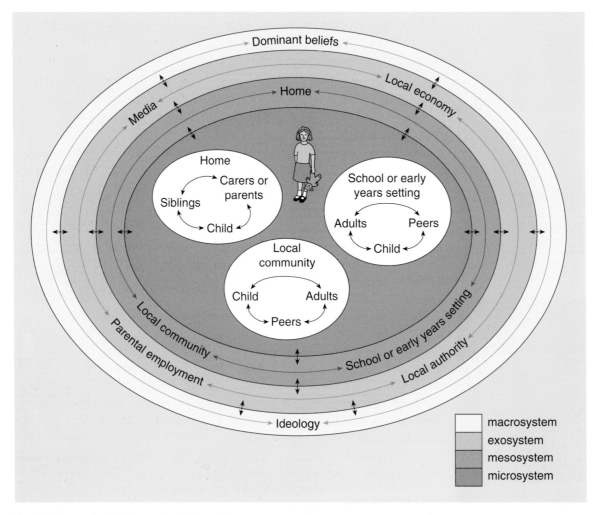

Bronfenbrenner's (1979) ecological model

workers and teachers. As children make transitions within and between each setting, they are expected to recognise and negotiate different social and cultural models.

> I remember when I was four I got told off for dropping stones in a pond at play school.
>
> (Boy quoted on At-Bristol, 2007, webpage)

Reflecting on the account from this child, it is possible to acknowledge the pleasure that he may have drawn from dropping a stone into a pond. Maybe he was replicating a happy memory from a family trip to the seaside. Yet within the play school environment he is presented with a new set of rules, or cultural model, which discourages his actions. The boy fails to comply with this and subsequently is 'told off'.

Earlier we saw how Brenda and Nicole were able to reflect on how difficult, confusing, and sometimes painful, these early transitions within the immediate environment can be. If they were adults with responsibility for the boy playing by the school pond their personal reflection might lead them to respond positively to his actions. Maybe they would have found him an alternative water play activity encouraging his interest and demonstrating their empathy with his situation.

Bronfenbrenner referred to the interrelationships that develop between each setting within the immediate environment as the mesosystem. The strength and quality of these interrelationships (for example between home and school) can have a bearing on how well or otherwise a child develops. It is likely, for example, that the play school workers would liaise with the boy's parents or carers and keep them informed about his progress. Workers in childcare settings are equally interested in being kept informed about children's home life and use this knowledge to create continuity between the two settings. Supporting children with their behaviour during transitions will be discussed in Chapter 7, where we will look more closely at the importance of continuity.

Some childhood transitions are influenced by interrelationships with systems in the wider environment, such as the local economy, the network of welfare services or the parent's workplace. Bronfenbrenner called this the exosystem. These wider environmental systems may directly influence family dynamics and, subsequently, a child's feelings and behaviour, as illustrated by the following example.

A girl's teacher contacted her parents, concerned that she was bullying other children. It transpired that this previously uncharacteristic behaviour coincided with a major disruption at home when the child's mother was forced by her employer to move to a new shift pattern. As a result, her mother was no longer available to tuck her in and read her a bedtime story. The child's behaviour at school appeared to represent her frustration at missing her mother's company.

Welfare services, as much as employment systems, are part of the exosystem and can consequently affect children's behaviour. In this example, the experience of being rehoused several times by the council is unsettling for the child involved:

> 'But when we were told we had to move from the flat to [... street], and then [... street] to here, it's like why? Why keep moving us? Can't you just put us in one place?'
>
> (Child quoted in Nettleton, 2001, p. 89)

Finally Bronfenbrenner identifies the influence of wider political and cultural beliefs or events (the macrosystem) in creating the context in which some transitions occur. Their influence can be both explicit (for example, formal rules or regulations, such as 'all children must go to school at age four') or implicit (for example, belief systems reflecting customs or cultural practices, such as 'childcare is shared between members of the extended family') (Colton et al., 2001).

One way of distinguishing between types of transition is to consider those which are commonly experienced by most children and those that only affect particular groups or individuals. Another is to divide transitions into those that can be expected (life course events like starting school) and those that are unexpected (life events such as the repossession of a home). A further differentiation can be between major transitional events, such as the birth of a sibling, and mini-transitions involving frequent but less obviously important events, like the journey between home and school.

1.2   Commonly experienced transitions

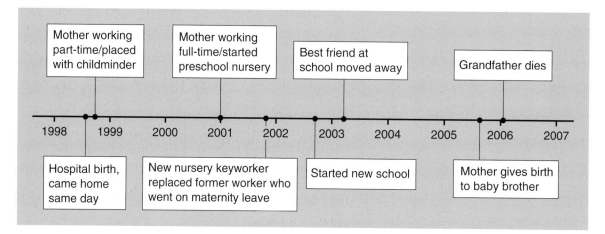

A child's timeline highlighting examples of transitions

This timeline represents one child's experience of early transitions. Many of these transitions are experienced by large numbers of young children.

Thinking point 6.3   What other commonly experienced transitions might be included if the timeline was continued until the child was twelve?

A common view of childhood is as a particular transitional phase in the life course. The tendency has been to use chronological models, such as the phases of infancy (0–2 years), childhood (2–12 years), youth (12–24 years) and adulthood (25 + years). Such a view, of course, is problematic because it is very difficult to determine, universally, where one phase ends and another begins – particularly as we carry our experiences with us as we progress through life. Factors such as biological changes, cultural rites of passage, legal entitlements and the subjective feelings of those involved can all be linked to the transition between childhood and adulthood (Maybin and Woodhead, 2003, p. 270).

Another way of thinking about transitions is to consider children as developing beings. It is assumed that all children pass through stages of development at a biological, psychological and socio-cultural level. Over time, most children will experience physical growth and the development of new and more sophisticated abilities. There may be cultural variations in how these changes are valued or understood, and individual differences amongst children resulting from their environmental and social interrelationships.

It has also been claimed that children influence their own environment and consequently play an active role in some aspects of their own development (Schaffer, 1992). Chapter 7 will examine how support for children in some circumstances can build on what they already have in terms of experience and resilience.

Universal education provision means that most children experience transitions into and through the school system. Some adults will recall their first day at school as a major life event. It is useful to reflect on how this may differ from more recent generations of children who have been affected by the expansion and wide take-up of preschool provision. The multifaceted nature of these transitions (considering the various part-time and full-time pathways through early years services including nursery, childminder and preschool) suggests children may start school already experienced at transitions, although this experience may vary greatly from one child to the next.

Much attention is paid to major transitions (such as starting school or nursery for the first time) by members of the children's workforce. Less consideration is given to the repeated day-to-day experience of moving back and forth between home and education and care settings in children's lives. This kind of mini-transition, which has also been labelled 'commuting' (Lam and Pollard, 2006, p. 123), requires children to adapt to the culture model of each place – a familiar experience for adults who spend time moving between home and the workplace.

Like adult workers, children will notice different ways of being between home and work. For both adults and children, work might demand different forms of dress, language, and general behaviour from home. For children this can result, as in our example of the boy playing by the play school pond, in situations where they unintentionally transgress unfamiliar cultural rules.

Most adults can adapt to these ways of being, although they may still cause them stress; generally adults learn the rules and adapt their behaviour to suit the environment in which they find themselves. Children, on the other hand, may need time and support in order to adapt.

1.3 Less commonly experienced transitions

We have identified that specific transitions are commonly shared by many adults and children within contemporary Western European society. Other kinds of transition are less frequently experienced yet equally important to understand. Some children have personal experience of poverty, disability, illness, bereavement, emigration, adoption, sexuality, family break-up and crime which entail specific transitions perhaps unfamiliar to many of their peers. These often result from unexpected or difficult-to-predict life events experienced by the child or their wider network. For some, like the children of armed forces personnel, relocation is a common yet still difficult-to-predict feature of their childhood, particularly during a time of war.

For other children, access to universal services may only be possible with the input of specialist support such as educational psychologists, Child and Adolescent Mental Health Services (CAMHS), physiotherapists or speech therapists. They may also require specialist community services, including adapted housing, transport, leisure and play facilities or after-school clubs. In some extreme cases children may rely solely on specialist services. For all of these families, accessing the right kind of support involves transitions across professional and agency boundaries and, whilst the trend is for children's services to aid accessibility by working more closely together, it has been claimed that 'a gap exists between what should be provided and what is provided' (Soames et al., 2006, p. 4).

As the following accounts demonstrate, transitions can be improved by providing more personal, accessible and local services and information about what is available in the community.

> 'There are times that having all different people in my life is too much. I spend a lot of my time up the hospitals. I wish there were less appointments and less doctors to see.'
>
> (Child quoted in Turner, 2003, p. 21)

> 'Having things a lot nearer and more of them would make things a lot easier. There should be a children's hospital closer.'
>
> (Child quoted in Turner, 2003, p. 22)

'There is not enough information around about lots of things. A friend told me about the service, I would never have known otherwise.'

(Child quoted in Turner, 2003, p. 26)

Key points

1 The concept of transition has many meanings and applications when applied to children's lives.

2 Ecological models are useful in helping us understand children's transitions.

3 It is useful to distinguish between commonly experienced and less commonly experienced transitions.

2 Different contexts of transition: status, time and space

This section will identify and analyse three common and interrelated contexts associated with transitions: status, time and space. It will be argued here that all transitions will relate to, and can be understood through, one or more of these contexts.

2.1 Age and status

Attaching a value to the concept of age

'I'm eleven and thirteen days!' This quote, taken from some research by Christensen et al. (2000, p. 2) will be familiar to anyone who knows a child. How often are adults corrected by a child who points out they are 'not six any more but six and three-quarters'? This confirms that children can attach a value to the concept of age – not a surprising finding if you consider the amount of time, effort (and in some cases money) adults invest in helping children celebrate their birthdays.

Informally, for many children, age may equate to new freedoms, such as being allowed to stay out late or being given more independence. In the UK, age also equates to moving up another year in the school system and is a prerequisite for other formal milestones of childhood.

Table 6.1 Different age-related milestones	
Age	Milestones
0–1	Children should be registered and provided with a birth certificate within the first 42 days after birth (21 days in Scotland).
	Children receive the following vaccinations at 2, 3 and 4 months of age: diphtheria, tetanus and whooping cough (triple vaccine), haemophilus influenza type B (Hib), meningitis C and polio.
	Exclusive breastfeeding is recommended by the Department of Health for the first six months of an infant's life. Six months is also the recommended age for the introduction of solid foods for both breast- and formula-fed infants.
	Early Years Foundation Stage (birth–5 years in England).
	Pre School Early Years Stage (ages 0–4 in Northern Ireland).
1	Children receive vaccinations against measles, mumps and rubella (MMR) between the ages of 12 and 15 months.
3	Children receive booster vaccinations against diphtheria, tetanus and whooping cough (triple vaccine); measles, mumps and rubella (MMR) and polio between the ages of 3 and 5.
	Foundation Phase (ages 3–7 in Wales).
	Scottish Curriculum Framework (3–5 years).[1]

4	Compulsory school education begins in Northern Ireland. Children start school on the September following their 4th birthday, providing it is before the previous 1 July – children therefore start school between the ages of 4 years 2 months and 5 years 2 months.
5	Compulsory school education begins in England, Wales and Scotland. Key Stage 1 (ages 5–7 in England and Wales). 5–14 curriculum in Scotland. Northern Ireland Foundation Stage Years 1 and 2.[2]
7	Key Stage 2 (ages 7–11 in England and Wales). Northern Ireland Key Stage 1, Years 3 and 4.[2] Children can draw money from a post office or savings account.
8	Age of criminal responsibility in Scotland – however, Scotland has its own unique Hearing System that deals with most offences by children below 16. Northern Ireland Key Stage 2, Years 5, 6 and 7.[2]
10	Age of criminal responsibility in England, Wales and Northern Ireland.
11	Secondary school education begins for children in England, Wales and Northern Ireland. Key Stage 3 (ages 11–14 in England and Wales), pupils in Scotland move to secondary education in the August following their 11th birthday. Northern Ireland Key Stage 3, Years 8, 9 and 10.[2]
12	Children are allowed to buy a pet. Children may rent or buy a 12-rated video or DVD. Children can see a 12A film at the cinema without being accompanied by an adult.

[1] From September 2008. Replacing Early Years Stage and Key Stage 1.

[2] Since August 2007. Revised Northern Ireland curriculum.

Thinking point 6.4   The list above represents a view of transitional milestones and status. If children themselves were to construct a similar list what milestones might they include?

Any list of age-related milestones is a snapshot in time representing a particular cultural and political construction of children's status and transitions. If we attempted to draw up a similar set of milestones for the UK a hundred years ago, for example, it would be very different.

Compulsory schooling for children from age five was introduced in the late nineteenth century, without consultation with educationalists or people with knowledge of child development (Woodhead, 1989). It was a political decision which reflected dominant views of the time about controlling the urban poor, protecting children and ensuring that they possessed sufficient skills and knowledge to eventually enter the labour market. The policy failed to consider cultural and economic variations in children's lives with the result that, for example, many rural children who were still involved in agricultural work at the turn of the twentieth century did not comply with the legislation.

This clearly contrasts with the twenty-first century, when most children in the UK start school at, or before, the compulsory starting age. Continuity exists, however, in the role played by government in constructing these milestones to reflect dominant discourses about childhood.

Despite a slight variation between the countries of the UK, school starting ages are low when compared to most European countries, where six is the norm, or to Scandinavia, where children must start school by age seven (Eurydice/Eurostat, 2005, p. 14). Younger school starting ages (children as young as four are in school reception classes) are the result of social policies attempting to give children (particularly those from disadvantaged backgrounds) an earlier start to formal learning and an opportunity for children's services to counter the effects of inequality. Earlier school starting ages have also supported the flexible employment market and governments' 'welfare to work' discourse by becoming a source of relatively cheap childcare for working parents.

It is notable that countries like Sweden provide a comprehensive range of childcare options for parents as part of a historic social policy commitment to children's welfare and gender equality. Parental pressure for earlier school starting ages is therefore not a major policy issue. This contrasts with the UK where, despite improvements to the availability and affordability of childcare, it remains an expensive option for many working parents. This results in frequent mini-transitions for children between several different formal and informal carers.

The early school starting age is a status or milestone imbued with economic and logistical significance for many parents because it provides a relatively stable and affordable source of childcare. A review of research, however, fails to uphold the key educational claims supporting the policy. Sharp (2002) suggests that children's long-term attainment in reading, writing and numeracy skills is much the same regardless of how early they started formal learning. 'There is also little evidence that an early start in school compensates children for lower achievement that may be associated with deficiencies in their home learning environment' (Sharp, 2002, p. 16).

In some countries (particularly in Eastern Europe) maturity replaces age as the status determining school entry. Maturity is variously assessed using procedures such as 'medical examinations, psychological examinations, aptitude tests' and the subjective views of teachers and parents (Eurydice/Eurostat, 2005, p. 69). Subjective determination of maturity as a basis for making a particular transition can present its own difficulties. Sharp (2002) is concerned that this creates a potential for equal opportunities violations. In one US study (Zill et al., 1997, cited in Sharp, 2002) boys and children from black and Hispanic families were over-represented in the numbers of children held back from starting school based on teacher recommendations or school assessments.

In the UK, maturity is usually bestowed with age status (for example, being allowed access to a 12A classified film).

> 'What I like about being 11 is some adults think you have matured so you can walk around by yourself and have proper discussions'
>
> (Girl quoted in Madge, 2006, p. 38)

Rarely is age challenged as a prerequisite for attaining specific milestones. A notable exception was the ruling by the House of Lords (Gillick v. West Norfolk 1985) which, for the first time, gave children and young people under the age of sixteen the right to consent to medical treatment if a General Practitioner (GP) assessed them as competent (described as sufficient understanding and intelligence). Thus, rather than using a straightforward age-defined threshold, GPs can use their discretion based upon the individual and the context.

Children's physical size is also a determining factor, alongside age, in relation to car seat use and as an entry requirement to certain fairground and theme park rides. In most areas of life, however, children still experience age as the dominant factor in attaining status. Consequently, there is a strong suggestion that children attribute status to age – with 'older' being a more desirable state.

Christensen et al. (2000) found, through listening to children's accounts, that they used specific markers as a way of defining changes of status linked to getting older. A particularly important marker was identified as the transition from primary to secondary school.

Physical height as opposed to age is used to determine access to fairground rides

> Almost all of the children felt that moving to secondary school made them feel more grown up. One explained:

> I'm around older people and I'm expected to be mature. At primary you're with four year olds.

> (Christensen et al., 2000, p. 2).

In the same study children also reported that they valued having more space, responsibility and a status associated with more freedom: ' "More friends, more freedom at dinner times – at primary school, I felt I was trapped in at dinner." ' (Christensen et al., 2000, p. 2). These accounts are a reminder that children attribute their own meanings to transitions.

Many of the key transitions are linked to age, and the associated opportunity to attain more desirable status positions associated with space, freedom and peer relationships. Many children value not being controlled by adults yet, at the same time, appear heavily influenced by their peers. Although age is key to unlocking many of these opportunities their realisation is not guaranteed and may be dependent upon other factors associated with the child's identity such as gender, social class or ethnic origin.

Childhood transitions can also impact on the identity and sense of self of other family members. Holland examined assessment reports as part of her research. One extract used in her fieldwork involved a six-year-old (referred to as Paige) who is consulted by a social worker regarding her family situation. It reveals how this child is affected by the imminent birth of a new sibling:

> Paige has talked at length about the baby expected in August, she is looking forward with enthusiasm to becoming a 'big sister.' Paige does, however, have fears regarding this child's birth, and these focus around her place in her mother's affections. She has stated that she hopes her mother will "still love me" when the baby is born, and she has expressed her anxiety that her mother will "look after the baby properly"

> (Holland, 2004, p. 75)

In this account it is evident that Paige is looking forward to attaining the status of 'big sister' while, at the same time, fearing that her present status of daughter in relation to her mother is in some way under threat. Similar tensions concerning status were noted in a study of how families cope at different stages in the diagnosis and treatment of childhood cancer (Woodgate and Degner, 2004). One female sibling of a child with cancer reported how 'during a good period' she was able to spend a weekend with her mother and was glad that she 'had her mother to herself' (Woodgate and Degner, 2004, p. 365).

Children's transitions, combined with their status and identity, can be the target of prejudicial attitudes and discriminatory practices at both individual and institutional levels. Refugee children may encounter racist bullying yet may avoid reporting it, believing that it may compromise their refugee status. Homophobic bullying may go unreported in schools because teachers lack the confidence or skills to confront it. Being in receipt of particular kinds of benefits or services may, in itself, be sufficient to leave a child vulnerable to bullying. This is particularly true of children in the Looked After care system, including the following child who describes what is bad about being in care:

> 'getting the mickey taken out of you at school ... other kids say where's your mum?'
>
> (Packman and Hall, 1998, cited in Kelly and Gilligan, 2002, p. 53)

Some children also demonstrate great loyalty and protection towards other children who they may perceive as vulnerable to discrimination. Shaw (1998) reports how children in mainstream education took time to get used to having disabled classmates. Initially they felt sorry for them and were afraid to make physical contact. Later they learned that they had a lot in common with these children and were prepared to defend the disabled children's right to be in inclusive education.

> 'When he came to school no one liked him that much. He kept being lonely but we learned to be friends with him and try to give him a chance. He's got one kidney, or one liver – something like that – but inside he's quite good.'
>
> 'They're doing all right here. There's no point sending them back to special school because they have got friends here.'
>
> (Shaw, 1998, p. 82)

2.2   Space and place

Transitions from preschool to school, between birth family and foster family, from the home to a local community park, are all situations where the transition itself involves children in moving from one space to another.

Space can be understood as more than just a physical or geographical area. For example, Strassoldo introduces the concept of 'lived space' which describes the way that people interact with and attach their own meanings to space (Strassoldo, 1993, cited in Törrönen, 2006, p. 130). 'Place' is a closely related concept and can be understood as a subjective attachment, or sense of belonging, to particular spaces. Place may relate to an individual, a family, a group or even a nation and is closely related to the development of

A child's bedroom acts as a familiar and secure place reflecting their identity

identity. 'It creates a feeling of security for children: they have a familiar place to which they belong and want to identify with' (Törrönen, 2006, p. 130).

Children can vary in how comfortable they feel about sharing space with others, it may depend upon their previous experiences or their familiarity with the new context. Some theorists (Hall, 1966) even suggest that cultural groups differ in the amount of personal space within which they feel comfortable. Some childhood transitions, such as migration, foster care or adoption, centre on the experiences of leaving behind or establishing a new sense of place. The following extract, from a poem written by a young person living in a foster family, indicates the challenges of finding a sense of place and the importance of adults and children working together to achieve this:

> In a family who
>
> Have a car, have fun, go away,
>
> Eat Popcorn in front of the telly.
>
> Laugh and cry without cruelty or abuse
>
> How can I be one of you?
>
> How can you absorb one of me?
>
> What do we need to make it happen?
>
> (Foster Care Associates, 2003, p. 31)

The following account indicates how ongoing success with transitions and life tasks can be enhanced by achieving a sense of place:

'Before I came to a foster home I was mixed up and confused – but now I am in a secure placement I feel my schooling is getting better'

(Boy quoted in Fletcher, 1993, cited in Kelly and Gilligan, 2002, p. 51)

Space: a site of control and resistance

In contrast to the relative freedom and belonging associated with place some children may experience transitions across space as changes in levels of adult control or surveillance. Both Brown (2007) and Gallacher (2005) draw attention to the subtle control of young children within nursery environments. Spatial layouts of classrooms and furniture (for example, the positioning and height of the teacher's chair) symbolically reinforce the power relationship between adults and children. Children know they are being watched by adults and most consequently self-regulate their behaviour to conform. In some cases surveillance is reinforced with verbal reminders to children:

Duncan was throwing toys into the play house. Nuala [adult carer] told him, 'Duncan, Duncan Jones; I'm watching you! That's all I'm saying'.

(Gallacher, 2005, p. 254)

When exploring these issues there is a danger of seeing power as a one-way process, with adults controlling children. In some cases children want adults to watch or see what they are doing and actively harness their own power and employ strategies that demand adult attention. Children also compete with each other and reproduce socially constructed inequalities as they access and control space. A girl reveals how boys resisted her attempt to be included in their football space on the school playground:

'... and when I used to play football, they used to make fun of me, because I can't really play.'

(Girl quoted in Smith and Barker, 2000, p. 325)

Both Gallacher and Brown also identify how children develop resistance to adult control. In some instances children were able to escape the adult gaze through the innovative use of space. The play house was particularly used for this purpose by children due to its small size and inaccessibility to adults:

The children were called over to the music corner for singing and stories. Some children went into the play house instead. Ashley [adult carer] told them to come out and join the other children in the music corner. Thomas and Louise came out reluctantly when told but Louise slammed the door as she came out. Kelsey still refused to come out, hiding in the far corner instead.

(Gallacher, 2005, p. 258)

Edwards et al. (2000) illustrate this point further in the transition between home and school. For the children in the study, home was seen as a haven in which they could relax and exercise a certain amount of control away from a heavily regulated school environment. Children demonstrated both their desire and a certain amount of ability to set boundaries between the two places and would employ innovative strategies to resist parental involvement in their schooling.

> Some [of the letters home from school] are just about things your mum and dad aren't going to want to know about ... so you just put it in your bag and forget about it.

(Child quoted in Edwards et al., 2000, p. 3)

The boundary of surveillance and control is, however, being pushed further into children's home lives (Shucksmith et al., 2005) transforming what has previously been a clear-cut home–school transition. Increasingly, adults are being encouraged to scrutinise, observe and control their children's behaviour, aided by new technology such as baby monitors, mobile phone tracking devices and computer software. At the same time, government policy is encouraging more parental involvement in education through monitoring children's homework and trying to ensure that children start school with certain basic skills.

It is likely that children's experience of this type of transition will also be influenced by the attitude and resources of their parents. Parents' confidence and familiarity with the educational process may be a factor inclining them to be more or less involved in their children's education. For some this may entail home schooling, while others may be restricted from involvement through competing family commitments such as working long hours to pay bills, or caring for other family members. Great variation in different children's experience of home–school transitions is therefore guaranteed, even in the same school.

Transitions into and through public space are a feature of some children's lives. This includes (Wooley, 2006) communal domestic spaces (for example, community gardens, housing spaces and allotments), neighbourhood spaces (parks, playgrounds, streets and incidental or natural spaces) and civic spaces (amenities related to transport, leisure and service delivery).

Children are placed into designated public spaces (including childcare, holiday playschemes, schools or family placements) by adults, in line with social conventions and expectations (James et al., 1998). They are also denied entry to some public spaces and can create anxiety by transgressing these adult-maintained boundaries by, for example, going into public houses or hanging around shopping centres or street corners (James et al., 1998, p. 38). Different types of transition would appear to relate to one, or both, of these interrelationships and this illustrates the extent to which transitions can be framed by both social structure and children's agency.

Children also pass through public spaces as part of other transitions, such as the journey between home and school. Transitions through such spaces, as in this nineteenth-century account of a journey to school, can become a time for children's agency, creative play and friendship development:

> The elder children would 'pick-a-back' their small brothers and sisters. A crippled boy who lived more than two miles from school was drawn by other boys in a truck made from a Tate's sugar box with perambulator wheels. His cart was always surrounded by boys who took turns at being the 'horse' between the truck shafts, with a string on each arm for reins which the crippled boy held
>
> (Horn, 1976, p. 43)

Thinking point 6.5   In what ways does this account contrast with contemporary children's experiences of the journey to and from school?

The early twenty-first century has witnessed a dramatic increase in the use of car journeys to and from school (Department for Transport, 2004). This suggests that the traditional 'walk to school' transition has been transplanted by 'the school run' in a car, an extension of domestic space. Consequently many more children now spend less time unsupervised in neighbourhood space.

Some attribute this change to parental anxiety and perceptions of risk and danger to children in public spaces (Furedi, 2001) perpetuated by sensational media coverage. It also reflects concern about increased traffic on the roads and the limited opportunities for children to develop road sense through direct experience. This, in turn, has been attributed to an increase in constraint and surveillance of children in public spaces (Wyness, 1994; Valentine, 1997; Valentine and McKendrick, 1997). Children also report that they are frequently excluded from their neighbourhoods due to 'lack of places to go, cost barriers and practical problems caused by traffic and other forms of fear' (Morrow, 2002, p. 170).

> 'More space, more space, more space to do things, more bigger things, bigger parks, things like that. More space to do things.'
>
> (Boy quoted in O'Brien, 2000, p. 2)

In the twenty-first century the 'school run' has replaced the traditional walk to school for many children

'Stop building so many houses and ugly buildings, 'cos children want space to play and they can't be expected to stay indoors for the whole of their time – children have to have space.'

(Girl quoted in O'Brien, 2000, p. 2)

It [the local area] is not a good place to play. Broken bottles and that

(Child quoted in Turner et al., 2006, p. 459)

Although some adult anxieties about stranger danger may be overstated, it is still the case that some children find themselves living in dangerous spaces. Rather than danger from strangers, these accounts reveal that children fear people who are visible members of their local neighbourhoods:

'there are people with drugs who drink and make trouble.'

(Boy quoted in Pain, 2006, p. 232)

Children's experiences and concerns are themselves mediated by poverty, gender, age, ethnicity, disability and geographic location. Avoiding unsafe spaces is easier for affluent children with parental transport and homes in relatively safe neighbourhoods. Children from disadvantaged neighbourhoods or poorer families have an increased exposure to environmental hazards and risks.

Negative outcomes associated with poverty include the increased likelihood of witnessing, or being the victim of, crime or violence and an increased risk of having an accident (Turner et al., 2006). For some children in poorer neighbourhoods participation in out-of-school activities creates a haven from perceived dangers in public space: 'it keeps us away from fights because we would be in here' (boy referring to his youth club in Turner et al., 2006, p. 459).

Others report their own streetwise avoidance strategies or individual and collective methods of fighting back:

> Fitba [football] teams keeps me aff the streets
>
> (Boy quoted in Turner et al., 2006, p. 459).

> I have learned to keep my head down, so I don't really get picked on cause I am just a person walking and I don't dress differently. I just dress in my school uniform.
>
> (Boy quoted in Turner et al., 2006, p. 460)

> We avoid [name of woods] because someone jumped out at my friend and attacked them.
>
> (Boy quoted in Pain, 2006, p. 231)

Interviewer: If you were being picked on, what would you do?

First girl: I'd batter them.

Second girl: So would I.

Interviewer: You would batter them?

First girl: Aye.

Second girl: Aye no bother ...

First boy: I'd just go and get all my mates and get a gang ... I'd go into the toilets and I'd get all them hiding in cubicles ... if he came in and started pushing me around I'd just whistle and they would all come out

(Turner et al., 2006, p. 461)

Girls are more likely than boys to report that certain spaces are 'scary', warranting some kind of precautionary behaviour, although it is suggested that boys are more likely to under-report this (Pain, 2006, p. 228). In many cases, precautionary behaviour involves avoiding public space altogether.

Children living in neighbourhoods lacking safe play spaces are often exposed to environmental hazards and risks

Boys, as they get older, also appear to have a wider 'spatial range' than girls and 'feel more comfortable in and in control of public places in their own neighbourhoods, and feel safer in numbers' (Pain, 2006, p. 234). This collective strategy creates a particular tension, with public perception and social policy working against children and young people who congregate together in public spaces.

Several studies (John and Wheway, 2004; Shelley, 2002) have identified numerous ways in which disabled children are denied access to public spaces, including facilities such as playgrounds and theme parks. A common barrier was the lack of adapted facilities or trained staff. Other barriers included overprotective parents or negative attitudes from members of the public.

2.3 Time

Transitions take place in temporal dimensions as well as spatial dimensions. Kagan (1992, cited in Lam and Pollard, 2006) examines this interrelationship by conceptualising horizontal and vertical transitions. Horizontal transition refers to movement across a number of unconnected settings that a child and their family may encounter within a similar time frame, for example, mini-transitions between a breakfast club, school, then a music lesson followed by Cubs. Vertical transition refers to sequential movement through a number of connected services over time, for example, special baby unit, neonatal care, health visitor, GP services.

Some children reflect on losses and changes that are produced through transitions through time. One girl's account reveals how ordinary life course transitions resulted in changes to interrelationships in her family:

> I think it's changed since we started going to school 'cos I used to go to playgroups and stuff like that with my mum, but now I miss the mornings and afternoons being with my mum – and my dads job's like gone higher – so he works more hours
>
> (Girl quoted in Christensen, 2002, p. 84)

It is possible to help children to plan transitions and use time as an asset. The concept of 'psychological travelling time' (Giddens, 1992, quoted in Flowerdew and Neale, 2003, p. 153) refers to 'the length of time it takes to accept and come to terms with a major life change'. The following account of one child's transition into a new foster family demonstrates how the passage of time enabled him to come to terms with the reality that he will not be returning to his birth parents. It suggests that effective transition planning should allow sufficient time for relationships to form and develop.

> I thought I'd be going home but after a while I knew it just wasn't going to happen
>
> (Foster child in McTeigue, 1997, quoted in Kelly and Gilligan, 2002, p. 47)

Time alone with adults may also be experienced as an asset for some children. Consider how a busy social worker might allocate space in her diary to a Looked After child who wants to talk about her forthcoming Statutory Review meeting. This is, in effect, a 'time transaction' and may appear to the child as a concession from the social worker who still retains the power to give or take back time.

It appears that children value the opportunity to 'have a say over one's time' (Christensen, 2002, p. 81). Rather than being allocated time slots, children show a preference for adults who can be there for them when they are needed (Christensen, 2002) and they expect adults to be honest about their time commitments.

> 'Today I had a review meeting and my social worker turned up an hour late. I tried to find out why he was late but he didn't tell me, he just dismissed me like I was nothing'
>
> (Dear Diary entry written by Looked After young person, Children's Rights Officers and Advocates, 2000, p. 44)

Children also value the opportunity to spend time on their own:

> 'My best thing on my own is I play with my rabbits, I give myself a makeover, believe it or not 'cos I don't look like one, I like doing that on my own. Its quiet and you get to do what you want to do'
>
> (Girl quoted in Christensen, 2002, p. 86)

For children experiencing transitions, time alone can be used for reflection or to switch off and divert their energies into something else. Time alone can also, however, be constructed as having no friends. In the conversation below, Joe has revealed that he spends time reading. Michael is concerned by this revelation because he equates reading to being alone. Joe denies this and is quick to emphasise his social connections:

> Michael: Did you spend a lot of time on your own over half term or ... ?
>
> Joe: Um, no not really. I was mainly outside most of the time and at my friend's house and everything.
>
> (Christensen et al., 2000, p. 174)

Key points

1   Time, space and status are useful concepts for analysing and understanding transitions.

2   Age bestows particular rights, entitlements and status on children; however, these socially constructed milestones can differ across both time and place.

3   Children's experience of transitions interrelates with their social position and identity and may, in turn, leave them vulnerable to discrimination.

4   Effective support and transition planning can be enhanced by listening to children's accounts and by providing them with a sense of place and psychological travelling time.

3 The experience of transitions

Children's accounts reveal that transitions can be experienced in different ways. Many such experiences can be understood with reference to concepts such as continuity, loss, change and liminality. This final section explores these concepts further.

3.1 Continuity and change

Continuity, in some accounts, is a key factor in providing the right kind of framework or context to support children with transitions. Continuity can be understood as some kind of stable force in a child's life which, during a transition, acts as an anchor of support, diversion or familiarity at a time of change. This could be represented by friends, family, pets, school, objects or environment. The concept of change (or discontinuity) can be perceived as exposure to unfamiliar experiences and is integral to all children's lives.

Candappa (2002, p. 229) states that 'for many refugee children the school, as a universalist service, is one of the few statutory agencies from which they could derive support in settling in to their new lives'. This is also the case for children with fragmented home lives, including children in the Looked After care system who have experienced multiple placements and children whose parents may be periodically absent for employment, health or social reasons:

> 'School helps me forget'
>
> (Child whose Dad was in prison, quoted in Boswell, 2002, p. 20)

Christensen et al. (2000) highlight the role of friendships during primary to secondary school transitions. 'Older children played a key role before the transition, through giving 'insider' information about the school, its conventions and routines. After transition to secondary school they continued to be a source of everyday support for the children' (Christensen et al., 2000, p. 3).

Peer friendships are also important in the transition from preschool to school: 'The presence of a familiar playmate in the same class is associated with children adjusting better to school' (Margetts, 2005, p. 42). Maintaining contact with friends during and after a transition can be difficult for children, particularly when their parents move house (Nettleton, 2001).

Transitions can result in changes and development that only become apparent in retrospect. They also provide children with opportunities to actively change or reinvent themselves:

> 'You can walk out of this school the person you've been for however many years you've been here and walk into this other school and it's good having friends because you've got friends there, so you know people, but you can also walk in and start being a different person.'
>
> (Girl talking about moving to secondary school in Lucey and Reay, 2000, p. 194)

In some cases, change in children's behaviour, relationships or wellbeing can be achieved with the support of therapeutic services. The following accounts demonstrate two children's willingness to change in different ways following play therapy sessions:

Interviewer: So do you think the fact that you don't fight with people now, has that got anything to do with play therapy, or is that something you did for yourself?

Legoman: It was both.

> (Carroll, 2002, p. 183)

> 'I've got a load of my confidence back. Before play therapy I used to be really scared of fireworks and balloons, but now I'm playing with balloons and one firework night I actually uncovered my ears and counted a load of fireworks.'
>
> (Girl quoted in Carroll, 2002, p. 185)

Flowerdew and Neale (2003) identify that the pace of change can be crucial in determining how well children adapt to transitions. Hurried changes may not leave sufficient 'psychological travelling time' (Giddens, 1992, cited in Flowerdew and Neale, 2003, p. 153) for children to come to terms with change.

Resource constraints, target-driven working methods and structural and organisational limitations can all also adversely affect support for children adapting to transitions. Highlighting how hurried admissions of children to residential care frequently occur on Friday afternoons or out of normal working hours, Milligan and McPheat (2006, p. 21) ask us to 'imagine what would happen if social workers worked seven days a week (in shifts!)'.

Thinking point 6.6   What structural and organisational factors have you encountered that limit work to support children with transitions?

Transitions can involve a complexity of continuities and discontinuities for children. Earlier we examined how ecological models can help us recognise that children are located within a multifaceted and intertwined set of relationships. Consequently potential gains resulting from transitions can also be experienced as losses, and vice versa. This is one of the issues involved in facilitating children's contact with parents following separation, divorce or entry into the Looked After care system. For some children, the discontinuation of parental contact may be fundamental to ensuring their safety. Separation for these children may result in a range of overlapping, and possibly conflicting, feelings such as relief and loss. Under such circumstances children may need support with their 'emotional literacy', that is, help with recognising, understanding, handling and appropriately expressing emotions (National Emotional Literacy Group, 2007).

In short-term foster care, where the intention is for the child to eventually return home, continued parental contact is usually considered necessary to support the child through their transition. Within long-term fostering and adoption the benefits of continued contact are subject to much greater debate. On the one hand, continuity of contact with birth families is considered important for maintaining attachment bonds. However, this is countered by the view that continuity with birth parents undermines the new relationship with foster parents (Browne and Maloney, 2001). (Different views from children concerning contact are presented in Chapter 7.)

3.2 Losses and gains

As we have discussed, change is closely related to loss. Much of the theoretical work around loss has focused on feelings of grief and bereavement following death. However, Holland et al. (2005) suggest that grieving can also be associated with other kinds of losses that correspond very closely with childhood transitions. These include a range of disparate experiences, relationships, states and emotions that can vary according to children's age and/or life context:

Friendship	Birth of a sibling
Home	Security
Starting school	Disability
Innocence	Relationship
Community	Stability
Parent	Illness
Faith	Mental health
Possessions	Emigration
Freedom	Having special educational needs
Divorce/separation	Dreams
Self identity	Culture
Sense of belonging	Self worth

(Holland et al., 2005, p. 11)

Thinking point 6.7   Consider how some of the losses in the list above could also be constructed as gains.

The following accounts show different extremes of childhood losses:

'We were children but we saw things you can't imagine, some of us saw our mothers, our fathers, our brothers or sisters taken away, tortured and killed. We lost our country, our families, homes, futures, everything'

(A young person living in London being interviewed about their experience of being a child refugee from North East Africa in Madge, 2001, p. 117)

'Things that you want to do, you just can't ... It is 'can't' if you want to go somewhere. Can't do that many things ...'

(Brother of a child being treated for cancer on the losses of personal freedoms associated with having an ill sibling in the family quoted in Woodgate and Degner, 2004, p. 364)

Some children's accounts reveal that losses can also present themselves as gains:

'I have the possibility to have free education here and the facilities are much better than in Somalia. But to be in your own country is better than anything else. I do not plan to be in Denmark for the rest of my life'

(Young Somalian refugee quoted in Ayotte, 2002, p. 36)

'My foster mother is very supportive ... Our relationship is very close and I feel more protected. The change has been huge, I feel more self confident and secure'

(Foster child quoted in Baldry and Kemmis, 1998, quoted in Kelly and Gilligan, 2002, p. 54)

'Before Mum and Dave got married, it used to be much more difficult. We used to get cheaper clothes, we didn't live in as good a house either as now. Yep, we kind of lived in a scruffy house and we just didn't get stuff we wanted as much. Things have got a lot better I reckon, a lot. We had a really big party when they got married. It was really good. And Dad's new partner is good, she's nice. She's a lot like Dad which I think is good.'

(Child's transition into a stepfamily, Flowerdew and Neale, 2003, p. 150)

Emotional reactions to loss are common in childhood. Children do not necessarily have the emotional literacy with which to understand or make sense of what is happening to them. Instead, they may act out their feelings, perhaps through introverted, aggressive or, in extreme cases, self-harming behaviour. Alternatively children's feelings may manifest themselves in other ways, such as becoming ill or running away. Douglas (2000) identifies some of the ways in which children react to parental separation:

> 'Just missing my Dad really. I mean it's all very well me seeing him twice a week, but that's really not enough. I mean, you'd like him there every day, you know.'
>
> (Child quoted in Douglas, 2000, p. 2)

> 'I keep my problems to myself because my parents have enough to worry about.'
>
> (Child quoted in Douglas, 2000, p. 4)

> 'It's very hard at first because you just don't want them to split up. You'll be very sad at the beginning because of not having your Dad around, but then it'll just come automatically that your Dad lives somewhere else and life will just be normal.'
>
> (Child quoted in Douglas, 2000, p. 2)

> 'I always used to get this temper and have tantrums and everything. I was mad at him and I takes my anger out on other people rather than my Dad.'
>
> (Child quoted in Douglas, 2000, p. 3)

> 'My dad makes me feel guilty for wanting to spend time with my mum.'
>
> (Child quoted in Douglas 2000, p. 4)

Thinking point 6.8   What other losses or transitions could result in similar reactions from children ?

Adults can help children by recognising the association between their behaviour and the losses they have experienced. For example, Holland (2003, p. 76) found that school teachers reported a range of changed behaviours in bereaved children 'including disruptive behaviour, anger, distress, crying, moodiness, depression and withdrawal'. He was concerned that teachers were not always able to make a connection between the behaviour and the child's experience of loss. Many also underestimated the time for which children would be affected by their loss.

The same study reported children's feelings about their experience of returning to school following bereavement. These included feeling:

- Ignored
- Isolated
- Embarrassed

- Uncertain
- Different

(Holland, 2003, p. 76)

Theorising about how people deal with loss has moved away from the assumption that people passively pass through a series of emotions on the way to accepting or coming to terms with their loss (Kubler-Ross, 1980, cited in Holland et al., 2005, p. 44). People's emotions do not necessarily follow a predetermined sequence: for some people loss is never resolved or accepted. An alternative model of loss, referred to as the 'continuing bonds model' (Klass et al., 1996; Bunce and Rickard, 2004, p. 45), is one in which the person experiencing the bereavement has:

- A continuing relationship with the deceased
- Detachment from the deceased
- A changing relationship with the deceased over time
- No resolution of the loss.

One of the merits of this model is that it may have more relevance across a range of cultures. It is also useful when considering transitions in which an individual may wish to retain some connection with the time, place or status they have moved away from. Henry et al. (2005) demonstrate its use in explaining how migrants assimilate to a new country whilst maintaining a bond with their homeland.

A further 'dual process model' (Stroebe and Schut, 1999, cited in Dent, 2005, p. 22) identifies an alternation between both accepting and avoiding a loss. The idea that people can take time out of grieving in order to concentrate on secondary losses has useful analytical potential when applied to children. In some cases, children cope with loss by avoidance or distraction.

3.3 Liminality

The earlier discussion about home–school transitions highlighted the mini-transition of the journey to and from school through an intermediate space. This supports the view that transitions are processes although, as the discussion on models of loss indicated, many transitions are experienced as fluid and may lack clearly defined beginnings or endings.

The idea of an intermediate, or in-between, experience is compelling as it can be found in many other types of transition. This has been conceptualised as liminality (Van Gennep, 1960). Liminal spaces are often not clearly defined because they are times, places or ways of being between two familiar states. For children these might include the dentist's waiting room, the journey in the car to meet their new foster parents, or the sleepless night ahead of the excitement of their birthday. They typically involve ambiguity or a suspension of normal ways of being.

The liminal spaces between adult-regulated spaces are often valued by children because they lack clearly defined adult control and surveillance. In nurseries, transitional spaces such as cloakrooms, corridors and stairwells used for changeovers in adult care, were observed to be used by children as sites to 'play up' (Brown, 2007, p. 106). Lucey and Reay (2000) identified how school-aged children's time away from adults was used to learn autonomy and independence skills:

> 'to get lots of choices, to get to make your own decisions so you can make your own mind up about things'
>
> (Girl quoted in Lucey and Reay, 2000, p. 198)

The liminal stage is where the core experiences of transition take place (Lam and Pollard, 2006, p. 131) and where powerful feelings, both positive and negative, are evoked for children. In some cases children may need help in confirming and understanding simultaneous, yet contrasting, feelings. Carroll found this to be the case when interviewing a girl about her feelings at the end of a play therapy session:

> 'I felt happy. Happy and sad, if you know what I mean. Happy because I've had a good time, and I'm sad because I don't want to stop having a good time.'
>
> (Girl quoted in Carroll, 2002, p. 182)

Similarly, Ayotte's (2002) interview with a young Somali refugee now based in Denmark reveals the liminal experience of uncertain and ambiguous identities and of being caught between boundaries: 'when she visited Somalia last year she "felt like a Danish girl there and yet also a Somali girl at the same time." She was relieved to return to Denmark' (Ayotte, 2002, p. 68).

The ritual transition of a Brownies investiture ceremony

Turner (1969) also drew attention to the part played by ritual in transitions. Most rituals involve a liminal or in-between experience. In uniformed organisations, such as Cubs and Brownies, this is represented through a period of induction during which the potential member is permitted to wear only part of the official uniform. In this way both their separateness from non-members and their lack of full status is confirmed. Only after an investiture ceremony are they permitted to wear the complete uniform and therefore make the final step in the transition.

Similar liminal experiences are observable in religious rituals and in the process of transition into new schools. In the latter, children are also known to instigate their own informal rituals.

Key points

1   Change and the pace of change can help children with transitions.

2   Observing and interpreting behaviour can help practitioners and other adults to understand children's experiences of loss and provide them with appropriate support, including help to express their feelings.

3   Transitions can involve liminal feelings of ambiguity and of being in-between for some children.

Conclusion

This chapter has promoted the view that transitions are significant processes in everyone's lives, linked to status, time and space. Certain childhood transitions are more common than others, with some children experiencing multiple transitions, but each child's experience is particular to them, as an individual within a specific ecological context.

Children have different capacities to deal with the gains, losses, changes and ambivalent feelings sometimes associated with transitions. Through listening to children's accounts, and reflecting on our own experiences of transitions, adults can develop effective ways of supporting children. As we shall see in the next chapter, the right kind of support, leading to positive experiences of transitions, can provide a basis for dealing with change throughout the life course.

References

at-Bristol (2007) *Memories of you*, available online at <http://www.at-bristol.org.uk/Explore/Memories.htm>, accessed 12 June 2007.

Ayotte, W. (2002) *Separated Children, Exile and Home Country Links: The Example of Somali Children in Nordic Countries*, Copenhagen, Save the Children Denmark.

Baldry, S. and Kemmis, J. (1998) 'The quality of childcare in one local authority – a user study', *Adoption and Fostering*, vol. 27, no. 3, pp. 34–41.

Boswell, G. (2002) 'Imprisoned fathers: the children's view', *Howard Journal*, vol. 41, no. 1, pp. 14–26.

Bronfenbrenner, U. (1979) *The Ecology of Human Development*, Cambridge, MA, Harvard University Press.

Brown, J. (2007) 'Time, space and gender: understanding "problem" behaviour in young children', *Children & Society*, vol. 21, no. 2, pp. 98–110.

Browne, D. and Moloney, A. (2001) '"Contact irregular": a qualitative analysis of the impact of visiting patterns of natural parents on foster placements', *Child & Family Social Work*, vol. 7, no. 1, pp. 35–45.

Bunce, B. and Rickard, A. (2004) in Harvey, R. (ed.) *Working with Bereaved Children: A Guide*, Essex, University of Essex Children's Legal Centre.

Candappa, M. (2002) 'Human rights and refugee children in the UK' in Franklin, B. (ed.) (2002) *The New Handbook of Children's Rights: Comparative Policy and Practice*, London, Routledge.

Carroll, J. (2002) 'Play therapy: the children's views', *Child & Family Social Work*, vol. 7, no. 3, pp. 177–187.

Children's Rights Officers and Advocates (CROA) and Department of Health (DH) (2000) *Total Respect Training Manual: Ensuring Children's Rights and Participation in Care*, London, CROA and DH.

Christensen, P. (2002) 'Why more "quality time" is not on the top of children's lists: the "qualities of time" for children', *Children & Society*, vol. 16, no. 2, pp. 77–88.

Christensen, P., James, A. and Jenks, C. (2000) 'Changing times: children's understanding of the social organisation of time', *Children 5–16 Research Briefing*, July 2000, no. 15, available online at <http://www.hull.ac.uk/children5to16programme/briefings/james.pdf>, accessed 12 June 2007.

Colton, M., Sanders, R. and Williams, M. (2001) *An Introduction to Working with Children*, Basingstoke, Palgrave.

Dent, A. (2005) 'Supporting the bereaved: theory and practice', *Counselling at Work* (journal of the Association for Counselling at Work), Autumn 2005, pp. 22–23.

Department for Transport (DfT) (2004) *DfT Policy Guidance and Research: School Travel*, available online at <http://www.dft.gov.uk/pgr/sustainable/schooltravel/schooltravel?page=1#1000>, accessed 12 June 2007.

Douglas, G. (2000) 'Children's perspectives and experiences of divorce', *Children 5–16 Research Briefing*, December 2000, no. 21, available online at <http://www.hull.ac.uk/children5to16programme/briefings/robinson.pdf>, accessed 8 August 2007.

Edwards, R., Alldred, P. and David, M. (2000) 'Children's understandings of parental involvement in education', *Children 5–16 Research Briefing*, April 2000, no. 11, available online at <http://www.hull.ac.uk/children5to16programme/briefings/edwards.pdf>, accessed 25 June 2007.

Eurydice/Eurostat (2005) *Data in Education in Europe 2005*, Luxembourg, Office for Official Publications of the European Communities.

Flowerdew, J. and Neale, B. (2003) 'Trying to stay apace: children with multiple challenges in their post-divorce family lives', *Childhood*, vol. 10, no. 2, pp. 147–161.

Foster Care Associates (FCA) (2003) *Rattle Your Cool. A Collection of Poetry and Art by Children and Young People Who Are Being Looked After*, Bromsgrove, Foster Care Associates.

Furedi, F. (2001) *Paranoid Parenting: Abandon your Anxieties and be a Good Parent*, London, Penguin.

Gallacher, L. (2005) '"The terrible twos": gaining control in the nursery?', *Children's Geographies*, vol. 3, no. 2, pp. 243–264.

Giddens, A. (1992) *The Transformation of Intimacy: Sexuality, Love and Eroticism in Modern Societies*, Cambridge, The Policy Press/Basil Blackwell.

Gillick v. West Norfolk and Wisbech Area Health Authority (1985) 3 All ER 402 (HL).

Hall, E.T. (1966) *The Hidden Dimension*, New York, Anchor Books.

Henry, H.M., Stiles, W.B. and Biran, M.W. (2005) 'Loss and mourning in immigration: using the assimilation model to assess continuing bonds with native culture', *Counselling Psychology Quarterly*, vol. 18, no. 2, pp. 109–119.

Holland, J. (2003) 'Supporting schools with loss: "lost for words" in Hull', *British Journal of Special Education*, vol. 30, no. 2, pp. 76–78.

Holland, J., Dance, R., MacManus, N. and Stitt, C. (2005) *Lost for Words. Loss and Bereavement Awareness Training*, London, JKP Resource Materials.

Holland, S. (2004) *Child and Family Assessment in Social Work Practice*, London, Sage.

Horn, P. (1976) *Labouring Life in the Victorian Countryside*, Dublin, Macmillan.

James, A., Jenks, C. and Prout, A. (1998) *Theorising Childhood*, Cambridge, Polity Press.

John, A. and Wheway, R. (2004) *Can Play Will Play: Disabled Children and Access to Outdoor Playgrounds*, London, National Playing Fields Association.

Kelly, G. and Gilligan, R. (eds) (2002) *Issues in Foster Care: Policy, Practice and Research*, London, Jessica Kingsley.

Klass, D., Silverman, P.R. and Nickman, S.L. (1996) *Continuing Bonds: New Understandings of Grief*, London, Taylor Francis.

Kübler-Ross, E. (1980) *On Death and Dying*, London, Tavistock/Routledge.

Lam, M.S. and Pollard, A. (2006) 'A conceptual framework for understanding children as agents in the transition from home to kindergarten', *Early Years*, vol. 26, no. 2, pp. 123–141.

Lucey, H. and Reay, D. (2000) 'Identities in transition: anxiety and excitement in the move to secondary school', *Oxford Review of Education*, vol. 26, no. 2, pp. 191–205.

Madge, N. (2001) *Understanding Difference: The Meaning of Ethnicity for Young Lives*, London, National Children's Bureau.

Madge, N. (2006) *Children These Days*, Bristol, The Policy Press.

Margetts, K. (2005) 'Children's adjustment to the first year of schooling; indicators of hyperactivity, internalising and externalising behaviours', *International Journal of Transitions in Childhood*, vol. 1, pp. 36–44.

Maybin, J. and Woodhead, M. (eds) (2003) *Childhoods in Context*, Chichester, Wiley.

McTeigue, D. (1997) 'The use of focus groups in exploring children's experiences of life in care' in Hogan, D. and Gilligan, R. (eds) *Researching Children's Experiences: Qualitative Approaches*, Proceedings of conference 27 May 1997, Dublin, The Children's Research Centre, Trinity College Dublin.

Milligan, I. and McPheat, G. (2006) '"What's the use of residential child care?" Changing lives: the power of residential child care', Scottish Institute for Residential Child Care, annual conference 2006 presentation.

Morrow, V. (2002) 'Children's rights to public space: environment and curfews' in Franklin, B. (ed.) *The New Handbook of Children's Rights: Comparative Policy and Practice*, London, Routledge.

Moss, P. and Petrie, P. (2002) *From Children's Services to Children's Spaces. Public Policy, Children and Childhood*, London, Routledge Falmer.

National Emotional Literacy Group (2007) *About emotional literacy*, available online at <http://www.nelig.com/about.htm>, accessed 13 June 2007.

Nettleton, S. (2001), 'Losing a Home through Mortgage Repossession; the views of children', *Children & Society*, vol. 15, April 2001, pp. 82–95.

Newman, T. and Blackburn, S. (2002) *Interchange 78: Transitions in the Lives of Children and Young People: Resilience Factors. Summary of Full Report*, Edinburgh, Scottish Executive Education Department.

Niesel, R. and Griebel, W. (2005) 'Transition competence and resiliency in educational institutions', *International Journal of Transitions in Childhood*, vol. 1, pp. 4–11.

O'Brien, M. (2000) 'Childhood, urban space and citizenship: child-sensitive urban regeneration', *Children 5–16 Research Briefing*, July 2000, no. 16, available online at <http://www.hull.ac.uk/children5to16programme/briefings/obrien.pdf>, accessed 8 August 2007.

Packman, J. and Hall, C. (1998) *From Care to Accommodation – Support, Protection and Control in Childcare Services*, London, The Stationery Office.

Pain, R. (2006) 'Paranoid parenting? Rematerializing risk and fear for children', *Social & Cultural Geography*, vol. 7, no. 2, pp. 221–243.

Rowling, J.K. (1997) *Harry Potter and the Philosopher's Stone*, London, Bloomsbury.

Schaffer, H.R. (1992) 'Early experience and the parent-child relationship: genetic and environmental interactions as developmental determinants' in Tizard, B. and Varma, V., *Vulnerability and Resilience in Human Development*, London, Jessica Kingsley.

Sharp, C. (2002) 'School starting age: European policy and recent research', Paper presented at the LGA Seminar 'When Should Our Children Start School?', LGA Conference Centre, Smith Square, London, 1 November 2002, available online at <http://dev.nfer.steel-hosting.co.uk/publications/other-publications/conference-papers/pdf_docs/PaperSSF.pdf>, accessed 13 June 2006.

Shaw, L. (1998) 'Children's experiences of school' in Robinson, C. and Stalker, K., *Growing Up with Disability*, London, Jessica Kingsley.

Shelley, P. (2002) *Everybody Here? Play and Leisure for Disabled Children and Young People – A Contact a Family Survey of Families' Experiences*, London, Contact a Family.

Shucksmith, J., McKee, L. and Willmot, H. (2005) 'Families, education and the "participatory imperative"' in McKie, L. and Cunningham-Burley, S. (eds) *Families in Society: Boundaries and Relationships*, Bristol, The Policy Press.

Smith, F. and Barker, J. (2000) 'Contested spaces: children's experiences of out of school care in England and Wales', *Childhood*, vol. 7, no. 3, pp. 315–333.

Soames, P., Gibson, C., Noble, R. and Summerson, U. (edited by McGahren, Y.) (2006) *About Families with Disabled Children*, London, Contact A Family. Also available online at <http://www.cafamily.org.uk/students.pdf>, accessed 13 June 2007.

Stroebe, M. and Schut, H. (1999) 'The dual process model of coping with bereavement: rationale and description', *Death Studies*, vol. 23, no. 3, pp. 197–224.

Törrönen, M. (2006) 'Community in a children's home', *Child & Family Social Work*, vol. 11, no. 2, pp. 129–137.

Turner, C. (2003) *'Are You Listening?' What Disabled Children and Young People in Wales Think About the Services They Use*, Cardiff, Welsh Assembly.

Turner, K.M., Hill, M., Stafford, A. and Walker, M. (2006) 'How children from disadvantaged areas keep safe', *Health Education*, vol. 106, no. 6, pp. 450–464.

Turner, V. (1969) *The Ritual Process: Structure and Anti Structure*, Chicago, Aldine.

Valentine, G. (1997) '"Oh yes I can." "Oh no you can't": children and parents' understanding of kids' competence to negotiate public space safely', *Urban Geography*, vol. 17, pp. 205–220.

Valentine, G. and McKendrick, J. (1997) 'Children's outdoor play: exploring parental concerns about children's safety and the changing nature of childhood', *Geoforum*, vol. 28, pp. 219–235.

Van Gennep, A. (1960) *The Rites of Passage*, translated by Vizedom, M.B. and Caffee, G.L., Chicago, University of Chicago Press.

Woodgate, R.L. and Degner, L.F. 2004 'Cancer symptom transition periods of children and families', *Journal of Advanced Nursing*, vol. 46, no. 4, pp. 358–368.

Woodhead, M. (1989) 'School starts at five ... or four years old? The rationale for changing admission policies in England and Wales', *Journal of Education Policy*, vol. 4, no. 1, pp. 1–21.

Wooley, H. (2006) 'Freedom of the city: contemporary issues and policy influences on children and young people's use of public open space in England', *Children's Geographies*, vol. 4, no. 1, pp. 45–59.

Wyness, M.G. (1994) 'Keeping tabs on an uncivil society: positive parental control', *Sociology*, vol. 28, no. 1, pp. 193–209.

Zill, N., Loomis, L.S. and Wesr, J. (1997) *National Household Education Survey. The Elementary School Performance and Adjustment of Children who enter Kindergarten: Findings from National Surveys (NCES Statistical Analysis Report 98-097)*, Washington DC, US Department of Education, National Center for Education Statistics.

Chapter 7

Working with children and transitions

Stephen Leverett

Introduction

Chapter 6 included some useful perspectives and ideas to underpin critical analysis and reflection on transitions in the lives of children and their families. This chapter will start by looking more closely at two contrasting types of transition and will then consider some ways of providing practical and emotional support.

In some cases providing support will require direct work, in others it will involve providing information, or referring people on to more appropriate specialist services. In many cases support involves connecting and engaging with children's family and social networks. We will suggest that, for many children, a positive transitional experience is useful preparation for further transitions throughout the life course.

Core questions

- How can an understanding of transitions be applied to work with children and their families?
- How can positive experiences with early transitions help children build resilience and confidence for the future?
- What are some of the different ways in which children and families can be supported with transitions?

1 Transitions: two contrasting examples

Across the UK, children's transitions have been targeted for more effective support by the children's workforce. 'Supporting Transitions' is one of the six headings in the English *Common Core of Skills and Knowledge for the Children's Workforce*. Specific groups of older children, including care leavers and disabled children moving between children's and adult services, are the subjects of social policy designed to improve their experience of transitions.

The expansion and diversification of early years services, the creation of extended schools and the requirement for multi-agency working, have redrawn the boundaries between health, social care and education. Consequently the pathways through services have evolved, creating a need for information and support to ensure a 'seamless' transition between each.

Other types of childhood transition are immersed within wider social and political issues and as a consequence receive less attention. Examples include highly mobile groups – such as refugee children or the families of armed services personnel – and children whose lives involve transitions into and out of poverty, often as a result of other socio-economic or health experiences.

To illustrate this distinction we will examine two situations involving transitions. The first is a commonly experienced transition into and through the day care and education system. The second, by contrast, is the less common experience of disability and its interrelationship with transitions into poverty. In both situations consideration will be given to methods of supporting children and their families.

1.1 Transitions into and through childcare and education

The first day at school: a common transition for most children

For many young children their initial experience of formal day care or education represents the first major transition away from their close family. Children can experience these early transitions as both losses (for example, because they miss their parents) and opportunities (for example, because they provide the opportunity for more interaction with peers, more space or more toys). This experience is particular to individual children and, as was suggested in chapter 6, subject to increasing variation due to the changing and diversified experiences of preschool care.

The provision of continuity is widely considered to be important in supporting children with transitions. This is difficult to achieve as children move into school from early years services, particularly where there is discontinuity in cultural model, ideology and pedagogy between each setting. Much preschool provision is influenced by early years' principles and pedagogy built around play, empowerment and a more flexible environment. Primary schools, in contrast, are more likely to have a rigid structure with far more teacher-directed activity (Einarsdottir, 2006).

Dunlop (2002) identifies the key elements of continuity into early years settings and on through to primary education:

- structural continuity provided by the system;
- continuity in the teaching process;
- continuity in curriculum;
- involvement of parents in supporting their child's transitions.

Part of the rationale for encouraging parental or carer involvement is to attempt to provide continuity of care and learning between home and education. Typically, transitions from the home into children's services will involve some kind of induction or orientation for parents and carers. However, there are limitations to what can be achieved at one-off events. Increasingly, service providers are moving towards more creative and open-ended approaches, such as that described by Mayo (2005) in Australia. Here both parents and siblings undertake a series of fun and interactive tasks designed to forge links and support transitions at a pace suited to the participants' individual needs:

> All children are photographed in the first days of kindergarten, and photos are compiled into a book along with children's comments and reflections about kindergarten. To support parents, as well as children, in getting to know more about each other, Family Stories are collated with photographs and information provided by parents. These books remain available to children and families throughout the year. Parents or grandparents are also welcome to stay with their children for as long as they want, to assist with, and support separation and attachment issues. Rarely does this exceed a month or so. If children have siblings at the school, visits to or from siblings are organised and this often helps anxious children to settle in better.
>
> (Mayo, 2005, p. 48)

Particular attention is required to meet specific transition needs, including disability or bilingualism. This can be achieved for hearing-impaired children by specialist input from a 'teacher of the deaf' who liaises between the child's home and the early years context. Similar support is possible for children with other physical, cognitive and sensory impairments. As the following quote shows, some children place a high value on learning support assistants. Mortimer (2004, p. 174) asked children, 'Why do you come to nursery?' 'Fola replied: "*SALLY!*" ' (Sally is a learning support assistant.) Early years settings can also promote continuity for bilingual children through having a mother tongue policy, and employing bilingual classroom assistants. These examples illustrate how specialist support for transitions can be integrated into mainstream provision.

Attention is also required in connecting with parents 'from culturally and linguistically diverse backgrounds' (Dockett and Perry, 2005b, p. 280). Some schools and early years settings implement straightforward solutions, such as providing information for parents in appropriate linguistic formats. Others try more ambitious approaches, such as employing Community Language Teachers (Dockett and Perry, 2005b) or undertaking outreach work promoting parent–child reading (Jordan, 2005).

Whilst attempts to create continuity between parents, carers and education providers appear important for children's transitions, some counter-arguments do exist. Adult–child relations are particularly influenced by a prevailing ideology that constructs children as passive, malleable resources who can help shape a better future for the state and the economy. It constructs parents and carers as the allies of the state, educating and transforming children into better future citizens. This is evident in the concept of 'total schooling' (Shucksmith et al., 2005, p. 61) used to explain a process in which the family home becomes an extension of the classroom. Parents are encouraged to be their children's 'first educators', to prepare children for school entry and to supervise homework. It has been reported that most parents want schools to set homework (Sharp et al., 2001) yet some may lack the confidence or skills to be able to help their children to complete it successfully. In response, the following project aimed to work with both parents and children around homework and claims some success in improving learning for both groups.

Practice box 7.1

A scheme that gets parents to share in primary school children's homework has been praised for the way it can get them back into education.

The scheme, Share (Key Stage 2) – aimed at seven to 11-year-olds – was developed by the education charity Community Education Development Centre to help primary schools in England develop homework strategies, which they are now required to have.

Dr Ann Lewis, from the University of Warwick's Institute of Education, says the scheme can motivate children to do their homework and can bring parents more in touch with schools.

In her assessment of the scheme Dr Lewis says it has inspired some parents to seek out other learning opportunities for themselves.

"Some Share parents began community or adult education classes such as first aid, computer skills and library courses and have gained confidence through Share work," she said.

(BBC News, 1999, webpage)

However, not all parents and carers wish to take on the total schooling role, fearing that it will encroach on their children's free time. Others lack resources and time. The following parental account represents how difficult it can be working, running a home and supporting children with homework:

You work till 5 and you try to make dinner. Then they're tired and they don't want to do it and you think, 'Boy, is it worth this?' They say it develops good study habits, but all it seems to do is help me develop good nagging habits. I nag them to do it.

(Owens, 2006, webpage)

In Chapter 5 we considered the benefits of children's participation in decision making. Total schooling and the drive towards more continuity between parents, carers and educators could be perceived as undermining children's rights. On the other hand, if this process involved children in a meaningful way, it could potentially promote children's rights to education. As was identified in Chapter 6, when consulted, children vary in their attitudes towards home–school links:

If I get stuck on my maths I normally ask my dad, and if I get stuck on anything else I normally ask my mum.

(Child quoted in Edwards et al., 2000, p. 2)

If I get into trouble at school I don't actually find it that useful telling [my parents], but I think they find it more annoying if I don't tell them myself, than finding it out from my Link Book.

(Child quoted in Edwards et al., 2000, p. 2)

These and other accounts reveal children as active agents who negotiate the daily transition between home and school.

Gregory (2005) introduces the concept of 'syncretism', whereby children use their agency to blend together both home and school experiences, adapting them, in collaboration with adults, to create and transform their own social space. For example, many children successfully share their learning from school about computers with their less technologically-proficient parents and family.

Children also bring values, language and ways of behaving from home to school which can, in turn, challenge the school's cultural model. Rather than constructing children's agency as a negative force, syncretism promotes the possibility that adults and children can work together, interdependently, to build continuity and solve the challenges presented during transitions. The concept also indicates the benefits of involving children in making decisions concerning the level and type of support they would like from adults.

Not all children are likely to exercise agency in the same way or to the same level. In some contexts children will need support to develop the necessary social and communication skills for successful transitions, not only into the classroom but also through liminal spaces, such as school playgrounds. For more on liminal spaces see Chapter 6. The following account of adjustment following the transition from an American kindergarten into school reveals that, even though the child appears to have developed a good relationship with her teacher, she is experiencing difficulties with her peers, particularly during recess (playtime):

O: What do you like about school?

C: Well, we do a lot of fun things. And in kindergarten it's so easy and now it's gotten a little harder.

O: It's gotten a little harder. Do you like it being a little harder?

C: Ya, I like to be challenged when I do things, 'cause then I can be better at things.

O: Is there anything else you like about first grade?

C: I have a good teacher.

O: Can you tell me about her?

C: Well, she's really nice and we have popcorn and poetry sometimes. But other classes don't really get to do that.

O: What don't you like about school?

C: Recess.

O: What don't you like about recess?

C: Well, there's nothing to do and nobody wants to play with me. My best friend doesn't even want to play with me.

(Donelan-McCall and Dunn, 1997, p. 172)

Thinking point 7.1   What strategies could be developed to improve the interaction of peers during playtime?

This account reveals the extent to which peers are a powerful force, both physically and psychologically, in children's lives. Peers can also play a positive role in transitions by providing friendship and emotional and practical support. For example, in one study, which asked children 'Why do you come to nursery?', one child replied, using sign language, 'To see my friend Callum' (Mortimer, 2004, p. 174).

Increasingly, people working with children are realising the value of peer support and seeking to make use of it as part of a strategy to support transitions. One idea is to enable more experienced children to pass on their experience to others. The following comments from older children were used in an induction booklet for new kindergarten students:

> 'I like it when we sing songs';
>
> 'We learn about interesting things like the old-fashioned days';
>
> 'I like it when we do puppets'.
>
> (Mayo, 2005, p. 47)

Practice box 7.2

Five further types of peer support strategy have been identified:

Peer mentoring: a peer supporter acts as a positive role model on a one-to-one basis or in a classroom. Peer mentors may also be seen as "buddies" or "befrienders".

Peer listening: peer supporters run a 'drop in' service, offering their peers a confidential listening service, often on a one-to-one basis.

Peer mediation: peer supporters are trained in conflict resolution strategies; they may be peer educators to others in acquiring these strategies, or may act as mediators in the playground or in response to bullying situations.

Peer tutoring: a peer supporter supports a peer with reading or other areas of academic work.

Peer education: peer supporters are trained in a particular subject area, e.g. drugs or bullying, and deliver training to their peers.

(Mental Health Foundation, 2002, p. 2)

Peer support can help some children make transitions into new environments

One buddying scheme, aimed to support preschool children with the transition into school, built on the idea that 'positive relationships' with experienced students can help new students adjust to, and engage in, school (Dennison, 2000, cited in Dockett and Perry, 2005a, p. 22). Older children (aged ten or eleven years) were trained and supported to act as 'buddies' to new school entrants (children aged from four-and-a-half to six years). Comments from buddies included:

> 'I got to learn how to play, comfort and act around kindergarten children and I liked that because I didn't have a buddy and anyone to comfort me so I want my kindy [kindergarten] buddy to have the best buddy.'
>
> (Child, quoted in Dockett and Perry, 2005a, p. 27)

> 'I learnt how to be a good buddy and I learnt to be cooperative.'
>
> (Child, quoted in Dockett and Perry, 2005a, p. 28)

> 'I learned how the kindergarten [children] would feel, e.g. scared, lonely, terrified and sad.'
>
> (Child, quoted in Dockett and Perry, 2005a, p. 28)

1.2 Disability, poverty and transitions

Reducing childhood poverty has been a striking feature of UK government social policy in the early twenty-first century. Carefully targeted initiatives and policies have helped move significant numbers of children above the poverty line. Transitions into poverty, however, take many forms, some of which are complex and resistant to these policies.

This section will consider the relationship between disability, children's lives and the transition into and out of poverty. Although this is a less commonly experienced transition it is one to which all children may be vulnerable. It is also a transition that receives relatively little recognition or support.

Poverty is both a social barrier in itself and the product of other social barriers. It also has direct links with disability: unemployment and low household income increase the likelihood that a person will become disabled during adulthood (Burchard, 2003). Having a disabled adult or child in the family also increases the likelihood that the family will experience poverty. Both disabled and non-disabled children can be affected, for example, in families in which a non-disabled child lives with a disabled sibling, parent or other family member.

Poverty does not exist as a fixed state. Instead, it is often experienced as a dynamic process involving transitions into, and out of, poverty mediated by other socio-economic factors. In some cases, particular life events or transitions can act as 'triggers' to poverty. Disability as an unexpected life event is one such trigger.

Ridge (2002) found that children who experience poverty often define it in relation to being excluded from peer activities:

> 'You can't do as much, and I don't like my clothes and that, so I don't really get to do much or do stuff like my friends are doing ... I am worried about what people think of me, like they think I am sad or something.'
>
> (Child, quoted in Ridge, 2002, webpage)

Young children's views on poverty and disability are under-researched, yet the comments of parents in families with disabled members, trying to survive on benefits, provide an insight into the frustration experienced by themselves and their children:

> 'They don't have things other children have'. 'They just get bits and pieces – we never buy them new clothes, people give us clothes – the children don't like it though' ... 'Our son wants to go to France [with the school] but it's going to cost £154 – I had to say no.'
>
> (Parents quoted in Preston, 2006b, p. 80)

Advocates of the social model of disability identify the many ways in which disabled people are confronted by social barriers that restrict their participation in society (Oliver, 1996). In some cases these barriers exist separately from poverty yet function in a similar way, by excluding children from opportunities. Disabled children report their frustration at being excluded from activities with other children and young people:

Carer: Sophie went to a local brownie group which she really enjoyed and she wanted to move up to the guides. And this is something that has upset Sophie a lot because they couldn't cope with Sophie's wheelchair, so she wasn't allowed to go, guides wasn't wheelchair accessible.

Researcher: And how did that make you feel Sophie?

Sophie: Angry!

(Mitchell and Sloper, 2001, p. 246)

Many of the issues associated with disability may be linked to discrimination in society as a whole – but this example demonstrates that everyone working with children has a responsibility to check their own practice to ensure that they are not colluding with this discrimination.

All children benefit from inclusive and non-discriminatory environments and opportunities

Thinking point 7.2   In what ways do the services for children, which you know about, ensure the inclusion of disabled children or disabled family members? Could these services do more to increase participation?

Although the Disability Discrimination Act 1995 resulted in the lifting of some barriers for disabled people, it is evident that children and their families still encounter a wide range of restrictions, many of which result in or result from poverty.

Such barriers include:

- Insufficient family support, practical help in the family home and too few breaks (with the most severely disabled children frequently receiving the least help because they may be viewed as *too disabled* for local services);
- The high additional costs of disability;
- The lack of key workers to ensure well coordinated services planned to meet individual family needs;
- Frequent delays in identification, diagnosis and provision of support;
- Lack of good accessible information on available services;
- Inequalities in access to health and other services;
- Limited expectations of children's educational achievements;
- Insufficient accessible sport, play, leisure and cultural activities;
- Lack of opportunities for young people moving to adult services;
- A limited range of culturally appropriate services for families from minority ethnic groups.

(Russell, 2003, p. 216)

Disabled parents or carers also experience barriers, particularly when trying to enter the job market, 'and emphasise that they are disabled by discrimination rather than their physical or mental impairment' (Preston, 2006b, p. 56). Disabled parents are less likely to benefit from 'welfare to work' strategies and more likely to remain unemployed; as a result, their chances of remaining in or falling into poverty are increased. A government report on child poverty confirms both that 'Among workless households with children the majority have at least one disabled parent' and that 'a quarter of children living in poverty have long-term sick or disabled parents' (HM Treasury, 2004, pp. 46 and 83).

Many other statistics highlight the link between poverty and disability. For example, of households with one or more disabled children, 31 per cent are at risk of living in poverty (after housing costs) compared with 27 per cent in households with non-disabled children (National Statistics, 2005, p. 59). Some suggest this underestimates the situation by not taking into consideration the additional costs of bringing up a disabled child (Preston, 2006a). Gordon et al. (2000) suggest that 55 per cent of families with disabled children are living on or close to the poverty line.

> Families with disabled children have considerable additional and ongoing expenses meaning that it can cost up to 3 times more caring for a disabled child than a non-disabled child
>
> (Gordon et al., 2000, p. 2)

> Families of disabled children incur considerable additional expenditure on heating, housing, clothing, equipment, and other items ... [they] are less likely to own a car or a telephone than families with non-disabled children.
>
> (Russell, 2003, p. 216)

For many families however 'the biggest cost of all is giving up paid work. Most accept that they will be out of employment for many years, or that they may never get a job. Unemployed parents not only miss out on additional income, but on paying for National Insurance credits, pensions and accumulating savings' (Preston, 2006a, p. 40). This can result in a continual cycle of poverty during which families may drift in and out of work as their caring responsibilities change. Many families are therefore dependent upon the benefits system. Despite government attempts to provide short-term extra benefits for poorer families with disabled children, information about entitlements is not readily available or easily understood. Some families feel stigmatised by having to apply for benefits and, when families do apply, sometimes their entitlements are reduced or removed (then reinstated again after an appeal) resulting in further fluctuations in family income (Preston, 2006a).

Trying to cope with such fluctuations and lack of money can have a negative impact on the whole family, resulting in uncertainty, distress and a range of unwanted transitions for children:

> It disrupts disabled children's access to services and social activities and generates anxiety among parents/carers, which in turn impacts on the wellbeing of all family members.
>
> (Preston, 2006a, p. 41)

Multiple transitions experienced by families with disabled members include:

- parents losing a job, with resulting lack of income and stress;

- loss of social and educational opportunities for children due to reduced income and extra expenditure;

- lack of money contributing to losing accommodation due to rent arrears or mortgage repossession;

- parental stress resulting from lack of money leading to separation and divorce;

- lack of money contributing to parental ability to cope leads to child being placed into foster care or moving away to residential school.

Providing support for families experiencing the multiple transitions associated with disability is challenging for people working with children, particularly where the needs lie beyond their particular specialism or area of responsibility. Children's centres, however, present new opportunities for overcoming this by locating different practitioners and services under the same roof. Tunstill et al. (2007) suggest that signposting people towards appropriate services is a simple but effective solution. They noted how people approach centres for specific information on one issue and, during the process, are enabled to identify other needs they might not otherwise have articulated. So, for example, a parent or carer seeking help with their disabled child's health may also find themselves being offered welfare rights or benefits advice. Children's centres also potentially have space and facilities that can enable people to form peer and self-help groups and access online sources of support, such as the *Contact a Family* website (http://www.cafamily.org.uk).

Providing appropriate information and signposting does, however, require effective systems. Tunstill et al. (2007) highlight the fact that, where specialist information is held only by a few people, there can be problems if personnel leave and knowledge is lost. In addition, due to the dynamic and fast-moving nature of service provision and policy, systems need to be in place to make sure that information is regularly updated and maintained. It is also essential to ensure that any peer-led activities or groups are considered in relation to the greater responsibility of safeguarding the welfare of any child users of children's centres (Tunstill et al., 2007).

Despite the fact that all children are vulnerable to disability, and transitions in and out of poverty, this is an experience that receives relatively little recognition or support. However, adults working with children can challenge discrimination and create inclusive access to services in which they are involved. Although the causes of transitions into poverty are located in wider society, practitioners can signpost families towards appropriate advice or services such as children's centres.

Key points

1   Different types of transition are influenced or created by wider social, economic and political factors, including discrimination.

2   Certain transitions are more commonly experienced by some children than others and as a result it is possible to overlook the types of support needed by children experiencing less common transitions.

3   Continuity is considered important in supporting some transitions and can be achieved by actively engaging with children, families and peers in an interdependent and inclusive way.

4   In some cases adults working with children can signpost families experiencing transitions towards appropriate advice and support.

2 Behaviour and transitions

So far in this chapter we have considered two contrasting experiences of transitions and begun to identify some of the ways in which children and the people they live with can be supported. Most people, including children, are likely to exhibit behavioural changes linked to experiences of transition. Being able to interpret and understand the causes of children's behaviour, and respond appropriately, are important skills associated with working with children.

Thinking point 7.3   Consider a transition from your own life, for example a situation where somebody abruptly ended an enjoyable activity (a party, hobby or conversation) in which you were participating. How did you feel and behave?

In Brown's (2007) study of nursery children it was noted that children 'played up' when their parents came to collect them. From the perspective of children, these transitions appeared to bring an abrupt end to their activities, such as watching TV, relaxing, or concentrating on a game (Brown, 2007, p. 106). We can thus interpret 'playing up' as a behavioural response reflecting these children's frustrations and disappointment at ending enjoyable activities. In this respect they are very similar to adults.

The following indicates some of the behaviours and associated feelings that childhood transitions may provoke.

Fun: Children, like adults, express fun and enjoyment in many different ways. Transitions, particularly into new environments, can result in some children becoming very excited and prompt them to make a lot of noise and run around. In some contexts this can be perceived negatively. Providing children with time and space to express their enjoyment and fun is very important.

New or unfamiliar environments can be a source of fun for children

Nervousness: Taking the first step into a new context can provoke nervous behaviour, such as shyness or avoidance. For adults supporting children it is hard to get the right balance between acknowledging their feelings and gently pushing them into taking a risk. The following account demonstrates the importance of fun and communication in helping some children assert themselves:

> 'On my first night of scouts I thought ... "nah this isn't going to work for me. I was nervous, scared, thinking will they like me?" Then I came back the next week and I talked, I felt great, from then I knew this is it, every Friday I'm going to have a great night with kids who just want to have fun.'
>
> (Child quoted in City of Edinburgh Scout Association, 2006, p. 1)

Behaviour considered disruptive or challenging: Wade and Smart asked children what a fictional child might do if a father failed to turn up for a contact visit. The responses included:

Kelly Marie (6):	Smack him
Adam (9):	He [child] might be ... flipping things around and getting bored
Sarah (7):	Kick in the door
Patrick (6):	[He] gets angry. Messes his bedroom up
Miriam (10):	He might get a bit angry and annoyed scream and shout and break things.

(Wade and Smart, 2002, p. 20)

Greenberg (2005) identifies several examples of disruptive or challenging behaviour linked to transitions:

- acting out feelings of loss or frustration;

- not following rules or crossing cultural boundaries; perhaps indicating the difficulties of moving into new situations and learning to decode the rules;

- attention-seeking: a child may not understand how to go about this in a socially acceptable way as they may lack experience of asking for help;

- a lack of impulse control: some children will develop this through practice over time.

Whilst challenging behaviour can be destructive, it is also an indication of a person's emotional state. In the adult world the concept of 'road rage' is often associated with the frustration of busy roads and exhibited by people who, in other circumstances, may present themselves as placid, relaxed, individuals. It is as much to do with the context as the person themselves. Likewise, being able to make a distinction between the child and their behaviour, and acknowledging the feeling behind the behaviour, are important goals for people working with children. The kinds of behaviour suggested above in response to a missed contact visit may be socially unacceptable. Yet if this was one of a series of parental let-downs it would be hard not to empathise with the child's frustration and hurt.

In chapter 6 we highlighted Holland's (2003) observation that teachers sometimes encountered anger and moodiness in children yet failed to make connections between this and the child's experience of loss. This indicates a worrying lack of knowledge and skill that should be a prerequisite for anyone working with children.

One of the indirect consequences of challenging behaviour is rejection by peers and the development of a particularly negative social status (Stormont et al., 2005). If this continues unchecked it can leave a child vulnerable to bullying, could lead to them being labelled and will inhibit their opportunities to learn and develop new skills.

Regressive, anxious and habitual behaviour: Fahlberg (1994) notes how separations and losses can cause temporary regression in children's behaviour. This may include becoming clingy, bedwetting or returning to baby talk.

She also identifies a range of behaviours found in anxious children, including 'whining, nail biting, hand-wringing, hair twisting or picking at face or fingers'. These behaviours can become habitual and, in the case of Jamie, affected his interactions and relationships:

> Jamie, nine, whined when making requests of his parents, when reporting interactions with peers and when responding to questions. His parents found this a very irritating habit. Siblings and friends frequently imitated him, leading to an escalation of the problem. Jamie himself seemed totally oblivious to his own tone of voice.
>
> (Fahlberg, 1994, p. 293)

Thinking point 7.4   What kinds of specialist behavioural supports are available to help children and families?

Adults working with children often encounter these habitual behaviours. They may need to reassure parents that such behaviour is a common response to anxiety, including domestic transitions, such as a house move or the birth of a new sibling.

Parents can be offered practical strategies to help change the behaviour. In Jamie's case, the parents were helped to develop a reward-based behaviour programme (Fahlberg, 1994). Such direct approaches can be successful at dealing with habitual behaviour yet may have limited impact where the underlying cause is not addressed. It is also important, from a children's rights perspective, that children are actively involved in negotiating these programmes and are not labelled as failures if no apparent behavioural change results.

Adults working with children should also be alert to other possible causes of unhappiness or anxiety. All adults have a responsibility to safeguard children's welfare and any relevant concerns arising from observing children, or talking to parents and carers, should be discussed with line managers or people in organisations with child protection responsibilities. Working with children and transitions therefore requires effective and accessible channels of communication and support.

Margetts (2005, p. 42) suggests that 'problems like hyperactivity, internalising or externalising behaviour in a clinical sense cannot be sufficiently dealt with through transition programs, but may need professional (family) treatment'. In such cases, parents or carers can be supported to refer the child on to more specialist support in the form of educational psychologists, or the Child and Adolescent Mental Health Services (CAMHS).

Resilient behaviour:

> I'm a foster kid. It's not much fun
>
> Because I miss my Mum.
>
> I'm a foster kid but I don't care,
>
> Because our family goes everywhere.
>
> I'm a foster kid; at first it was a bit of a scare.
>
> I thought they didn't really care.
>
> Now I know they do and I love them too.
>
> (Laura's poem, Foster Care Associates, 2003, p. 70)

Children's voices convey powerful messages about their experiences. The poem above describes the experience of a particular transition: moving into a new family. For the poet, being a foster child is not much fun. Perhaps it is the loss of a previous life, or perhaps it is the unsettling experience of having to move. Possibly it's the stigma that the status of being 'in care' can produce. A combination of any of these would be sufficient reason to feel unhappy and scared. But the words also convey something that we can refer to as resilience.

Despite the position the child is in, the poem expresses a defiant 'I don't care' attitude. The poem acknowledges that despite early prejudices and uncertainty about the foster carers, it is possible to take risks, build bridges, move forward and develop loving relationships. But how do children who experience transitions reach a point where they are comfortable with themselves and their new situation? We can assume that the success of the child who wrote the poem has emerged from strength of character and experience of life. But this would be telling only part of the story. To make transitions children also require supportive environments and people.

The capacity and strength of the child who wrote the poem is an example of what some people have described as resilient behaviour involving 'the capacity to resist or "bounce back" from adversity' (Newman and Blackburn, 2002a, p. 4). Some children seem better than others at overcoming barriers encountered in their lives. These resilient children are better equipped to resist stress and adversity, cope with change and uncertainty, and to recover faster and more completely from traumatic events or episodes (Newman and Blackburn, 2002a, p. 1).

One way of thinking about resilience is as an asset or characteristic that some people possess, either individually, within families or within wider social systems.

Rutter identifies three factors associated with resilience:

- A sense of self esteem and confidence
- A belief in own self efficacy and ability to deal with change and adaption
- A repertoire of problem solving approaches

(Rutter, 1985, cited in Aldgate et al., 2006, p. 27)

Involvement in communal projects (such as a community garden) may help some children develop resilience

Other factors which promote resilience in family members include parental harmony, high warmth/low criticism family structures, and good parent–child relationships. Resilience can also emerge through experiences within wider social systems and networks, including successful school experiences, valued social roles (helping neighbours or community activities), religious affiliations and friendship networks (Newman and Blackburn, 2002b).

The child who wrote the poem quoted above is likely to have benefited from the sensitive care and attachment formed with foster carers. Children in this position might also gain benefits from the support of a social worker and help from teachers, siblings or friends. The part played by voluntary organisations and extended school activities in resiliency building is illustrated in this account from a boy in a study asking what can help some children, despite difficult lives, full of risk factors, to live conventionally-defined successful lives:

> 'With Scouts and First Aid and all that, they learn something and I know with Scouts and all that, you do camps and it could teach you to do stuff that they might feel a bit better about themselves'
>
> (Child, quoted in Howard and Johnson, 2000, p. 333)

The dynamic interaction between many of the systems in children's lives can help build resilience and, in turn, protect children during transitions and from risk and adverse experiences. Resilience is a useful concept because it can act as a focus for practice. People working with children can identify situations and approaches that both build and further develop the capacities, strengths and protective factors of children, families and communities. Newman (2004) lists a range of effective resilience-building strategies related to different age groups:

Practice box 7.3

Effective strategies for the early years (antenatal to 4)

In the antenatal period:

- adequate maternal nutrition throughout pregnancy
- avoidance of maternal and passive smoking
- moderate maternal alcohol consumption
- social support to mothers from partners, family and external networks

- good access to antenatal care
- interventions to prevent domestic violence

During infancy:

- adequate parental income
- social support for mothers, to moderate perinatal stress
- good-quality housing
- parent education
- safe play areas and provision of learning materials
- breastfeeding to three months
- support from male partners
- continuous home-based input from health and social care services, lay or professional

During the pre-school period:

- high-quality pre-school day care
- preparatory work with parents on home–school links
- pairing with resilient peers
- availability of alternative caregivers
- food supplements
- links with other parents, local community networks and faith groups
- community regeneration initiatives

Effective strategies for middle childhood (5 to 13):

- Reception classes that are sufficiently flexible to accommodate a range of cultural and community-specific behaviours.
- Creation and maintenance of home–school links for at-risk children and their families, which can promote parental confidence and engagement.
- Positive school experiences: academic, sporting or friendship-related.
- Good and mutually trusting relationships with teachers.
- The development of skills, opportunities for independence and mastery of tasks.
- Structured routines, and a perception by the child that praise and sanctions are being administered fairly.
- In abusive settings, the opportunity to maintain or develop attachments to the non-abusive parent, other family member or, otherwise, a reliable unrelated adult; maintenance of family routines and rituals.
- Manageable contributions to the household that promote competencies, self-esteem and problem-solving coping.

- In situations of marital discord, attachment to one parent, moderation of parental disharmony and opportunities to play a positive role in the family.

- Help with resolving minor but chronic stresses as well as acute adversities.

- Provision of breakfast and after-school clubs.

(Newman, 2004, pp. 2–4)

Thinking point 7.5 How many of these strategies can you identify in children's services with which you are familiar?

Building services around protective factors that promote resilience is an important strategy – but it is likely to overlook the needs of some children. Resilience is rare in children experiencing severe, multiple and enduring adversities (Newman and Blackburn, 2002b). These children might find more normative approaches at building resilience impossible to achieve or even painful and damaging.

Resiliency is a popular concept and links closely with contemporary multi-targeted welfare approaches. Yet early evaluations of projects such as Sure Start reveal a failure to access the families, and, in turn, the children with the greatest need (Taylor, 2005). There is also concern that the adoption of resilience into some educational programmes has been 'inflected with normative middle class values' making these programmes less helpful to children from ethnic, cultural and class groups which may not share these values (Howard et al., 1999, p. 317). It could also be argued that resilience is simply conceptualising what would otherwise be viewed as straightforward good practice (Newman and Blackburn, 2002b).

Key points

1   People working with children should be alert to the different types of behaviour that can be associated with transitions.

2   Responding to children's behaviour may involve direct work with the child and sometimes their parent or carers; referrals can be made for specialist support.

3   Resilient behaviour is an asset found in some children, as well as a capacity that can be built through appropriate forms of support in different parts of children's systems.

4   Enduring, multiple transitions and severe adversity can have a negative impact on children's ability to develop resilient behaviour.

3 Attending to children's feelings

Transitions can result in fear and anxiety; consequently adults can be reluctant to expose children to such feelings. In chapter 6 we highlighted concerns that adults sometimes overprotect children. There are of course some children whose previous traumatic experiences demand that they are helped to avoid certain transitions. Many children, however, have the capacity to deal with their emotions if provided with space, time and empathy from adults.

One child expresses his fear about being abandoned by his parents when he goes to secondary school:

> When you get older, when you go to secondary school, like, if your mum and dad take you to school they might change and say 'You've got to go to school on your own, you're old enough
>
> (Boy quoted in Lucey and Reay, 2000, p. 196)

Thinking point 7.6   How would you attend to fears like these and what practical steps could you take to help with the transition to secondary school?

The experience of overcoming fear can, in itself, help some children build the self-confidence and strength to take on other challenges

In the account above we can detect fear. Although often presented as a negative emotion, fear can also 'be a creative force as it generates energy to handle threat' (Cairns, 2002, p. 98). The experience of overcoming fear can, in itself, help build self-confidence and the strength to take on other challenges. Although affective conditions, including anxiety and fear, 'can be a driving force' they do not *always* drive children to a `bad place' or 'pathology '(Lucey and Reay, 2000, p. 192). Feelings of fear, anger or anxiety can be 'self assertive' emotions and consequently force children into using their own resources to deal with them (Cairns, 2002, p. 98).

Joely (9):   I just scribble on some paper, or stamp on some paper and screw it up when I'm really, really angry ... It gets all the feeling away.

(Wade and Smart, 2002, p. 22)

For some children handling the feelings and emotions associated with transitions can be a positive experience. Anxiety, for example, is 'essential in helping to mobilise adaptive responses to sometimes disturbing circumstances and change' (Barbelet, 1998, quoted in Lucey and Reay, 2000, p. 192).

It has been suggested that children exhibit three types of response to their problems, including those related to transitions:

- trying to alter their external world
- trying to alter their internal world
- doing nothing

(Thurber and Weisz, 1997, in Wade and Smart, 2002, p. 18)

Wade and Smart (2002) found some children lacked sufficient power to achieve the first of these and were therefore more likely to alter their own states of mind through either diversion or expression:

Elise (10):   There's nothing children can do [if parents split up]. It's because it's their parents. There's no point getting involved because it might make it worse.

Q: So what's the best thing to do?

Elise: Try and forget what's happened and get on with normal life.

(Wade and Smart, 2002, p. 19)

Kara (9):   I've got a secret diary where I put all my, you know like you're talking to me about, I'm talking to you about my family, I've been putting things in there, in my diary.

(Wade and Smart, 2002, p. 19)

Supporting children may involve strategies that help children express or avoid their feelings. Cairns (2002) writes about her experience of living with foster children, some of whom face extreme traumas and emotional feelings associated with many difficult and complex transitions in their lives. She encourages adults to help children become emotionally literate and put words to their feelings:

> Children need to be encouraged and enabled to speak the feelings, and adults also need to be open and authentic with the children about their own feelings and thoughts. Carers and teachers, social workers and therapists, play leaders and child minders all need to be aware of the need to keep exercising the words-for-feelings bits of the brain. Games, stories, mealtimes, bedtimes, rides on buses, playtime in the park, anything and everything can be an entry point to speaking the feelings.
>
> (Cairns, 2002, p. 125)

In some cases children may choose their own way of expressing their feelings that runs contrary to that being offered:

Buffy (10):   My teacher's really nice about it. She said that if ever I want to talk to her I can.

Q: And have you ever?

Buffy: Er ... well, I wrote this story about someone that ... mum and dad had split up, but I've never actually spoken to her about it.

(Wade and Smart, 2002, p. 31)

This highlights the importance of tuning in to the different methods of communication chosen by children to express their feelings. The Children and Family Court Advisory and Support Service (CAFCASS), working to prepare children for family court proceedings, has had success in helping children express their feelings through the use of play, art, media and computer-assisted software (CAFCASS, 2006, p. 5). Drawing and, in this case, writing poetry can be useful channels for communicating feelings:

With no mum or dad

The children are sad,

Away from home

You feel alone.

No sisters to fight with,

No clothes to share,

No second hand shoes for me to wear.

My life seems empty, nobody's around;

Then things change and carers are found.

The nights I've cried

The door opens wide,

I stop and stare,

Suddenly I'm aware

Everythings going to be alright

My Foster Parents are here tonight.

(Poem by foster child, Foster Care Associates, 2000, p. 57)

However children choose to communicate, it is important that adults listen and acknowledge their feelings. Children value adults who have time to listen and who convey genuine empathy. Children who are coping with loss or transitions that leave them feeling angry or sad may have difficulty in rationalising how they feel. It is possible sometimes to 'scaffold' children's communication by demonstrating strategies and ideas to them about how to express themselves. In some cases it may be helpful to refer the child for specialist help, such as bereavement counselling or cognitive behavioural therapy.

3.1 Reluctance to talk about feelings

Every time when I go in the house [my parents] always go 'David, how was your day?' I go 'don't ask', and they don't. And then the next day they don't ask, and then the next day they do and I go 'don't ask', and it carries on like that. I don't want to tell them about the day 'cos it's boring.

(Child quoted in Edwards et al., 2000, p. 3)

Feelings belong to the person who is having them. We should not assume therefore that children will want to talk about their feelings or experiences. The child quoted above may prefer to do something more exciting than talk about his 'boring' school day. Providing space for children like him to switch off and divert their attention is important. Sometimes time spent with peers can help children with this.

Some children suppress feelings of hurt or pain, others wait for the right time and place or an appropriate confidante.

Michael: He'd tell a friend after a few days when he got used to it.

(Wade and Smart, 2002, p. 28)

Adults can support children by creating safe places and trusting relationships and, when children do choose to express their feelings, by taking them seriously. Some contexts, however, are just not the right place for children to talk:

Miriam: You can't really talk to a teacher because you have to see her every day, or him, and if you break down crying in the middle it's very embarrassing. So I mean, I wouldn't, I'd just talk to my mum about it or an understanding adult.

(Wade and Smart, 2002, p. 31)

Some children may need to be referred on to counselling or therapeutic help in order to unload painful experiences. It is important that children are offered rather than forced into counselling. The reaction of the child quoted below indicates the danger of children not being involved fully in deciding what support they would prefer.

Ocky: That one mum did [send me to] didn't work ... All I did was play with the toys they had there and I never talked once.

Q: Why didn't you talk to the counsellor?

Ocky: Because I don't like talking.

Q: Is there anything the counsellor could have done that would have made it better?

Ocky: I don't think they can. They say they can but I don't think they can. I think that's a load of crap but I'm not allowed to say that ... Well, it didn't work for me.

(Wade and Smart, 2002, p. 40)

Thinking point 7.7   At what times, and in which places, do you prefer not to talk about how you feel to others?

3.2 Ambivalent feelings

Part of me feels sad and part of me feels mad

(Child quoted in Fahlberg, 1994, p. 140)

Feelings of ambivalence are an expected response to childhood transitions (Fahlberg, 1994), reflecting liminality and inbetweenness. A Looked After child may be coming to terms with leaving behind previous family problems or rejection while, at the same time, missing members of their families, friends and perhaps pets. Part of the task for people working with children is to help them to recognise that it is OK to have ambivalent feelings. Liminal spaces are often times of creativity and encouraging children to write or draw may enable them to express how they feel. Providing younger children with reading books, such as *Double-Dip Feelings* by Barbara Cain, can help reassure them that what they are feeling is OK.

> They are called "double-dip" because they are two different feelings that happen at the same time, sort of like two flavours of ice cream scoops right on top of each other. With an ice cream cone, double dips are fun, because you get to have twice as much ice cream as a single scoop. But with feelings, double dips usually aren't so much fun. When kids have these kinds of feelings, they often feel confused and uncomfortable. It bothers kids to feel two different ways at the same time because they don't quite know what to do. Here are some ideas to help you with your double-dip feelings ...
>
> (Extract from *Double-Dip Feelings*, Cain, 2001, p. 30)

In chapter 6 we introduced an understanding of how loss and change can be a feature of transitions. Work that prepares children for feelings, including those related to loss and change, can be undertaken as part of day-to-day learning in schools and other educational contexts.

Practice box 7.4

There are many ways of addressing loss, depending on the age and experience of the child. The following examples all develop children's awareness that life involves endings and new beginnings:

Circle time – talking about seeing a hedgehog run over or the death of the class hamster

Science – the difference between living and non-living

History – past lives and events

English – literature, including separation and illness

Music – associated with rites, requiems and meditations

(Holland et al., 2005)

The idea of ending relationships or experiences can itself invoke powerful feelings of loss. On the other hand it can also be used as a marker to signify change or moving on. Mayo (2005) describes how group work can be used with children to reflect on their transition into kindergarten and to prepare them for their next transition into school. 'We discuss how children won't all be together next year, nor in the same class and how children could maintain contact especially for children moving to other schools' (Mayo, 2005, p. 49).

Another popular strategy is to develop rituals and symbolic gestures representing an ending. Birthday parties and the practice of leaving baby teeth for the tooth fairy are common examples of marking significant endings and new beginnings. Children are being encouraged to learn that transitions are part of a circular life pattern. These approaches also encourage them to use the experience and confidence of previous transitions as a scaffold for future transitions.

Birthday parties and other rituals can help signify and celebrate key transitions in children's lives

Key points

1 Children have a range of feelings associated with transitions.

2 Children possess capacities to deal with their feelings, although with very maltreated children these can be deep-seated.

3 Adults can support children with their feelings by providing them with space and time to express them, keep them private or just switch off.

4 Children should be provided with opportunities to choose and consent to support.

5 Preparatory work and rituals can help children dealing with loss and endings.

4 Supporting children's connectedness and transitions

The discussion so far has highlighted the potential complexity of some children's relationships and how they involve transitions across and within a network of systems. One way of helping children make sense of these relationships is through the use of genograms (family trees) and ecomaps. These are creative ways of working alongside children of different ages and in different contexts. Social workers find them useful when undertaking assessments and they can also be adapted by teachers and after-school play workers interested in exploring the child's wider social network.

Genograms are very similar to the ancestry or pedigree charts used by family historians. In school they could be integrated into a history lesson. A genogram can use colour or symbols to indicate different types of relationship – children can have fun choosing their own. In the following example Clare has chosen to show her parents' divorce by crossing out the line that connects them. Notice how extended family members, and even pets, feature in her representation of family.

Genograms can help children visually represent key family relationships

Ecomaps enable children to represent a wider range of networks and information. Children can be encouraged to be creative by using colours, symbols and photos, for example. The following example (used in a social work assessment) uses a prepared format and extends beyond the social network to incorporate information about the child's feelings and preferences.

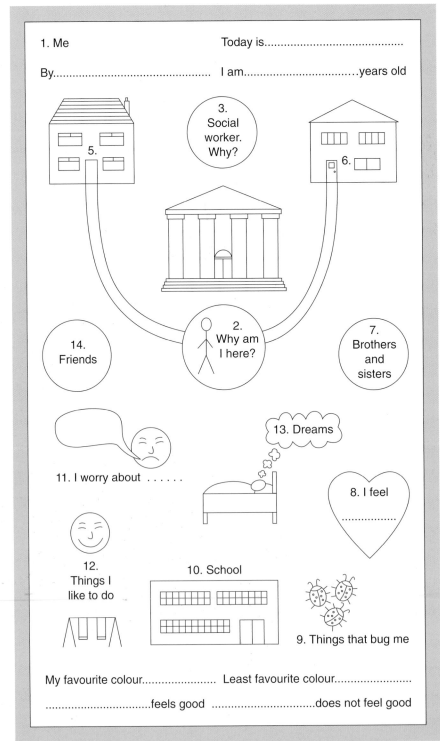

1. Me

Today is...

By.. I am................................years old

3. Social worker. Why?

5.

6.

2. Why am I here?

14. Friends

7. Brothers and sisters

11. I worry about . . . . . .

13. Dreams

8. I feel
....

12. Things I like to do

10. School

9. Things that bug me

My favourite colour....................... Least favourite colour.......................

................................feels good ....does not feel good

Ecomaps enable children to represent a wider range of networks and information. (Fahlberg, 1994)

As we discussed in Chapter 6, achieving a sense of place is particularly important for children who make transitions. A child's potential to grow and change can be enhanced by providing a secure emotional and physical base from which to explore an uncertain dynamic world. The following extract from a primary school induction booklet indicates how one setting goes about making children feel welcome and able to claim the school as a place of their own:

> School life can be quite exhausting for some young children with new friends to make, a new environment to explore and a new structure to their day. To make the transition easier, we arrange a couple of mornings in the summer term for new pupils to come to school to get to know what school is like. They will then attend school for half a day for the first six weeks. By then they are usually keen to stay all day. School starts at 9.00 am, but the door is open from 8.40 am. On the first day, each child will be given a peg to hang their coat on and a tray to put their belongings in.
>
> (Cunningsburgh Primary School, 2004, webpage)

The temporal dimension is attended to by gradually introducing children to the school. Children are also provided with a small place of their own in the form of a school peg and a tray for private possessions. Often children are encouraged to personalise these places, perhaps with a drawing or photograph of themselves. A sense of place can also be achieved if children are empowered to be involved in decision making about their environment.

Personalised coat hooks are one of many creative ways of providing children with a sense of place

4.1 Continuity during multiple transitions

In the earlier discussion about home to education transitions we highlighted how connectedness with children also involves reaching out and working with families and other important figures in their lives. Providing continuity, however, is more difficult when children do not live with their birth families, in particular for adopted children, and children in the Looked After care system. The child quoted below reveals a high level of disruption, uncertainty and discontinuity during her six years in the care system:

> 'I've been in care five times since I was 6, I had my seventh birthday in care then a few months afterwards I went back. That happened another four times. When I was nine I came for the fifth time, then the court said I had to stay in 'til I am eighteen. Then six months later my two sisters were adopted and my brother was put in long term foster.
>
> When all my friends found out they were all sorry for me, but I'm not allowed anywhere on my own at night and all my friends are. When my friends are still out talking on our street me and Nikita have to go in, which is not fair.
>
> Foster Homes are not fair on young people. What happened to me to get me in care is my mum used to hit us and I told my school, they told the Social Services and I thought it was so unfair. Now my mum has learnt her lesson, so I want to go back.'
>
> (A National Voice, 2006, webpage)

Some of the children in the Looked After care system have suffered harm and as a result may find it difficult to connect with others. This in turn can increase the likelihood of placements breaking down. Providing continuity and connections with a stable base for these children is particularly important, yet maintaining contact with birth parents is not always possible or desirable. Even where children have found a permanent placement, the trend towards maintaining contact with birth families can be challenging for children and adults alike.

Thinking point 7.8   What kinds of challenges arise when children living away from home maintain contact with their birth families?

The level and form of contact with birth families for these children is dependent on the circumstances of each individual case and frequently subject to decisions made by a court. Contact, whether direct or indirect, has to be considered to be in the best interests of the child and, in some cases, a contact order can be changed or ended in the interest of promoting the child's welfare. Unsurprisingly some children who live away from their birth parents report feeling homesick:

> 'I wished I could go home ... but I couldn't and I just wanted to hide'
>
> (Child in short-term care, quoted in Aldgate and Bradley, 2004, p. 79)

Consequently contact visits with birth parents are important for many of these children. Some children see contact as a realistic alternative to moving back full time, others want more contact, or even the chance to be reunited permanently.

> 'I don't want to go back and live with her, but I want to go back and visit ... why ... because she's my Ma'
>
> (Child quoted in McTeigue, 1998, cited in Gilligan, 2000, p. 45)

> 'I wish that I got seeing my real mummy more often ... I wish that all my real family was all together again and not living separately'
>
> (Child, two years into care placement, quoted in McAuley, 1996, cited in Gilligan, 2000, p. 45)

Aldgate and McIntosh (2006) interviewed some children who had no desire to maintain contact with birth parents, particularly where they had been placed in a stable foster family since early childhood or had experienced severe neglect from birth parents:

> 'Mum couldn't look after us properly – she wasn't coping. It was never suitable for us to go back. Then we haven't wanted to go back – we don't want contact with mum'
>
> (Child quoted in Aldgate and McIntosh, 2006, p. 64)

It is important that contact visits are carefully planned and supervised. Both children and adults may need emotional support before and after visits. Contact visits can be a source of anxiety and stress for children and impact negatively on their education and health. They can also undermine the work and achievements of foster carers:

> 'I sometimes feel embarrassed as she shouts and still drinks a lot'.
>
> (Child talking about contact with birth parent in Aldgate and McIntosh, 2006, p. 68)

'Mum promised to come at Christmas and didn't come'

> (Foster carer quoted in Aldgate and McIntosh, 2006, p. 67)

'Chloe has flaky skin which is brought on by seeing her mum, although she is dying to see her'

> (Foster carer quoted in Aldgate and McIntosh, 2006, p. 67)

'The school can always tell if Ian has seen his mum because his behaviour goes right down'

> (Foster carer quoted in Aldgate and McIntosh, 2006, p. 67)

Even where contact with birth parents is not possible, the law encourages Looked After and adopted children to maintain connections with siblings and extended family members through both joint placements and continuing contact. Continued contact with a sibling is one way of helping a child maintain a sense of belonging. Children identify the importance of contact with siblings and extended family, but also demonstrate a mixture of consequential emotions:

> 'I wasn't happy that my brother and sister weren't coming to stay here ... I would like to see them once a week but I don't get to see them now'
>
> (Child quoted in Aldgate and McIntosh, 2006, p. 71)

> 'I like holding my wee brother but I hate going to my mum's'
>
> (Child quoted in Aldgate and McIntosh, 2006, p. 71)

It is likely that children will also form new relationships, perhaps with other Looked After or adopted children or with the birth children of their foster carers. Both sets of children are likely to need support with such transitions. The account below reveals both the challenges and the benefits of living in a house through which sixteen children have passed in the previous four years. We could suggest that this experience of multiple transitions has occurred against the backdrop of a consistent and stable family home that, in turn, accounts for the balanced response:

> 'At first it was hard to share my parents and my bedroom – I used to get a bit annoyed – but now I'm used to it and I don't mind at all. The best thing about living with fostered kids is the fact I always have someone to play with'
>
> (Child quoted on Newsround, 2004, webpage)

Multiple transitions are also experienced by refugee children who may move between several temporary forms of accommodation before finally settling in a permanent placement. For travelling children, mobility is embedded within their lifestyle and culture, but there are occasions when their families may be forced to move to new locations by councils or the experience of discrimination. Other children, including some disabled children or those with medical conditions, may experience frequent moves between home, residential care and hospital. Ensuring continuity and connectedness for all of these children can be challenging.

4.2 The importance of memories

One of the many functions of families is to become 'the repository of knowledge about the child' (Fahlberg, 1994, p. 353). This involves keeping safe important documents about children such as their birth certificate, passport and health details and collecting photographs or DVD footage of children's life events. Some parents go further by keeping artefacts such as their baby's first lock of hair or plaster casts of their hand or foot prints. Families also develop and re-tell narratives of significant events which help keep alive important memories and construct an oral family history. For migrant families, such stories also help maintain links with their original homeland or culture of origin. For a child, these activities and processes all contribute to a developing sense of self and give them an insight into 'how the past influences present behaviours' (Fahlberg, 1994, p. 353). It could be argued that adults supporting children have a responsibility to keep alive children's personal histories.

This form of knowledge retention would appear to be particularly important for children who experience multiple transitions. It would be very easy to lose track of important parts of a child's history where they are moving from one carer to the next. Attempts have been made to keep official paper records for children in the Looked After care system that can be updated as the child moves between placements. Whilst such official documents are welcome, they can be enhanced by providing children with opportunities to help construct their own life story (or journey) books.

Life story books are a visual compilation of important memories in a child's life and, unlike official records, can allow children's creativity and personality to be represented more easily. They can consist of pictures, maps, genograms, records, timelines and written narrative, all helping to construct a chronology of a child's journey. Sometimes creating a life story book can involve practical activities, such as tracking down an old nursery teacher and writing down her memories of the child when they were younger, or photographing the child's first school. Different formats are used, depending on the child's choice, experience or ability. Some children enjoy using a scrapbook, others a software package. Experience suggests that children are more likely to make use of a life story book if it is written 'in neat legible script' (Fahlberg, 1994, p. 359). Organisations such as the British Association for Adoption and Fostering (BAAF) and National Children's Homes (NCH) provide advice and consultancy to professionals who wish to help children compile life journeys.

Life story books are designed to be added to by the child, either alone or with the support of an adult such as their carer or social worker, and carried with them if they move to a new home. In some cases, particularly where a child has experienced a painful past, they can be used within a therapeutic intervention. Going back into the past can invoke powerful feelings for some children and they will need help and support to contextualise and come to terms with these feelings. They can also help new carers to empathise with a child's past.

4.3 Connecting to wider networks

Supporting connectedness also means helping children and their families connect to wider social and support networks. Family and children's centres would appear to be designed with this in mind, bringing together a wide range of support services under one roof. Tunstill et al. (2007, p. 74) found users of family centres to be people with 'limited social and support networks'. Their social isolation often resulted from a lack of social connectedness and different types of transition involving space, time and status, for example:

- Moving to a new area;
- Geographical distance from, or lack of, extended family;
- Having more than one preschool child;
- Having mental health problems.

(Tunstill et al., 2007, p. 74)

There has been a tendency to place children's services at the heart of communities (Sure Start centres aimed to be within 'pushchair distance' of most families). However, community is a difficult concept to define and it is not always the case that people in a particular geographical area identify themselves as belonging to a community. It may be possible to encourage interest in community services through paying attention to the quality and form of communication with families. Improving the quality of communication may involve adapting written communication into linguistic forms that are familiar to parents, or undertaking consultations to ensure local people's views inform service development.

Connectedness also depends on the extent to which issues from the macrosystem, including prejudice and discrimination, are addressed:

Nazeera is an Asian British Muslim woman living in a neighbourhood in which a children's centre has been built. The centre prides itself of being located close to a residential area and attracts a large number of low-paid and unemployed families. An evaluation of its effectiveness revealed that it was not attracting families from minority ethnic groups in numbers proportionate to the local demography. In response, the centre produced a leaflet in a number of minority ethnic languages and distributed it around the community.

Nazeera's attention was drawn to the leaflet and she was very interested in the types of service being offered by the children's centre. She particularly liked the idea of a crèche for mothers integrated with a woman-only adult literacy class. Although it was only a ten-minute walk away from her home, she decided not to attend the children's centre, despite its attractive programme. In order to reach the children's centre she would have to walk through two streets in the neighbourhood where in the past she, and other Asian friends, had been subjected to racist comments and stone-throwing from local residents.

Thinking point 7.9   What parts of the wider ecological network need to be addressed in order to make Nazeera and her children feel connected to the children's centre?

Key points

1   Providing a sense of place to which children can connect may help them with transitions.

2   Building connections with close family, siblings, peers and extended family can help some children cope with transitions but they may need support to maintain these links.

3   Connectedness and transitions can be represented and shared by children through visual media, including ecomaps and life story books.

4   Connecting children and their families to social networks requires careful attention to discriminatory processes and other forms of social exclusion.

Conclusion

Supporting children with transitions is increasingly viewed as part of the role of everyone working with children. Because children's experiences are very particular, it is necessary to provide support that is responsive to both their wider ecological system and their own individual capacities and choices. Support may involve working closely with other professionals, including specialists, and with family members and peers. Effective and adaptable observation, communication and information-providing skills are required to ensure that responses to feelings, behaviour and requests for help are inclusive and fair.

Although some transitions are unexpected and difficult to negotiate it is reasonable to assume that everyone will experience change and loss in their lives. By providing positive experiences for children with their early transitions we are helping them develop resilience and confidence that will support them into the future.

References

A National Voice (2006) *My Life Story About Being in Care*, available online at <http://www.anationalvoice.org/contributions/articles/article1.htm>, accessed 9 August 2007.

Aldgate, J. and Bradley, M. (2004) 'Children's experiences of short-term accommodation' in Lewis, V., Kellett, M., Robinson, C., Fraser, S. and Ding, S. (eds) *The Reality of Research with Young Children and Young People*, London, Sage.

Aldgate, J., Jones, D., Rose, W. and Jeffrey, C. (eds) (2006) *The Developing World of the Child*, London, Jessica Kingsley.

Aldgate, J. and McIntosh, M. (2006) *Looking After the Family: A Study of Children Looked After in Kinship Care in Scotland*, Edinburgh, Social Work Inspection Agency, available online at <http://www.scotland.gov.uk/Resource/Doc/129074/0030729.pdf>, accessed 9 August 2007.

Barbelet, J.M. (1998) *Emotion, Social Theory and Social Structure: A Macrosociological Approach*, Cambridge, Cambridge University Press.

BBC News (1999) *Sharing homework benefits parents*, available online at <http://news.bbc.co.uk/1/hi/education/452286.stm>, accessed 29 August 2007

Brown, J. (2007) 'Time, space and gender: understanding "problem" behaviour in young children', *Children & Society*, vol. 21, no. 2, pp. 98–110.

Burchard, T. (2003) *Being and becoming: social exclusion and the onset of disability*, CASE report 21, November 2003, York, Joseph Rowntree Foundation, available online at <http://sticerd.lse.ac.uk/dps/case/CR/CASEreport21.pdf>, accessed 9 August 2007.

CAFCASS (Children and Family Court Advisory and Support Service) (2006) *Children's Rights Policy, Final Version*, London, CAFCASS, available online at <http://www.cafcass.gov.uk/english/Publications/policies/06Oct06ChildrensRightPolicy.pdf>, accessed 9 August 2007.

Cain, B.S. (2001) Double-Dip Feelings: Stories to Help Children Understand Emotions (2nd edn), Washington DC, Magination Press.

Cairns, K. (2002) *Attachment, Trauma and Resilience: Therapeutic Caring for Children*, London, British Association for Adoption & Fostering (BAAF).

City of Edinburgh Scout Association (2006) *CESAN newsletter*, vol. 39, no. 2

Cunningsburgh Primary School (2004) *Induction Booklet 2004/2005*, available online at <http://www.cunningsburgh.shetland.sch.uk/induction_booklet.html>, accessed 9 August 2007.

Dennison, S. (2000) 'A win-win peer mentoring and tutoring program: a collaborative model', *Journal of Primary Prevention*, vol. 20, no. 3, pp. 161–174.

Dockett, S. and Perry, B. (2005a) ' "A buddy doesn't let kids get hurt in the playground": starting school with buddies', *International Journal of Transitions in Childhood*, vol. 1, pp. 22–34.

Dockett, S. and Perry, B. (2005b) 'Starting school in Australia is "a bit safer, a lot easier and more relaxing": issues for families and children from culturally and linguistically diverse backgrounds', *Early Years*, vol. 25, no. 3, pp. 271–281.

Donelan-McCall, N. and Dunn, J. (1997) 'School work, teachers, and peers: the world of first grade', *International Journal of Behavioral Development*, vol. 21, no. 1, pp. 155–178.

Dunlop, A-W. (2002) 'Continuity in transitions', *Early Years' Matters*, online newsletter, issue 2, Summer 2002, available online at <http://www.ltscotland.org.uk/earlyyearsmatters/previousissues/issue2/index.asp>, accessed 8 August 2007.

Edwards, R., Alldred, P. and David, M. (2000) 'Children's understandings of parental involvement in education', *Children 5–16 Research Briefing*, April 2000, no. 11, available online at <http://www.hull.ac.uk/children5to16programme/briefings/edwards.pdf>, accessed 25 June 2007.

Einarsdottir, J. (2006) 'From pre school to primary school: when different contexts meet', *Scandinavian Journal of Educational Research*, vol. 50, no. 2, pp. 165–184.

Fahlberg, V. (1994) *A Child's Journey Through Placement*, London, British Association for Adoption and Fostering (BAAF).

Foster Care Associates (FCA) (2000) *It's Mad That's All. A Collection of Poems about Being Looked After*, Bromsgrove, Foster Care Associates.

Foster Care Associates (FCA) (2003) *Rattle Your Cool. A Collection of Poetry and Art by Children and Young People Who Are Being Looked After*, Bromsgrove, Foster Care Associates.

Gilligan, R. (2000) 'The importance of listening to children in foster care' in Kelly, G. and Gilligan, R. (eds) *Issues in Foster Care Policy Practice and Research*, London , Jessica Kingsley.

Gordon, D., Parker, R., Loughran, F. and Heslop, P. (2000) *Disabled Children in Britain: A Reanalysis of the OPCS Disability Surveys*, London, The Stationery Office.

Greenberg, P. (2005) 'The child who always starts trouble', *Early Childhood Today*, vol. 20, no. 3, p. 24.

Gregory, E. (2005) 'Playful talk: the interspace between home and school discourse', *Early Years*, vol. 25, no. 3, pp. 223–235.

HM Treasury (2004) *Child Poverty Review*, Norwich, HMSO.

Holland, J. (2003) 'Supporting schools with loss: "lost for words" in Hull', *British Journal of Special Education*, vol. 30, no. 2, pp. 76–78.

Holland, J., Dance, R., MacManus, N. and Stitt, C. (2005) *Lost for Words. Loss and Bereavement Awareness Training*, London, JKP Resource Materials.

Howard, S., Dryden, J. and Johnson, B. (1999) 'Childhood resilience: a review and critique of the literature', *Oxford Review of Education*, vol. 25, no. 3, pp. 307–323.

Howard, S. and Johnson, B. (2000) 'What makes the difference? Children and teachers talk about resilient outcomes for children "at risk"', *Educational Studies*, vol. 26, no. 3, pp. 321–337.

Jordan, A.B. (2005) 'Learning to use books and television: an exploratory study in the ecological perspective', *American Behavioral Scientist*, vol. 48, no. 5, pp. 523–538.

Lucey, H. and Reay, D. (2000) 'Identities in transition: anxiety and excitement in the move to secondary school', *Oxford Review of Education*, vol. 26, no. 2, pp. 191–205.

Margetts, K. (2005) 'Children's adjustment to the first year of schooling; indicators of hyperactivity, internalising and externalising behaviours', *International Journal of Transitions in Childhood*, vol. 1, pp. 36–44.

Mayo, J. (2005) 'Passing on the baton', *International Journal of Transitions in Childhood*, vol. 1, pp. 46–51.

Mental Health Foundation (2002) *Peer support manual. A guide to setting up a peer listening project in education settings*, available online at <http://www.mentalhealth.org.uk/publications/?EntryId=38728&char=P>, accessed 9 August 2007.

Mitchell, W. and Sloper, P. (2001) 'Quality in services for disabled children and their families: what can theory, policy and research on children's and parents' views tell us?', *Children & Society*, vol. 15, no. 4, pp. 237–252.

Mortimer, H. (2004) 'Hearing children's voices in the early years', *Support for Learning*, vol. 19, no. 4, pp. 169–174.

National Statistics (2005) *Households Below Average Income: An Analysis of the Income Distribution 1994/5–2003/04*, Leeds, Department for Work and Pensions.

Newman, T. (2004) *What Works in Building Resilience?*, Ilford, Barnardo's Policy and Research Unit.

Newman, T. and Blackburn, S. (2002a) *Interchange 78: Transitions in the Lives of Children and Young People: Resilience Factors. Full Report,* Edinburgh, Scottish Executive Education Department.

Newman, T. and Blackburn, S. (2002b) *Interchange 78: Transitions in the Lives of Children and Young People: Resilience Factors. Summary of Full Report*, Edinburgh, Scottish Executive Education Department.

Newsround (2004) *I share my bedroom with foster kids*, available online at <http://news.bbc.co.uk/cbbcnews/hi/club/your_reports/newsid_3480000/3480143.stm>, accessed 26 June 2007.

Oliver, M. (1996) *Understanding Disability; From Theory to Practice*, Basingstoke, Macmillan.

Owens, A-M. (2006) 'Parents rebelling against homework', *National Post* [Canada], 2 September 2006, available online at <http://www.canada.com/nationalpost/news/story.html?id=72983a12-e347-4a19-ba37-786d28113ebd>, accessed 9 August 2007.

Preston, G. (2006a) 'Families with disabled children, benefits and poverty', *Benefits*, vol. 14, no. 1, pp. 39–43.

Preston, G. (2006b) *A Route out of Poverty. Disabled People Work and Welfare Reform*, London, Child Poverty Action Group.

Ridge, T. (2002) 'Listening to children: their contribution to anti-poverty policies', *Poverty*, vol. 111, Winter, Child Poverty Action Group, available online at <http://www.cpag.org.uk/info>, accessed 9 August 2007.

Russell, P. (2003) 'Access and achievement or social exclusion. Are the government's policies working for disabled children and their families?', *Children & Society*, vol. 17, pp. 215–225.

Russell, P. (2004) *Disabled Children, Their Families and Child Poverty Briefing Paper*, End Child Poverty and Council for Disabled Children, available online at <http://pegasus.xssl.net/~admin315/assets/files/reports/Child_Poverty_and_Disability_A4.pdf>, accessed 9 August 2007.

Rutter, M. (1985) 'Resilience in the face of adversity: protective factors and resilience to psychiatric disorders', *British Journal of Psychiatry*, vol. 147, 1985, pp. 163–182.

Sharp, C., Keys, W. and Benefield, P. (2001) *Homework: a review of recent research*, Slough, National Foundation for Educational Research (NFER).

Shucksmith, J., McKee, L. and Willmot, H. (2005) 'Families, education and the "participatory imperative"' in McKie, L. and Cunningham-Burley, S. (eds) *Families in Society: Boundaries and Relationships*, Bristol, The Policy Press.

Stormont, M., Beckner, R., Mitchell, B. and Richter, M. (2005) 'Supporting successful transitions to kindergarten; general challenges and specific implications for students with problem behaviour', *Psychology in Schools*, vol. 42, no. 8, pp. 765–778.

Taylor, A. (2005) 'Special report: Sure Start evaluation analysed', Community Care, 9 December, available online at <http://www.communitycare.co.uk/Articles/2005/12/09/52106/special-report-sure-start-evaluation-analysed.html>, accessed 9 August 2007.

Thurber, C.A. and Weisz, J.R. (1997) '"You can try or you can give up": the impact of perceived control and coping style on childhood homesickness', *Developmental Psychology*, vol. 33, no. 3, pp. 508–517.

Tunstill, J., Aldgate, J. and Hughes, M. (2007) *Improving Children's Services Networks. Lessons From Family Centres*, London, Jessica Kingsley.

Wade, A. and Smart, C. (2002) *Facing Family Change: Children's Circumstances, Strategies and Resources*, York, Joseph Rowntree Foundation.

Acknowledgements

Grateful acknowledgement is made to the following sources:

Text

Page 36: Foster Care Associates (2000) 'The Park' in *It's Mad That's All. A Collection of Poems about Being Looked After*, Foster Care Associates; Page 50: Storey, C. 'Answer back: Children's views on family breakdown' on http://www.headliners.org/storylibrary/stories/2001/answerbackchildrenviewsonfamilybreakdown.htm Reproduced with kind permission of Headliners; Pages 145 and 146: Bransby, D. 'Junior Jury: children's rights' on www.headliners.org/storylibrary/stories/2001/juniorjurychildrensrights.htm. With kind permission of Headliners; Pages 145 and 146: Mather, G. 'Junior Jury: the police' on www.headliners.org/storylibrary/stories/2002/juniorjurythepolice.htm. With kind permission of Headliners; Pages 176 and 177: Foster Care Associates (2000) *It's Mad That's All*, Foster Care Associates; Page 222: Foster Care Associates (2003) 'Let me be one of you' in *Rattle Your Cool. A Collection of Poetry and Art by Children and Young People Who Are Being Looked After*. With kind permission of FCA Publications; Page 262: Foster Care Associates (2003) 'I'm a foster kid' in *Rattle Your Cool*. With kind permission of FCA Publications; Pages 269 and 270: Foster Care Associates (2000) 'Someone's there' in *It's Mad That's All*. With kind permission of FCA Publications.

Figures

Page 46: Schaffer, H. R. (1996) Figure 17, 'The relationship of parental belief systems to rearing practices and children's development' in *Families, Parents and Socialization in Social Development*, John Wiley and Sons; Page 52: Hinde, R.A. (1992) 'Human social development: An ethological/relationship perspective' in *Childhood Social Development*, McGurk, H. (ed.) Taylor and Francis Books Ltd. With kind permission of Lawrence Erlbaum Associates Ltd; Page 104: Dunn, J. and Deater-Deckard, K. (2001) *Children's Views of their Changing Families*. Reproduced by permission of the Joseph Rowntree Foundation; Pages 150 and 151: Madge, N. (2006) 'Getting along together', *Children These Days*, The Policy Press; Page 167: Hart, R. (1992) 'Children's Participation: From Tokenism to Citizenship', Florence: UNICEF (Innocenti Research Centre - *Innocenti Essay*, 4). Reproduced with kind permission of UNICEF Innocenti Research Centre Florence; Page 170: Fajerman, L. and Treseder, P. (1997) *Empowering Children and Young People*. Reproduced with kind permission of Save the

Children Fund. Page 193: Kirby, P. and Gibbs, S. (2006) 'Facilitating participations: adults' caring support roles within child-to-child projects', *Children & Society*, vol. 20, John Wiley and Sons; Page 197: Shephard and Treseder (2002) 'Evaluation targets' in Holford, A.(2002) *Participation Spice it up!*, Save the Children Fund.

Illustrations

Page 12: © Getty Images; Page 23: www.johnbirdsall.co.uk; Page 27: www.johnbirdsall.co.uk; Page 30: www.johnbirdsall.co.uk; Page 31: Dialogues with places: spatial simulation at school from *Rechild* – Reggio Children newsletter – © Preschools and Infant-toddler Centers – Istituzione of the Municipality of Reggio Emilia, Italy, published by Reggio Children, April 2007; Page 33: © Janine Wiedel Photolibrary/Alamy; Page 34: Hoyles, M. and Hemmings, S. (eds) *More Valuable Than Gold*, With kind permission of Martin Hoyles; Page 37: www.johnbirdsall.co.uk; Page 46: www.johnbirdsall.co.uk; Page 53 © Paul Harris/Getty Images; Page 59: CLEO Photo/Alamy; Page 59: www.johnbirdsall.co.uk; Page 62 © Nick Daly/Getty Images; Page 68: Hantler, A. (1994) 'Children's views of bullying', *Health Education*, December 1994, vol. 94, issue 5, Emerald Group Publishing Limited; Page 89: www.johnbirdsall.co.uk; Page 90: Adams Picture Library t/a apl /Alamy; Page 94: www.johnbirdsall.co.uk; Page 98 © Alamy Images; Page 106 © Alamy Images; Page 116: www.johnbirdsall.co.uk; Page 134: © David White/Alamy; Page 138: © Spencer Platt/Getty Images; Page 139: © Abode/Beateworks/Corbis; Page 141: www.johnbirdsall.co.uk; Page 169: JAMES JIM JAMES/PA Archive/PA Photos; Page 176: Pugh, J. (2003) Cartoon belittling children's strikes, *The Times*. NI Syndication Ltd; Page 176: Martin, S.W. (1972) Cartoon belittling children's strikes, first published by the *Sunday Express*, 14 May 1972. With kind permission of Janet Slee and The British Cartoon Archive, University of Kent; Page 177: Austin, D. (2003) Cartoon about communication and text messaging, in the *Guardian*; Page 191: © Roger Bamber/Alamy; Page 209: © Shaun Egan/Getty Images; Page 219: © Wyatt Photography/Alamy; Page 222: © Profimedia International s.r.o./ Alamy; Page 226: © Acestock Stock Limited/Alamy; Page 228: www.johnbirdsall.co.uk; Page 238: © Sally and Richard Greenhill/Alamy; Page 246: © Jennie Hart/Alamy; Page 252: © Tim Platt/Getty Images; Page 254: © Don Smetzer/Getty Images; Page 259: © Seymour Hewitt/ Getty Images; Page 263: © Sally Greenhill/Alamy; Page 267: © BananaStock/Punchstock; Page 273: © Taxi/Getty Images; Page 276: Fahlberg, V. I. (1994) *A Child's Journey Through Placement*, British Agencies for Adoption and Fostering (BAAF); Page 277: © Rex Features.

Index